T0206480

Mastering Software Project Requirements

A Framework for Successful Planning, Development & Alignment

Barbara Davis

J.ROSS
PUBLISHING

Copyright © 2013 by Barbara Davis

ISBN-13: 978-1-60427-091-4

Printed and bound in the U.S.A. Printed on acid-free paper.

10 9 8 7 6 5 4 3 2 1

Library of Congress Cataloging-in-Publication Data

Davis, Barbara, 1969-
   Mastering software project requirements : a framework for successful
planning, development & alignment / by Barbara Davis.
      pages cm
   Includes index.
   ISBN 978-1-60427-091-4 (hardcover : alk. paper) 1. Information technology
projects--Management. 2. Computer software—Development—Management.
3. Management information systems. I. Title.
   T58.64.D37755 2013
   005.068'4—dc23
                              2013028702

Direct all inquiries to J. Ross Publishing, Inc., 300 S. Pine Island Rd., Suite
305, Plantation, FL 33324.

Phone: (954) 727-9333
Fax: (561) 892-0700
Web: www.jrosspub.com

Dedication

"If the only tool you have is a hammer, you tend to treat everything as a nail."—Unknown

This book is dedicated to:

Robert, my husband, for all the years of discussion we shared about requirements. I'm looking forward to many more.

Tonya, my sister, for helping edit the manuscript for this book.

Mr. James Canter, for his contribution to this book on the importance of requirements from a testing perspective.

Mr. Tony White, for his contribution to the Agile discussion in this book.

Mr. Klassen, my favorite high school English teacher.

And this book is dedicated to every business analyst who works hard every single day and works for something more. Don't give up; you'll get there.

Table of Contents

Preface

"*Mastering Software Project Requirements* is a must read for the successful business analyst. Barbara has provided tried and true solutions for situations that BAs run into every day. The information is current, insightful, and based on real project experiences. After reading it, I applied lessons learned from the *Setting and Managing Expectations* section on a current project and was able to successfully align project expectations. I highly recommend this book as part of your analyst's toolkit."
— Caprice White, Business Analyst, BC Liquor Distribution Branch

THE PURPOSE OF THIS BOOK

One of the key issues that I have personally witnessed over the past thirteen years, on various projects and with varying levels of experience and responsibility, is that there seems to be an overall lack of context to the tasks that are performed in business analysis. This is certainly true in requirements.

When you think about it, business analysis has evolved from its establishment as a means of translating business needs into technical terms for development teams. Early on, the business analyst was often considered to be a "jack-of-all-trades" who was tasked with everything from project coordination, to requirements, to testing. The reality today is that the analyst is no longer the "jack-of-all-trades and master of none." A qualified analyst is the critical differentiator between project success and failure. The analyst is the one resource with the information, details, and knowledge to implement solutions that align to long-term strategies. Of course, that suggests that the analyst is a driver of the solution and the path of the project in a way that no other resource could possibly be. The project manager is tasked with budget and completion. The architects are tasked with design. The developers are tasked with building, and the testers are tasked with quality assurance. Who, then, is left to be tasked with the alignment of the solution to the long-term strategy—the stakeholders or the business user community? No, and they should not be.

The stakeholders and users often have a limited perspective of the solution and certainly of the underlying technology required to make their business function throughout its daily operations. The analyst is tasked with authoring specifications that define the solution, which will meet the needs of the business or resolve its problems. These specifications are consumed by the architects, developers, and testers in the performance of their tasks. In doing so, the analyst becomes privy to information about the business, its industry, and its inner workings in a way and depth that no other resource is. This length and breadth of information pushes the analyst into a unique position to offer advice about the solution, its alignment, and its feasibility. But all of this assumes that the analyst can perform the primary task of requirements, which forms the fundamental objective of the business analysis role.

The purpose of this book is to provide the much needed context to individual tasks, which constitute the daily due diligence of requirements activities, and to provide analysts with the step-by-step instruction they need to be effective and proficient in their roles. Within the pages that follow, the full end-to-end process of requirements is detailed. I have also highlighted some of the project methodologies an analyst may work on to better adapt the methods of requirements to suit the particular situation.

The three focal points that span this book are:

- How and where requirements activities begin, what they look like, and how they can be estimated, measured, and benchmarked.
- How to plan, manage, and deliver great software project requirements.
- How to adapt requirements development techniques and tasks to the project methodologies being utilized to address the needs of the project.

The objective of this book is simple: to redefine the requirements process in pragmatic detail and to enable technology and business organizations to maximize the return on investment (ROI) of every implemented business solution, by providing detailed task descriptions, key performance indicators (KPIs), and benefits realization planning. Together, these are a means to improving the results for the project and achieving that value proposition.

WHO WILL BENEFIT FROM THIS BOOK?

Business analysts and project managers who are interested in elevating their performance through due diligence in requirements, utilizing better techniques for requirements activities, and having the ability to adapt requirements tasks to meet the particular needs of a given project without sacrificing quality, scope, or project schedules.

Business analysis managers and leaders who are looking to improve the results of their existing requirements activities by adding a context to their daily routine, establishing realistic performance expectations for requirements activities, as well as garner a measurable efficiency in all of these tasks.

Students, professors, and instructors of business analysis and project management college courses, continuing education, and training programs, who focus on learning the specific and detailed steps of requirements development and management, which forms the foundation of all business analysis activities.

Chief information officers who are looking to accomplish at least one of the following objectives: more accurately estimate requirements activities; establish performance-based key performance indicators for requirements activities and resources; reduce operating costs; increase alignment between technology products and business needs; and obtain peace of mind, by establishing a functional framework for requirements activities that effectively reduces break-and-fix cycles on projects and the problematic defect rates that cause post-implementation headaches.

Consulting firms that are interested in establishing a requirements framework for their organization or clients that will enable them to accurately estimate requirements activities, establish performance-based KPIs, reduce operating costs, increase alignment between technology products and business needs, and obtain a higher ROI for their technology projects and solutions.

Recruiters who are interested in improving their assessment and selection processes by gaining a better understanding of the detailed steps and stages for potential business analysis candidates, improving the management of business analysis resources across all engagements through productivity KPIs, and improving the quality and consistency of candidates who are being placed in client organizations.

HOW THIS BOOK IS ORGANIZED

This book is organized in a step-by-step approach to building and establishing the frameworks and models for the management and development of requirements. To this end, this book follows a simple formula from start to finish—across the full requirements life cycle, from vague concept to detailed design-ready specifications.

In Section 1, the reader should gain an understanding of how to define the solution. Regardless of whether the analyst is a part of the activity that determines the solution to meet the need or resolve the problem, the analyst must be able to understand what to do and why in great detail. This detail enables the analyst to decompose the high-level solution into its granular requirements. Further, the reader should also gain an in-depth understanding of stakeholder engagement and management in this section. It illustrates how to attract, lead, and involve stakeholders in a way that so many projects today are missing.

In Section 2, the discussion moves on to how to manage requirements and the specific requirements tasks to be accomplished throughout the project so that the foundation is laid for effective and productive requirements tasks. Section 2 further outlines the detailed set of metrics and benchmarks that can be utilized to quantitatively assess requirements quality, effectiveness, and resource productivity.

In Section 3, the full and detailed end-to-end requirements process is presented for the reader. This process covers every shred of documentation that an analyst will consume and produce (as either deliverable or artifact) throughout the project. This description and detailed walkthrough will provide context for each document and enable the analyst to make well-informed decisions about which document to apply in a specific situation—depending on the project, the timeline, the stakeholders, and the team capabilities and capacities. The objective is to provide each analyst with the ammunition to make critical project-impacting decisions without losing the integrity and quality of the requirements themselves.

Finally, Section 4 describes the considerations that must be made to accommodate the project methodology, as well as the corresponding methodologies or frameworks—such as Waterfall, Agile, WAgile, TOGAF, and DO-178—in order to ensure that the integrity of the requirements is maintained across multiple project frameworks. Section 4 also helps the reader to develop a solid understanding of strategies for adapting the requirements activities to each of these frameworks.

THE KEY TAKEAWAYS

The strongest takeaways can be found in the answers to each of the following questions:

1. How can any analyst improve performance in conducting requirements activities? This takeaway is formed through an in-depth review

of the varied documentation that the analyst consumes, coupled with a detailed review of every document that must be produced and, above all, *how* these documents must be consumed and produced.

2. How can requirements and requirements activities be quantitatively measured and assessed for consistent improvements? *Mastering Software Project Requirements* proposes a detailed benchmarking model for requirement quality, activities, and productivity by prescribing a set of metrics and formulas for analyzing these attributes. This baseline provides any business analyst, project manager, or CIO with the ability to more accurately target areas for improvement within requirements.

3. How can requirements and requirements efforts be more accurately estimated? This takeaway is provided by a detailed discussion on estimating requirements, based on complexity in a marriage of standard estimating models. These are functional complexity and three-point analysis.

4. How do you write great requirements, and what do they look like? Above all else, any book about requirements should teach the reader how to consume the information and analyze it, how to write detailed requirements, and how to validate those requirements. It takes more than defining a process and describing a collection of inputs and outputs; there are so many nuances of stakeholder management, taxonomy, and semantics that must also be addressed. These nuances can dramatically impact a project by altering the time and effort required to complete each task, which can throw a project schedule out the window.

A PERSONAL MESSAGE

My analytical nature and desire to consistently improve are undeniable. This book is intended to share every technique, trick, and tip in business analysis that have not only helped me and my clients over the years but also enabled me to gain a strong foothold in job satisfaction. It is my hope that, through sharing this knowledge, others will not only thrive as business analysts but will gain a strong sense of that same pride in accomplishment that I have felt over the years.

It is also my hope that companies will gain the knowledge, tools, techniques, and insight to end a large part of the financial waste and personal frustration associated with information technology. I am convinced that we could have technologies far beyond the current means, if we simply changed the way in which business analysis is performed. In order for that to happen, business analysis must become a quantitatively managed and measured set of tasks, which can be consistently improved through targeted efforts.

Barbara Davis

About the Author

Barbara Davis is the author of *Managing Business Analysis Services: A Framework for Sustainable Projects and Corporate Strategy Success* and a champion for technology standards and infrastructure for over 13 years. She is also an international speaker and works with Fortune 500 companies to realign business analysis services, critical and struggling projects, and establish operational infrastructure in order to ensure successful outcomes in the face of conflict and very challenging circumstances. Barbara has launched business analysis portfolios and grown them from $500K to over $8 million. Over her career, she has grown other service portfolios to over $51 million and enabled clients to reduce operational spending by salvaging struggling projects and driving operational changes for clients in excess of $220 million. She has been published in *Strategize Magazine*, created the world's first university-accredited Business Analysis diploma program, and spoken at Project Summit/BA World conferences across Canada, the United States, and India.

Barbara came into technology with over fifteen years of functional business experience—including professional training, project management, community development, business ownership, change management, and conflict resolution.

She has drawn on these experiences throughout the course of her career and become a champion by defining organizational capability through infrastructure (such as career paths, assessment tools, competencies, and key performance indicators), training (such as educational programs and workshops), and the creation of centers of excellence and management frameworks. She audits and redefines operational management of key practice areas and methodologies.

Throughout her career, Barbara has interviewed and assessed hundreds of resources and held various titles and roles—including Business & IT Portfolio Manager, IT Operational Manager, Methodologist, Solutions Consultant, Project Manager, Business Analyst, Author, and Professional Skills Trainer. Her experiences include operational management, organizational change management, document management, vendor management, configuration management, change control, practice management, business analysis, project management, and auditing project management office methodologies.

Web
Added
Value™

This book has free material available for download from the
Web Added Value™ resource center at *www.jrosspub.com*

At J. Ross Publishing we are committed to providing today's professional with practical, hands-on tools that enhance the learning experience and give readers an opportunity to apply what they have learned. That is why we offer free ancillary materials available for download on this book and all participating Web Added Value™ publications. These online resources may include interactive versions of material that appears in the book or supplemental templates, worksheets, models, plans, case studies, proposals, spreadsheets and assessment tools, among other things. Whenever you see the WAV™ symbol in any of our publications, it means bonus materials accompany the book and are available from the Web Added Value Download Resource Center at www.jrosspub.com.

Downloads for *Mastering Software Project Requirements* include templates for every aspect of requirements including estimation, and materials for academic instruction.

SECTION I

IDENTIFYING AND UNDERSTANDING THE BUSINESS SOLUTION

Identifying the Solution

DEFINED VERSUS UNDEFINED SOLUTION STARTING POINTS

While it is usually true that by the time the average business analyst joins a project the solution has already been defined, this is not always the case—especially on projects where the analyst is more experienced as senior business analysts tend to be brought in earlier in the initiation of a project. In fact, sometimes the analyst is a part of the discovery team who goes in to define the solution, even before the project has been initiated. Both of these starting points, which will be called "predefined solution" and "undefined solution," present different sets of challenges for the business analyst. Each challenge must be overcome and mitigated if success on the project is to be achieved.

Challenges that may be present when the solution has been defined by others include (but certainly are not limited to): a preexisting escalated level of commitment; a lack of fundamental understanding of the problem to be solved; an incorrectly defined solution; a lack of business planning (such as benefits realization, vision or mission definition); a limited operational perspective on the problem to be solved; as well as limited exploration of various alternative solutions.

An escalated level of commitment occurs when people and companies are heavily invested in the success of the project because they have spent a lot of money, time, and effort on it, or have done a lot of promotional and marketing work to "talk up" the new solution to employees, clients, and vendors. The best example of an escalated level of commitment is when gamblers refuse to leave their seats at the table because they have spent a lot of money and believe they will (or MUST, as the case may be) get it back, if they simply play long enough.

The problem is that the gambler is not only sitting there. Spending more and more money in the pursuit of getting back the investment becomes a no-win cycle.

Sometimes, before an analyst joins the project, the business is already in this mode. They have spent a lot on the solution and are in the process of forcing it. "Failure," in their minds, is not an option—whether this is a realistic goal or not, and whether or not they are on a path to correct the situation. In this case, sometimes it is best to either shut down the project altogether or get the right resources in to fix it and let them have the authority to fix it. If the business analyst is a part of the team to fix the broken project, they must have the authority to do the whole job and to help the business make some tough decisions, or they simply will not be successful and the company ends up as a sad gambler waiting for the right cards and doing nothing but losing.

Believe it or not, there are times when a business analyst comes on board and there is a lack of fundamental understanding of what the problem to be solved actually is. It can be difficult for a business analyst (more so when this is a junior to intermediate analyst) to get a clear picture of the reason for the project, when the business stakeholders themselves are not clear.

The Great Divisional Divide

A consulting firm was engaged by an energy company to define a solution and provide an estimate for this solution. The consulting firm brought together an account team, a senior business analyst, and a project manager to define this solution.

The team met with executives from the energy company in order to understand what the problem and the needs were. During the meeting, the executives openly argued (loudly and angrily) with each other in response to questions about the problem, how this problem impacted the business, and the results needed to fix the problem.

Since the energy company could not afford a complex solution, and it was important not to build a mammoth solution that could not be tested, the executives could not agree on what the most significant impacts of the problem were and how to prioritize them. While in this example the disagreement took place before initiation, it is not uncommon for this situation to exist when the project has already started and the business analyst is working to elicit the requirements. The average business analyst can spend a lot of time working with and mentoring the stakeholders through this process so that they can start the requirements.

Unfortunately, the biggest danger from this situation is that the perception of the problem can change and the analyst will later see excessive and unnecessary changes to requirements throughout the remainder of the project life cycle. This problem can be compounded when the analyst was not a part of the solution definition and is viewed as an order-taker by the business.

Another problem analysts face when they were not a part of the solution definition is that the incorrect solution can be defined. Unfortunately, when this happens, the business has an escalated level of commitment, and it falls to the analyst to make the best of the situation. In this case, the analyst may have little control or influence and will still get the lion's share of the blame when things fail.

To further compound the problems already described (many of these problems could be present in any given project in varying degrees), many stakeholders and project sponsors forget that some basic business planning must occur in order to ensure the success of a project. It takes more than a timeline, a budget, and resources to be successful.

DEFINING THE BUSINESS NEED, VISION, AND MISSION

In reality, building a new process, infrastructure, or system means building a new part of the organization and must be planned as such. These plans should include (and yet rarely do): a benefits realization plan, a clearly defined and articulated vision (*SHARED* across the team and stakeholders), and a clearly defined and articulated mission (again, *SHARED* across the team and stakeholders).

One of the primary issues, as cited previously, which impacts projects and the success of business analysis, is that the solution is often defined before the analyst comes on board, and it has been defined by inappropriate resources (executives, employees, contract, or other). These resources may be well-intentioned, however, this does not mean that they have done the due diligence required to develop a great solution to the problem or even to fully understand the problem.

What often happens is that an executive, a team of executives, or a group of managers from a single division identifies a problem within the purview of their responsibilities (the teams for whom they are responsible and accountable). They may then investigate a few solutions and invite a couple of solution vendors or consulting firms in to estimate the development and implementation. The business team will not necessarily consult other groups about their perspective on the problem. They are not asked about how, or if, the problem impacts them and what results or changes they need to see. This leads to a limited business perspective on the problem to be solved and ultimately, can lead to developing and implementing the wrong solution.

The consulting firms and vendors will make their respective presentations and the stakeholders will choose a solution. This choice is not always based on a sound investigation of the decision or (business) case for the solution. Unfortunately, this will also lead to a limited exploration of alternative solutions that may be available. Certainly, there is good evidence to suggest that business analysts should—no, *must*—be involved in the solution definition. The benefits to the solution far outweigh any costs associated with additional perspectives of the trained problem-solver supporting the solution definition.

Alternatively, there are challenges that arise when the business analyst is involved in the discovery and definition of the solution. These challenges include: an inconsistent framework for discovery activities; mismatched expectations between the business stakeholders and information technology; the availability and commitment of resources before financial commitment to the project; as well as the occurrence of the "snowball effect" during needs analysis and problem definition sessions.

One of the biggest challenges that a business analyst will face, if they are included in discovery and definition of the solution, is that (as with business analysis as a practice area) there is little in the way of industry standards. This leads directly to an inconsistent framework for the performance of discovery activities. It cannot be stressed enough that processes (*all* processes) must follow the Capability Maturity Model (CMM), as illustrated in Figure 1.1, in order to be truly successful. The CMM illustrates how processes go from chaos to managed and optimized through careful management and the application of consistent frameworks and improvement principles.

Several years ago, I put the average consulting firm discovery process under a microscope and examined it from start to finish. Unbelievably, I found in excess of fifty seemingly small and insignificant errors that ultimately led to problems in the execution of the project. Having an analyst on the team during the discovery phase will significantly reduce the problems caused—when this analyst is truly analyzing and advising the business about the solution. This involvement and the discovery must be repeatable, measured, and assessed consistently across the board. *No* exceptions!

Another challenge business analysts will face in discovery is a set of mismatched expectations between the business stakeholders and information technology. They will have to understand and embrace their role as mediator in order to overcome this and build bridges between the two groups.

Requirements Disconnect

On a project to replace a legacy insurance program, the first phase was so defective that it broke everything when it was first implemented. In fact, the first integration of the software to support the program had 396 defects.

It took a lengthy root cause analysis to determine what had happened and how it could be fixed. As it turned out, the requirements and the architecture design were created in complete isolation from each other and then approved by two completely different stakeholder groups and sponsors, neither of whom had ever read the other set of documents.

In this case, disconnect led to a complete misalignment of expectations for what was being built and delivered. Incidentally, it also led to high levels of conflict on the team because people were being ignored and had no influence on the project.

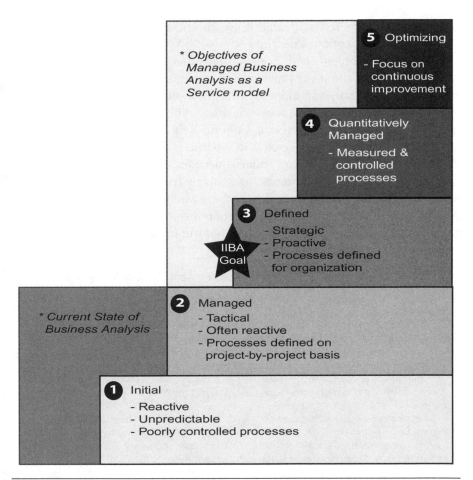

Figure 1.1 CM model

Another significant challenge the business analyst will have during discovery and solution definition is the availability and commitment of resources before the company's formal and financial commitment to the project. In other words, the company may not be willing to spend money up front because the return on investment (ROI) has not yet been established or proven.

It is also important to understand the level of personal commitment from the resources in this situation. Simply because the company may have allocated appropriate funds and resources (personnel), it does not follow that those resources have buy-in. Thus, when the company does make those resources available, they may not perform the work with any degree of skill or dedication.

Part of the problem could come from outside the project. For example, if a company has a track record of starting and stopping projects in the early stages—regardless of justification—the buy-in and dedication of the resources may drop, simply because they feel as though it does not matter what they do: it will be dumped and their work will be fruitless.

One of the problems with needs analysis and problem definition sessions is that discussions about the problems can turn into one big "venting" session, and the business analysts will be overwhelmed with an avalanche of information. In essence, it becomes a "snowball effect," with the amount of information increasing as the session progresses. Unfortunately, much of this information is unnecessary. However, to a degree, a wise business analyst will allow it to occur before taking control and asking pointed questions. When a problem has existed for a long time, people have become increasingly frustrated; above all, they have probably been complaining and when nothing was done, they did not feel heard. Allowing a degree of venting and then responding to it helps those people to feel heard and may also reveal critical details that will impact the solution.

Vent Session Replaces Project Kickoff

The project team was assembled at the client site. The project objective was to replace a legacy insurance claim system. On day one, the team met and filed into the conference room with the client stakeholders and sponsors. The consulting firm project manager started the kickoff by introducing everyone. From there it went downhill.

A typical format for a kickoff is to discuss the project objectives and the approach the team will use. This means that the consulting firm should have laid out a clear plan and identified the objectives. However, in this case, the client stakeholders and sponsors took over and started complaining about what they did not like about the existing system.

Now, venting for a few minutes and then directing the discussion towards the objectives of the meeting and back to the agenda would have been far more productive. Eight long hours of venting left the project team still wondering about the information the stakeholders and sponsors were to have shared in the meeting.

This story illustrates how venting, if left unchecked, can simply turn into chaos. The best way to get past frustration and the need to feel heard is to *listen*. Listening does not mean that the meeting facilitator should simply let people go while they sit there like a lump, saying nothing. It means letting them release some of the anger and frustration and then guiding them towards the solution with active listening techniques.

Active listening is the process of engaging participants by asking questions about the problem and the solution they see. This is the only way to help people feel heard. When people feel heard, their satisfaction with the solution goes up, even if the solution does not address all of their complaints. In addition, when people feel heard, it is easier to get their overall buy-in because they feel they are working on the same team.

All in all, in spite of the challenges, there is a reason for business analyst involvement at each of these starting points. However, it is important to know and understand how each of these challenges can and will impact the quality of the requirements that are produced in the final document. Again, the reasons for analyst involvement at each of these starting points is to reduce the amount of time it takes to define the solution, to ensure that the solution defined is the right one, and to increase the buy-in of the stakeholders.

The goal of this material is to attempt to address these challenges in more detail, since it is important not only to identify but also to address each one. Well-known business analysis expert, Glenn Brule, once asked, "If you were only able to ask stakeholders three questions about their solution, what three questions would you ask?"[1]

My response to this question is swift and simple:

1. What is the solution intended to resolve or do (this is to say, what are the RESULTS that the solution must produce)?
2. What other solutions/systems do they already have in place that works well?
3. What do they like and dislike about those solutions?

First and foremost, a business analyst must be able to identify the problem that needs to be solved, no matter what type of start they made on the project (defined or undefined). Unfortunately, not every analyst can identify the problem quickly and easily. For some analysts the inability to answer this simple question comes from having a defined solution before they arrive. For other analysts it may be attributed to the egos of the management team, and for still others, it results from a lack of clarity within the business and the other team members about the real problem to be solved.

Often, when the solution was defined before the business analyst became involved, the expectation is that this information has served its purpose of laying the foundation for the business analyst to follow in defining the requirements for the solution. This expectation exists because the solution has already been selected or identified. So, how can the business analyst ensure that the solution actually resolves the problem? Further, how can the analyst ensure that the requirements they write to define the detailed specifications to create this solution will actually align to the right solution (even if it is merely customizing and implementing a commercial off-the-shelf software solution)?

To be clear, verifying that the solution is going to solve the problem is one thing, and validating that the defined requirements actually support the development of this verified solution is quite another. These are discussed in depth in chapter 9, "Validation."

The bigger question, which often arises here, is whether it is the business analyst's job to verify that the solution is the right one to meet the need or to address the problem. After all, the business analyst, who arrives after the solution has been selected, has been allocated to define the requirements to create this defined solution. The answer is "yes." It is the business analyst's job to ensure that the identified solution is actually the right solution for resolving the problem or meeting the need. In the development of the requirements, the analyst must ensure that those requirements not only create the identified solution but also address all aspects of the problem.

Again, in some cases the business analysts are unable to clearly identify the problem, and sometimes this inability stems from an ego issue with the management team. In other words, management may be treating the information as if it is on a "need to know basis" and—to them—the business analyst does not need to know. When there is ego involved, questioning and researching the problem (its roots and impacts) can be interpreted as questioning the management decision about the solution. However, the business analyst is simply working to maintain alignment between the final solution and the business objectives through complete and accurate requirements.

Finally, the inability to identify the business problem to be solved may stem from a lack of clarity on the part of the business and management team. In other words, management has not clearly articulated the problem to the business analyst. When management has difficulty articulating the problem, the business analyst must work with the business and management team to help them clearly articulate the problem before any requirements activities can begin. After all, the analyst is accountable for defining the right requirements in order to ensure that the final solution meets the objectives and resolves the problem.

At the end of the day, if the analyst cannot articulate and identify what the problem is, it will be impossible to document the requirements. Moreover, why should the business spend money on it? The project will be riddled with interpersonal conflict, change requests, defects, and budget and schedule overruns. The project will probably only end up like so many other projects before it: digital roadkill along the information technology highway.

This being said, not every project is initiated to solve a "problem." However, defining the best solution can still be considered a "problem to be solved." Let's think about this for a moment.

Consider that the role of the business analyst is to enable strategy. Is strategy a problem to be solved? Well, kind of. The business defines its strategy for where it wants to be in a few years. Within this strategy, the business defines specific goals, either as a part of this future position or as the means to achieve this position. When the business is not on track or does not have the means to achieve the strategy, it is a problem.

The business analyst must always conduct some degree of needs and stakeholder analysis when joining a new project, even if it has been done already. The reason for this is simple: the needs and stakeholder analysis is not simply a tool for defining a solution; it is also actually a trust-building activity. An effective needs and stakeholder analysis consists of five basic steps:

1. Identify the stakeholders
2. Identify stakeholder needs

3. Build a trust bond with each stakeholder
4. Build trust bridges between the various stakeholder groups
5. Document the business needs of all stakeholders into a single document

First and foremost, in order to conduct an effective needs and stakeholder analysis, the business analyst must identify the stakeholders. It is crucial to know who these stakeholders are as people, and not merely as individuals with some input into the project. In order to identify the stakeholders, the business analyst must answer these basic questions:

- What are the areas and business units impacted by this project?
- What does each of these impacted areas do (what functions are they responsible for)?
- What are the main concerns for this area?
- How does each area fit into the organization?
- How is each area going to be impacted?
- How much is each area going to be impacted?
- What will be impacted in each area?
- How many people are in this impacted area?

Once the stakeholders have been identified, it is important to determine and understand their needs, so that these needs can be translated into project success through appropriate involvement. Remember that there is a difference between needs, wants, and expectations. It is crucial to be able to identify each of these needs, wants, and expectations for the stakeholders in order to build a successful plan for involvement.

The differences between needs, wants, and expectations are not always apparent. The stakeholder *needs* to see business results. This same stakeholder *expects* the business analyst to produce those results. Further, this stakeholder also *wants* the analyst to get along with the business and the project teams. If they do not get along, the stakeholder will *want* the business analyst replaced. While projects are initiated to meet business needs, the project team must recognize that they are dealing and working with people.

In understanding the differences, the business analyst can be more successful in navigating toward successful delivery. The analyst identifies stakeholder needs by answering the following basic questions:

- What types of language does each stakeholder use?
- What types of body language does each stakeholder use?
- What does the problem to be solved look like for each stakeholder/group?
- What kinds of things does each group say about the problem?
- What frustrates the stakeholder the most about it?

- What are the stakeholders' fears and concerns about a solution?
- What should this solution look like?
- Can you classify each stakeholder as: "Active," "Non-Participant," "Heckler," or "Hijacker?" (more on these in Chapter 2)
- What are the personal needs of each stakeholder in relation to the work environment?
- What are the stakeholders' expectations of you/the project team?
- Can those expectations be accommodated?
- What are the business analysis team's expectations of each stakeholder?
- What are the stakeholders' expectations for the project?
- Are there any differences?
- Can these differences be negotiated?
- How can the business analyst manage/leverage these expectations to support the project?

The next step is to build trust with each stakeholder. This is crucial, but is often overlooked by project teams and sometimes by the individual members of those teams. Remember that the best stakeholders are engaged participants because they will sign off on the requirements and support their implementation. However, there can be no engagement without involvement, and both of these require trust. The stakeholder will be neither engaged nor involved if this stakeholder does not trust the business analyst or the project team. In order to build trust, it is important to look for, understand, and perform the following:

- Meet with each stakeholder individually when possible.
- Ask each stakeholder to talk about the project.
- Know the stakeholder's success and fail criteria?
- Know the stakeholder's personal concerns?
- Understand the results each stakeholder needs to see?
- Set up an informal communication plan to reassure each stakeholder as the project progresses.
- Above all else, **follow through**.

The next thing for the business analyst to do is recognize what each stakeholder/ group brings to the project. Unfortunately, sometimes these groups bring conflict and office politics. This can be the result of poorly managed mergers and acquisitions, interpersonal relationship breakdowns (e.g., friendships and marriages), poorly managed technology projects, and interdivisional competitions.

As a direct result of these conflicts and office politics, it is crucial for the business analyst to leverage the newly developed trust with each stakeholder to rebuild team morale and trust by building "trust bridges" between the stakeholders/groups. The reason for this is, quite simply, that these conflicts and politics can adversely affect the level of involvement from the business, regardless of how much trust these stakeholders may have in the analyst. In effect, these conflicts must be managed in order to prevent issues from impacting the project. In order to build these bridges, the analyst should answer each of the following questions and perform each of the following tasks:

- Are there any stakeholders/groups who are in conflict with each other about what is needed?
- What is each group saying?
- What are the similarities between each group's needs or what they are saying?
- Talk to the groups in a combined meeting and point out similarities at every opportunity.
- What are groups that are not in conflict saying?
- Point out similarities in concerns, needs, and interests between all groups.
- Identify and talk about how each group will benefit from the new solution and how this aligns with overall business needs.

The final step in the needs and stakeholder analysis is to write the business needs of all of the stakeholders into a single document. This is simple. The following basic steps will guide the development of the needs analysis artifacts:

- Create a mission and vision statement for the project (if not already done) from the results-based needs.
- Put the vision and mission statements in the front of this document.
- Post these statements in your workspace.
- Distribute this document.

Once the needs and stakeholder analysis has been completed, the business must look at where it is now and identify the impediments or barriers to achieving the desired position. This information is used to define solutions (with or without the help of information technology), and these solutions become the projects that analysts will work on. The business utilizes these projects in the process of creating the desired position. This is done by building the new processes and tools that will help them resolve the problems (impediments and barriers). This is exactly how the analyst enables strategic plans and resolves the problems that would otherwise restrict the business's ability to achieve its strategic goals.

It is crucial to remember that there is a difference between needs and wants. At this stage, business analysts are heavily involved in identifying the needs of the business and identifying the vision and mission of the project, which will result in their ability to perform at their best and to create quality results.

A Server Named Bob: Needs Versus Wants

During a project to migrate multiple Windows platforms over to Windows XP, an employee ("user") sent several requests to the help desk using the automated system, indicating that he wanted the project team to change the name of the system he logged into every day on his computer. The user wanted this server to be named after himself so that he could log into something with his own name on it. The project team had to explain to him several times that the server could not be named after him because he was not the only employee who logged into it every day.

In this story, it is easy to see the difference between what the user wants and what the business needs, but it is not always so easy to differentiate between them. A business "need" is essentially the problem to be solved, the tangible results that are required, or the strategic goal to be achieved. A "want" is personal. It is something the stakeholder or user would like to see in terms of functionality. This often has little to do with (or can even be in conflict with) the business's needs.

To be clear, expectations and wants may look the same, but they are not. An expectation is really like a service level agreement for how the product will look, feel, and operate; how the service will be delivered; and how much communication will occur (and when) throughout the development process. A want is a personal need such as a desire to belong, to be important or recognized, and has nothing to do with the business need, but everything to do with ego.

Many business analysts (and stakeholders and project managers alike) confuse needs with wants. Often, this confusion shows up in requirements and development as poor requirement definition, unused features, and a flurry of subsequent change requests. Remember that "wants" are very personal and individual. These wants will change dramatically depending on the stakeholder or user group the business analyst talks to. Here is where the confusion between wants, needs, and expectations get compounded. Business analysts do not merely assume that needs and wants are one and the same; they also approach stakeholders and ask them what they want instead of what they need or why the problem really is a problem and what should happen instead.

An Example of Needs and Wants

The business *needs* to replace a legacy system, which uses too many manual work-arounds, simply to get the job done. The sponsor *needs* to see a 25% efficiency increase in the overall processing. The stakeholders *want* the system to also perform the functions of ten other systems. And finally, the users *need* the screens to be easy to use and *want* the system to perform the functions of another fifteen systems. The users *want* this additional functionality because they know those systems will not get replaced and, once this new system is in, they will be stuck with it.

In this example, the business analyst would consider each of these needs to be a part of the overall solution, and they would develop requirements for each of them. However, the wants are not necessarily feasible.

Because the wants in this example seem to be related to project outcomes, the analyst must assess the feasibility of each, identify risks and impacts and then raise those to the stakeholders and the sponsors in order to educate them. It is then the responsibility of the stakeholders and the sponsor to address priority and criticality of the wants and to determine if they should be included.

MANAGING TO THE EXCEPTION

According to communication and management thought leader Marty Clarke, managing to the exception is when one of two situations occurs. These are:

1. "Any time a person or group of people allow an idea to be shot down because it's not perfect, this is overt managing to the exception."
2. "Any time a manager lets a matter of small consequences dictate decisions on matters of large consequences, this is unconscious managing to the exception."[2]

Unfortunately, business analysts also sometimes manage to the exception. When eliciting requirements, the analyst must be decisive and guide the group to a consensus without simply acquiescing to the will of every person by saying, "sure we can do that," to every request. The analyst should be wary of simply including everything in the solution and the requirements because this is how "monster systems" are built. Monster systems are a nightmare to develop, test, implement, and use because they are often hobbled together and overly complicated versions of the old systems.

However, by focusing on the features and functionality that will meet the needs, the analyst defines the best solution and generates an accurate set of requirements to design and build it. Would stakeholders and user groups ask for things they "want" over what the business "needs?" Well, maybe. And, would they be dissatisfied if they did not get it? Actually, the answer here is probably "yes," and there are a couple of reasons that they would be dissatisfied when it is not delivered.

First, business stakeholders are often frustrated and looking for a greater sense of control over the work they perform. The systems they are using may be broken, or there may be a company history of not fixing problems with the system. So, people tend to get disengaged, frustrated, and often disenfranchised.

Second, the egos of the stakeholders often come into play, especially when there are strong personalities and opinions involved. There are times when the stakeholders may believe that the business analyst and the project team are there to serve them and to create their vision of the new solution, but these stakeholders do not necessarily go outside of their own department or division to find out what makes the most sense across the company. In this situation, it is not uncommon to see multiple projects across a single company designing, building, and implementing similar solutions (overlapping functionality) to resolve similar problems. Ultimately, this increases the total cost of ownership and introduces a whole host of other problems, which the stakeholders (and perhaps even the business analyst and project teams) are not aware of.

There is, however, a way to have a conversation with the stakeholders about their visions without having the business analyst proceed to work on all of the things individual stakeholders and users want. This still makes the stakeholders, sponsors, and user groups happy. Again, once the analyst understands the business *needs*, they start framing their questions around the *RESULTS* they would like to see or need to see. The business analyst would talk about how the new solution meets some of their personal needs for lower project frustration and discuss the logic behind not including certain things in the final solution. In doing so, the analyst will be able to help the business focus on its priorities, to understand how their work life will improve, and to show how the business will achieve its real goals.

As a result of this collaborative process, the business analyst will take the needs and the vision—as expressed in the overall strategic goals—and define the mission for the project to achieve the vision and meet the defined needs. Many project teams do not have a mission statement. Unfortunately, this means that the various sub-teams (development, test, business analysis, and architecture) are not necessarily all focused on achieving the same goal. This leaves a lot of room for interpretation, by the individual or sub-team, of the problem to be solved, and ultimately leads to discrepancies in what is defined, designed, developed, and implemented.

UNDERSTANDING BUSINESS ARCHITECTURE

Wikipedia defines business architecture as "the functional structure of an enterprise in terms of its business services and business information." It further elaborates on the importance of business architecture, stating: "By following the governance and articulating business information, the business architecture considers all internal and external actors to an enterprise (including its customers, suppliers, and regulators), to ensure that flow in and out of the enterprise are captured."[3] In basic terms, this means that the core "who, what, where" and "which" (according to the National Institutes of Health, or NIH, model shown in Figure 1.2) enables the business and technology teams to articulate the abilities

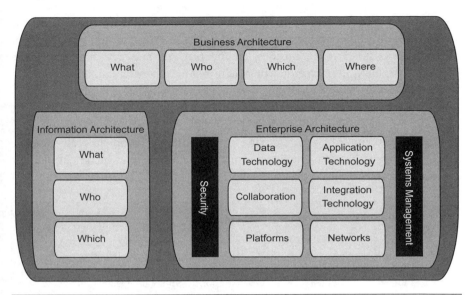

Figure 1.2   NIH business architecture model

of the company. Business architecture articulates these abilities in terms of what they do (products and services), for whom they work (customers), where the company provides those services or sells those products, and which data ties all of those elements and pieces together.

In terms of requirements, it is crucial for an analyst to know and understand the business architecture information as they become acclimated to the project (if they were not already familiar with this architecture). The knowledge of the architecture is a key contributor to developing the requirements themselves. In fact, this business architecture could be a part of the problem to be resolved. At the very least, the business problem exists within the context of the architecture. This means that each (problem and architecture) is impacted by the other and the solution.

First, the business architecture itself could be a part of the problem the project is intended to resolve. For example, the processes that formulate the basis for a key area of the business architecture may not be properly documented, managed, and governed. As a result, these processes may be circumvented by employees throughout the workflow. The business must address the broken processes in an effort to create efficiencies and to improve compliance. To address these issues, the business initiates a project. When this happens, the analyst must develop the requirements that will automate the processes, in order to address key problem areas and to establish and control workflow.

In the case where the problem exists within the context of the business architecture, the problem itself is outside of the architecture but interacts with it in some way. For example, when the source of the problem is external to the business, the problem may only be evident once the transaction, data flow, or process flow passes into the business architecture and begins to interact with it. While the problem itself may not be able to be directly rectified, it is important to address the impacts of the problem as they occur within the business architecture. This helps to both define the best solution and to further decompose this solution into its atomic requirements. While it can be argued that, as in a case where the problem only occurs during transactions, the problem really does lie within the business architecture and is merely the result of an incompatibility or an inconsistency, it is not necessarily the case.

Spam

In a small firm a number of years ago, it was obvious that there was no firewall in place because every employee got approximately one hundred spam e-mails per day. The information technology manager insisted that nothing could be done to correct the problem because the Internet services provider had consistent security issues.

In this case, the problem originated outside of the business architecture, but the impacts were apparent from within. In order to correct this problem, a project could have been initiated to establish increased security protocols on the company's servers.

Finally, business architecture can impact the solution being implemented. This is especially obvious when office politics and the "way things are done" interfere with the development and implementation of the solution.

They Make Us Money

A project to implement Windows XP Service Pack 2 was well underway within a large company a number of years ago. This particular company had acquired five other smaller companies and had been running them as divisions. One of those divisions was an investment firm.

During the implementation, it was discovered, through some routine joint application design sessions with the technology department, that the network for this division was unsecured. It was unsecured so that independent contract brokers could have access to the trading folders and to manage their client accounts. Further, it was decided that the company was choosing not to address the situation because the brokers earned money for the company.

In this situation, the brokers and the investment division represented pieces of the business architecture. This business architecture impacted both the information technology group and the specific project (and ultimately the solution) simply because the business architecture element was determined to take precedence over the security needs of the organization.

The analyst must be able to identify and articulate the problem to be resolved. When starting any project—especially when starting any requirements activities—it is crucial to start by digesting and learning the business architecture so that the best solution can be defined through the most accurate and complete requirements. This architecture information provides specific details about workflow across departments (what, how, and which data) and identifies the stakeholders and impacted groups (who). It is these details that identify who will need to be involved and how, but they also identify who the primary audience will be for change management activities. These details also identify the various integration points with the appropriate business units and how the work flows across those units. This information ensures that the analyst can understand and define the business rules and processes for a new solution, but most importantly, it allows the analyst to write more complete requirements for the final overall solution.

In terms of the solution, knowing and understanding the business architecture enables the analyst to identify the best solution, including features and functionality to meet the needs that have been identified (resolve the problem).

BENEFITS REALIZATION PLANNING

Benefits realization is the planning, delivery, and subsequent management of positive benefits across the life cycle of a particular product from a specific financial investment. Basically, this means that the business identifies specific benefits, plans how and when those benefits will be realized, and determines what those benefits mean to the company (i.e., how the benefits relate to or impact the top and bottom lines). Unfortunately, many businesses are not doing this type of planning, and I believe this stems from a gap that business analysts are in a unique position to close.

It is possible that at least some of this lack of benefits planning originates in mismatched expectations and a lack of experience on the business side. The business may be relying too heavily on the consultants to provide guidance about all of the planning and steps that must occur in order to be successful in delivering and implementing a solution. In many cases, the consultants arrive and are given a preselected solution, so there is an assumption made that the business must have already conducted this in the solution definition and selection stage (i.e., the business case). However, as Ahmad Al Mulla articulates in his article, "The Most Common Mistakes Made By CIO's," he cites both simply overlooking the big picture and inexperience as causes. One of the criticisms of technology made for the business is that chief information officers often miss the big business picture. "This eventually results in not being able to present the justifications for investments in a convincing business context. In other words, decisions must be ably supported with business reasoning rather than limiting them to technical enhancements or features."[4]

In either scenario, by not performing benefits realization planning, the business is unable to justify the investments in a convincing business context. It should be stressed here that a business case is by no means a benefits realization plan.

A business case simply justifies the expenditure from a cost-benefit perspective under three basic situations: doing nothing; doing something to fix the existing; and replacing "it" entirely. All of these prospective situations are assessed against the estimated costs of each, compared to a high level set of tangible results as well as a calculated ROI. In addition, the business case does not contain a timeline or baseline, with milestones to measure the achievement and realization of defined benefits. There are very few identified benchmarks in place to ensure that the full benefits are being realized, and there is no real total cost of ownership being assessed.

By contrast, a benefits realization plan lays out the estimated ROI; an estimated total cost of ownership; other anticipated benefits, such as increased revenue, decreased costs, or decreased service times; and milestones for the achievement of those benefits, returns, and costs against a timeline. This plan is used to assess and analyze the progress of the system in meeting those milestones and benefits.

One of the latest trends in information technology is to attempt to formalize benefits realization planning under the auspices of portfolio management (where groups of related products and/or projects are managed at a strategic level instead of merely at a tactical level). It is portfolio management that provides both the business and technology sides a greater ability to see the project or product within the context of the overall business and strategic objectives. Within the context of business analysis, benefits realization planning enables more full and complete specifications, which include requirements for business readiness and long-term business objectives and ensures alignment between all of the moving parts of the planned and implemented solution.

An estimated 40% of software features are never used.[5] This means that either information technology is over-engineering the solution or business analysts are simply not defining the right requirements before the project teams develop, test, and deliver it. Ironically, one of the reasons for the high volume of project challenges and failures, which are cited in The Standish Group's annual *CHAOS Report*, is the lack of user involvement. If there is a general lack of user involvement, it can be inferred that there can be no significant effort to conduct benefits realization planning because the planning process requires user involvement. Further, many project managers and sponsors would probably also add that the budget is a major factor in what can be delivered. The ability to budget all needs into a single project will impact the benefits realization plan, so it is even more critical to conduct this planning.

While budget and the lack of benefits realization planning does play a major role in the implementation of specific features and solutions, it can be argued that business and project teams have an inability to prioritize features and operate within budgetary confines because projects do not have enough user involvement.

Effectively, benefits realization plans contain benefit statements, baselines, and timelines for both tangible and intangible benefits. These include: financial, quality, service (customer experience), products development process, team competency, and emotional benefits.

There are seven basic steps I recommend for business analysts to follow when conducting benefits realization planning. These are:

1. Identify the problem or need
2. Identify the desired outcomes and results
3. Define the benchmarks
4. Determine priority
    a. Plan the new or changed capabilities
    b. Plan any additional investments
    c. Optimize the plan
    d. Complete a risk/impact assessment
5. Create the plan
    a. Design and obtain agreement
6. Communicate the plan to the team
7. Consistently review planned versus actual realizations

By now, the business analyst should have a solid understanding of how to identify the solution. This was achieved by identifying the two primary starting points for business analysis activities on projects and the different tactics the analyst must use when starting at each point. It is critical that business analysts take the time at the start of a project (or when they come onto a project midstream) to identify the solution and go through the steps identified in this chapter so that they can develop a solid understanding of the solution to be defined through the business analysis activities. This understanding is required, whether the business analyst was the person who actually defined the solution for the business and whether the analyst is the team lead, because it enables business analysis activities to be conducted successfully.

REFERENCES

1. Brule, Glen, 2011, *CRRSP Business Analysis Forum* on LinkedIn.
2. Clarke, Marty, 2005, "Leadership Land Mines! 8 Management Catastrophes and How to Avoid Them" (Martin Productions).
3. Object Management Group, Business Architecture Working Group, 2009.
4. Ahmad Al Mulla, "The Most Common Mistakes Made by CIOs" on LinkedIn.
5. Cook Enterprise Corporation, 2009, "Building Requirements Consensus" at http://www.building-requirements-consensus.com/.

Stakeholder Involvement and Management

THE SEINFELD APPROACH TO REQUIREMENTS

Software industry statistics clearly show there is an urgent need for dramatic and immediate improvement to the way that information technology develops its products. Only 32% of software and technical projects are successful,[1] and of this successful 32%, only 20% of the implemented features are used all the time, and 40% are never used at all![2]

First of all, this means that only 6.4% of all proposed features are actually implemented *and* used. Further, it also means that 12.8% of all proposed features are implemented but never used.

One of the more common reasons for these alarming statistics is poor quality of requirements. Both a lack of practice formalization and a holistic view of the causes and effects of failure have led to the shotgun approach to requirements development. This has been further compounded by the communication skills, both written and verbal, of those performing business analysis activities. In the past, there was little understanding and definition of what the business analyst did, so there was no way to assess skill levels and identify the needed competencies. While periodic successes with this approach have, in turn, led some business analysts to believe that the fault lies elsewhere in the process, the truth is that business analysts do play a role and cannot deflect the entire responsibility for these statistics onto other involved groups. Rather, analysts should be asking, "What is my role in this?" and "How can I contribute to making it better?"

In a nutshell, business analysts approach requirements in the same way that human beings approach any other communication or conversation: most communications and conversations are often one-sided and egocentric. The sitcom, *Seinfeld*, back in the nineties, was an excellent example of the impacts of multiple people carrying on conversations in the same room without either listening or being heard. This demonstrated how effective human beings really are at conversations and communication in general. Translate this into business analysis and requirements activities, and the result is ambiguity, miscommunication, and above all, missed requirements.

The solution to this communication problem is that business analysts need to learn to utilize such techniques as active listening and effective written communication. This will enable them to streamline the requirements process and follow the SMART ideology. The process itself must be Specific, Measureable, Achievable, Repeatable, and Timed.

Think of requirements as a recipe. If the recipe called for "some" flour and a "little bit" of sugar, and said to cook "until done," could anyone possibly make the product? No, unless this person also took the time to go through countless trial and error cycles and created a prototype in each cycle. The recipe must be exact in order to be successful. Business analysts would have better luck creating recipes and requirements in the same way that science experiments are conducted. Define the expected outcome, determine the specific measures to be used, and then verify the results.

While many people would argue that requirements are verified in testing (regardless of who does it and how), the fact is that testing verifies the product against the defined requirements. When the product differs or the requirements are wrong, then testers wonder whether they should be testing the product as it was developed or testing the product against the defined requirements. The truth is if the product defined in the requirements were the product actually developed, there would be nothing left to wonder (except maybe what they are going to do with all this free time they get from significantly fewer defects). Unfortunately, what happens is that requirements are poorly defined, validated, and communicated; then development occurs based on the misunderstood requirements; and finally, testing exposes the gaps between them and struggles to reconcile the differences.

It is one thing to define and document requirements, but this is really only a part of the task. Business analysts also have to verify the requirements before the project team starts the design and development process.

SETTING AND MANAGING EXPECTATIONS

In Chapter 1, one of the considerations for defining the needs, vision, and mission, was to be able to identify and to differentiate between needs, wants, and expectations. It further elaborated on how to frame conversations with the business in order to ensure that people were feeling good about the solution and the results they would see, while at the same time allowing the business analyst to focus on defining the solution and the requirements for this solution.

This was really the first step in setting and managing expectations. The truth is that while many business teams and people will come in with their own preconceived expectations, it is the job of the business analyst (and arguably, everyone on the project team) to level set those expectations. Ultimately those expectations must align with what is going to be achieved by the project team, the functionality the business will see in the solution, and the impacts this solution will have on the business.

The most critical ingredients to setting and managing expectations are: having the up-front and frank discussions to present the mission and reinforce it, keeping communication lines open, using the same language as the business, demonstrating consistency of messaging, demonstrating cohesiveness of the project team, conducting communications and escalation planning, and finally, planning for communication in crisis situations. By having the up-front and frank discussions and presenting the project mission to the business, the analyst clarifies that the mission is indeed in line with the business objectives and demonstrates that the various business groups have been heard. By providing this recognition of the business needs and wants through the mission, the business analyst instills confidence that they will be successful to the business groups. Having this confidence from the business is crucial to success.

Anatomy of a Failing Project: Week 1

Recently, a short discovery project was initiated to define the solution to replace a legacy claims system, which was so broken that the entire workflow had to be considered manual for the purposes of defining the workflow and estimating the final solution. After week one, the business was not sure about the vision and mission of the project. Further, they did not know how the work was going to progress, and what the results of the discovery process would be.

This was a key indicator that expectations had not been properly set. In fact, due to circumstances beyond the control of the business analyst, the first meetings they had with the business were the kick-off meetings, and the agenda was to define the objectives, vision, and mission of the discovery project.

Why are expectations not set at the start of a project? Sometimes they are overlooked, sometimes they are assumed, and quite honestly, sometimes the project team is merely inexperienced or does not want to be held accountable for not delivering in case they fail to meet expectations.

It is very important to maintain the set expectations by using open and consistent dialogues throughout the project. This is accomplished by having similar discussions throughout the project development life cycle in order to reinforce the mission and the overall objectives and to keep people focused. When this consistent messaging does not occur, the business begins to feel as though there is a lack of transparency from the project team, and begins to mistrust and lose confidence.

Anatomy of a Failing Project: Week 2

Now, recall the discovery project where everyone walked out of the kick-off meeting not knowing the objective, vision, and mission for the project. Throughout the subsequent weeks, there were many conversations between the business analyst and the business about what was going to be delivered, how it was going to be created, and what the solution should look like. This demonstrated that the initial expectations were not set, but also that the team was not working to maintain those expectations.

The next step in managing expectations is to keep communication lines open. As the foregoing discovery project story demonstrated, there was no way to maintain expectations, not only because they were not set but also because there was no consistent and ongoing dialogue with the business. Unfortunately, what starts to happen in this situation is that the lines of communication break down. As in Figure 2.1, the lower the confidence levels, the higher the mistrust; the higher the level of mistrust, the more rapidly communication breaks down.

Anatomy of a Failing Project: Week 3

As the discovery project progressed, the trust and confidence that the business had for the project team broke down, and it became a contentious environment to work in. Not only was there an increasing amount of gossip and conflict, but also little in the way of positive team communication.

It is important in communication to demonstrate that the original message was heard and understood. This is done by ensuring that all team members consistently use the same language as the business does when they are meeting and sharing information back to the business. Not only does this demonstrate that the business has been heard, but it also instills confidence as the project team makes progress, that the project is going to deliver on the initial expectations.

One of the hallmarks of escalating conflict is repetition in the message as an indicator that the person does not feel heard. What also happens when a person does not feel heard is that they begin to raise their voice. The quickest way to de-escalate any conflict situation is to recognize and clarify what the other person has said. By demonstrating listening and understanding about the person's issues,

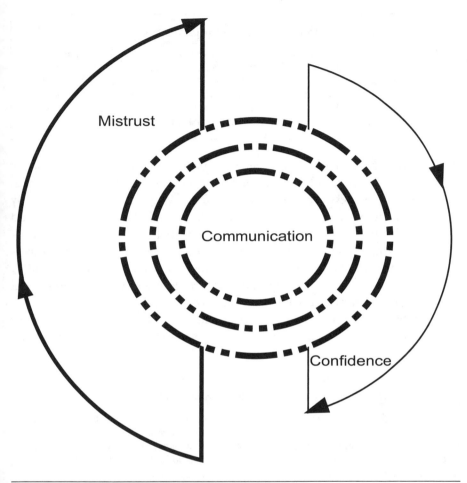

Figure 2.1 Mistrust and confidence cycle

the person begins to open up and share in the conversation. They also begin to calm down and trust the listener.

In the case of business and technology collaboration and the overall working relationship, it is critical to write and communicate with the business in the words they have used in meetings or their own documentation. For example, in a discussion about data storage, if the business calls it a data warehouse, the business analyst must also call it a data warehouse and nothing else. This not only eases any potential conflict and ambiguity, it also demonstrates listening, showing the business they will get something they need and something that fits into what they already have. Throwing around different and grander terminology (using $5 words) only serves to browbeat the business, put them on edge, and increase the need for more change management efforts later.

Anatomy of a Failing Project: Week 4

With little communication within the project team, divisions grew among the team members and as a result, the business did not get the same version of the objectives, work progress, and anticipated outcomes from the different team members. The team did not consistently communicate the same version of objectives, progress, and outcomes, nor did they use the same language that the business had used, which only compounded the frustration and confusion for the business about what was going on.

While it is important to use the same language as the business, it is equally important that all project team members are delivering the same message about the objectives, process, progress, and outcomes. When the team consistently delivers the same messages to the business, it not only builds confidence and trust, but also helps to maintain the expectations that have been set. By consistently delivering the same message, the project team demonstrates cohesiveness and buy-in to the solution. In other words, they believe in what they are doing, and they are all on the same page about how to do it and what the results will be. This leads directly to the business being more accepting of the project and the expected results. It also means that no one could possibly get to the end of a six-week discovery project without knowing what was done and what is going to be delivered.

Anatomy of a Failing Project: Week 5

One of the problems, which became evident as the project team and the relationship with the business collapsed, was that the project manager was telling one story while the business analyst, enterprise architect, and data architect, were giving another story about what was going on, and what the outcomes would be to the business.

First of all, this situation demonstrated a lack of confidence from the project manager in the resources they had selected to accomplish the work on the project, which did nothing to instill confidence in the business that this team was capable of delivering. Further, it created a deep divide between the team and the business. The project manager was consistently intervening between the team and the business in an effort to control the flow of information. Unfortunately, this made it impossible for the team to perform the necessary or appropriate activities and to create the needed results. Finally, one of the most critical areas to be established, in order to set and manage expectations, is a communication and escalation plan. For many projects, this occurs at the project level and falls under the purview of the project manager. However, it is recommended that business analysis team leads also develop a communication and escalation plan for the business analysis team, as this will provide needed guidance to the team about the expectations upon them for delivery and reporting progress.

Setting and managing expectations is a "two-way street," whether the business analyst is dealing with the business or with the rest of the analysis team. In the long run, the setting and management of expectations helps everyone because there is confidence, transparency, and comfort with what is going on around them. The communication and escalation plan is merely a way to ensure that everyone knows what to report and when, and how to raise issues so that they can be mitigated quickly, keeping both the momentum and project on track.

The communication plan identifies the types of communications that will be utilized to relay information to and from the business analysis team and to the stakeholders and the project team. Table 2.1 depicts a sample of the most common example of the communication matrix. This matrix forms the crux of the communication- and escalation-planning document. The table identifies not only the types of communications that will occur but also when they will transpire and how often. In addition, it identifies who will initiate the communication and who will receive it.

The escalation part of the plan maps out the escalation process throughout the project. It accounts for events that are to occur not only during standard business operating hours but also after business hours, during vacations, and during other major events that would not be considered a full-blown crisis. These events may include minor upgrades, patch rollouts, or moving the code into production (implementation).

Escalation planning not only outlines the process for escalation but also identifies who is to be contacted, under what circumstances, and how they are to be contacted. For example, when a manager is on vacation, the escalation plan will identify the temporary point of contact, identifying when and why they should be contacted. The plan should also list the contact details for each person. If the contact is listed as an after-hours point of contact, the plan should include a personal cell or home phone number.

One of the other areas to be considered in developing the communication and escalation plan, is how to communicate in crisis situations. On a project, a crisis could be anything from nasty letters being sent out to 60,000 customers over Christmas, to breaking a seemingly disparate system during deployment. The crisis plan on the other hand, typically identifies a central point of contact, the key messaging to be utilized during a crisis situation, how that messaging will be distributed, and who the primary audience is expected to be. In addition, on highly visible and complex projects, it is also important to locate a crisis control room. This control room will be utilized for the coordination of communication and crisis management that will need to be enacted. A crisis on a project could be anything from break and fix cycles, which occur after implementation, to poorly

Table 2.1 Sample communication matrix

Communication Type	Communication Purpose	Delivered By	Audience	Communication Format	Frequency
Status Updates	Inform of status of requirements activities	Analysis Team	Project Manager	E-mail, Use the Weekly Status Report Template	Weekly, Friday, 12:00 P.M.
Review	Discuss current progress and set weekly goals	Analysis Team	Analysis Team Lead	Meeting	Weekly, Monday, 9:00 A.M.
Status Reports	Inform of status of project activities	Analysis Team	Analysis Team Lead	E-mail, Report	Weekly, Monday, 12:00 P.M.
In Process Reviews (IPRs)	Inform of status of project activities, provide updates to work plan, and provide performance reports	Analysis Team	Analysis Team Lead, Project Manager	PowerPoint Presentation, Report	Work Stream Milestone Deliveries
Quality Review(s)	Provide objective review of projects to ensure adherence to policies, processes, standards, and plans	Analysis Team	Analysis Team Lead	Report, Meeting, 1-on-1	Work Stream Closure

managed communication, which causes excessive time to be diverted from the project's positive progress.

By having a crisis communication plan in place, should the call center, which was supposed to be on minimal staffing levels over the holidays, suddenly have to manage an influx of 60,000 angry phone calls, the business and the project team will know exactly what should be said, to whom, and how it should be phrased in order to ease the situation. In addition, there will be a plan in place that determines who the extra resources will be, when they should be in place, and at what locations they should appear to support the effort.

Anatomy of a Failing Project: Week 6

On that discovery project, it was clear early on that there was no communication plan in place. Granted, it was only a six-week project; however, there was no solid commitment to the business for progress reporting (status updates) and keeping the stakeholders in the loop about what was being worked on, by whom, and how much effort it was taking to get the job done.

For the project manager, this was not done for two reasons: so that if progress fell behind schedule, they would not really be accountable because they had committed very little in terms of milestones; and so that they would not overburden such a short project with additional documentation, which was seen as unnecessary when they could provide "water cooler" updates to the sponsor on an ad-hoc basis. Unfortunately, this led to diminished trust, confusion for the business, and "watermelon" reports (green on the outside but red on the inside).

The essence of setting and managing expectations is appropriate communication with the business at all levels and among the project team. Again, the key elements of communication for the purpose of managing expectations are: to have open discussions at the outset to present the mission, to continually remind people about it, to keep the communication lines open, to maintain the language of the business, to demonstrate consistency of messaging, to showcase cohesiveness among the project team, to conduct communications and escalation planning, and finally, to plan for communication in crisis situations.

BEYOND RACI: GETTING SPONSORS, BUSINESS OWNERS, AND USER GROUPS INVOLVED

The key to any successful project, business analysis, and requirements activity is to ensure that the business is involved. As previously mentioned, setting and managing expectations, and maintaining them throughout the project, is a critical part of the foundation for this involvement. However, for a variety of reasons, many of which are outside of the control and purview of the analyst or even the project team, it can be a challenge to rally the business, getting and keeping it involved. The results, when this challenge becomes too much for the business analyst or the project team to overcome, are that there are increased numbers of change requests, and schedule and budget overruns. Ultimately, this means that inappropriate software features are developed, implemented, and then never used.

RACI Matrix

One of the ways projects work to support the business and ensure it is actively involved throughout the project is to define the RACI matrix. As in Table 2.2, this matrix outlines who is "responsible" (R) for performing key tasks, who is "accountable" (A) for ensuring that it is completed, who "contributes" (C) to key tasks, and who is merely "informed" (I) of the results.

Why Some People Contribute and Others Don't

Outlining roles and expectations using the RACI matrix is no guarantee of involvement by the business. Again, many factors go far beyond the scope and control of the analyst and the project team. At any given time, there could be a number of inhibiting factors at work: office politics, family issues, personality issues, overloaded work schedules, feeling cheated by the company, a lack of buy-in about the need for any changes, leftover grudges from past mergers, and so on. The point is that the analyst still has a responsibility to get the business involved and contributing. This is more than simply marking names in a RACI matrix; it means working with people and all of their personal baggage to ensure that they contribute so that at the end of the day, the project is a success and develops a quality solution for the business.

Table 2.2   Sample RACI matrix

Name	Position	R	A	C	I
Sally Smith	Project Manager		X		
Antonio Johnson	Testing SME			X	
John Doe	Interface SME			X	
Jane Doe	Resource Center			X	
Barbara Davis	Business Analyst Team Lead	X			
Raj Smith	Forecasting/Bidding			X	
Vic Tran	Call Center CSR Mgmt		X		
Skippy Jackson	Call Center QA			X	
Allie Melon	Call Center IT				X

In addition to working with personalities, the analyst must also work to create opportunities for both the business as a whole and as individuals to contribute to the project. By creating opportunities to contribute, the foundation has been laid for this contribution to occur.

One of the main issues that arise on projects is the lack of contribution, which results from the assumption that merely inviting the business to meetings or asking questions in requirements sessions creates the opportunity to contribute. The core assumption is that the business will show up and contribute without active engagement. Many analysts then proceed to struggle with getting "time with the business" throughout the rest of the project. To a degree, this goes back to setting expectations and building a RACI matrix, but it also goes back to working with individual personalities.

On projects, creating opportunities to contribute takes the form of respecting people's time, asking for clear and specific inputs or feedback, and providing adequate time to contribute.

To respect people's time, their involvement must be limited to those things they need to be involved in. This means that when a meeting is held, the organizer must ensure that those who will actually be contributing are invited as "required" attendees and anyone else who needs to be informed is invited as an "information only" attendee. Let's face it: business stakeholders and users are not usually sitting around waiting for project meetings so they can come and grab some free coffee and pastries. They have more things to do in a day, especially when they also have to make time for projects, which do not include attending unnecessary meetings.

Why Opportunity Alone Does Not Equal Contribution and Increased Participation

Have you ever been to a party where a couple of people are sitting off on their own and not really interacting with anyone? They seem content, simply being in the same room with people who are laughing, dancing, and having fun. However, looks can be deceiving. Seeming to be content does not mean that they actually are, and it does not mean that they would prefer to sit there alone. In fact, it could be that they do not really feel welcome, they feel left out, or they do not know how to participate. Of course, it could also be that they were having a great time and interacting a lot before a certain other person arrived, or even that some event occurred that caused them to shut down.

In reality, people will participate or not for a variety of reasons, which may be completely out of the control of the business analyst. The opportunity to contribute to the conversation or input ideas may sometimes go over like a ton of bricks and will not necessarily get a person to contribute an idea or share a perspective.

In fact, if this kind of opportunity is presented in a meeting with heavy tension to participants who are already shut down, they may feel confronted and could shut down even further.

Types of Participation

There are several ways in which any business analyst can overcome personality conflicts and tension, and even reach those who are shut down. First and foremost, the analyst must identify the types of participation they expect from the business before planning each meeting. Once the business analyst knows the specific outcomes from a particular meeting, it should be fairly simple to identify who and how each person can help to create them. It is important to identify the specific decisions to be made, questions needing to be answered, and information needed from the session. Next, the analyst must be able to identify the different types of participants they will be meeting with. There are four primary types of participants that every business analyst should become acquainted with in order to be successful in their role. These are: the Active Participant, the Non-Participant, the Heckler, and the Hijacker.

Active Participant   Active participants come to the meeting prepared to contribute and get work done. They are not usually quiet and play well with everyone else in the room. Active participants have no problem contributing ideas and are open to discussing the ideas of others to explore the value of each idea. Active participants need to be in an environment where everyone is encouraged and welcomed to contribute. They are concerned with the ideas and the merit of those ideas and do not take criticism of their ideas personally. Active participants will, however, become frustrated when the goal of a meeting is not met, the work to be done in a meeting is not accomplished, or when attendees are not contributing or pushing others around. Active participants will lose respect for a meeting facilitator or manager who cannot manage the other personalities in the room because they want to work on and complete tasks.

The best way to manage active participants is to encourage them to contribute and take the lead from time to time. They are usually good mentors who are well respected, so having them lead sessions gives them the opportunity to work with the team and manage others, which allows them to demonstrate the collaborative and cohesive qualities of the team.

Non-Participant   Non-participants sit at the back of the room and do not contribute. They are shut down and do not want to be in the meeting; they would prefer to be back at their own desks, doing work they may feel will not be recognized. If non-participants are asked for input in a round-robin meeting, they will usually opt to pass and not say anything. Non-participants are people whose egos have been injured in some way at work, or even in the very meeting going at the moment. Perhaps they contributed ideas several times in the past and their ideas were ignored by the group. No matter what the scenario, the fact is that with a little bit of digging, the business analyst will uncover that they generally feel unimportant, disengaged, disempowered, and disenfranchised.

Active participants and non-participants are a good pairing for breakout sessions because active participants will acknowledge and explore the ideas of all others as well as their own and will help non-participants feel included and important.

Non-participants are easily managed by being given specific opportunities to contribute. The facilitator must ask them specific questions and, if they are going to be asked to contribute information at a meeting, the more notice given to them, the better prepared they will be. In this way they are more likely to contribute. Again, round-robin discussions do not work to get these people talking, but then again, neither do general questions to the group, because they will merely let someone else answer. The facilitator must address them by their names and ask the question, or for their opinion, if non-participant contributions are desired. Another way to get non-participants involved is to approach them, get into their physical space, and then pick up something in their reach because it gets their attention. Non-participants are often a million miles away until they hear their own names being called, or someone addresses them and makes eye contact. Again, the facilitator must personally ask non-participants to get involved in the meeting.

Heckler   Hecklers openly and loudly dispute ideas and attack credibility. They will attack and dispute the credibility of the facilitator, the manager, the solution, the company they work for, the department they work for, and even others in the room. Hecklers are deflecting attention away from themselves because they do not want anyone (including the facilitator) to know that they may not be able to understand or believe in what is going on. Of course, they could be bored, but an adept facilitator will quickly find out the situation.

Hecklers need clarity, guidance, and support. However, they need this to occur *outside* of the meeting. They are good at calling others out but do not want to be called out in return. In fact, calling the heckler out in a meeting may cause the heckler to shut down and become a non-participant. If bored, the behavior will cease once the facilitator has taken them aside and spoken to them about it. Hecklers need extra attention so the best way to manage them is to give them a personal demonstration, to coach and mentor them, and to ask them for questions while they are out of the group setting. Once hecklers have started feeling they understand and buy-in, or at least that the facilitator is a person they can trust, they will begin to contribute during meetings.

Hijacker Hijackers try to take control of the meeting. Typically, hijackers feel they—rather than the facilitator—should be at the front of the room, so they will make every effort to take control over the room by directing the conversation, steering the agenda off course, or having side conversations. It is simple: hijackers do not respect the authority of the manager or facilitator because they want to be in their shoes (role). They usually feel a degree of supremacy but could also be feeling jilted. Perhaps hijackers feel passed over in some way.

Hijackers need ego boosts, public recognition, and public attention. Ironically, most of all, they need to feel the facilitator is their ally. Remember that hijackers may be feeling passed over and want recognition, so if the facilitator gives it to them, they will respond positively. This recognition does not always work on the first few tries, but keep going and it should have a positive effect once trust has been established. The best way to manage hijackers is to give them some time to speak during the meeting, give them public praise, offer them time after the agenda items are covered to discuss their burning issues, ask them to facilitate when there are breakouts or the facilitator is going to be away, and set limits on off-topic discussions.

Hijackers want to be leaders but do not necessarily know how. Generally, others do not respect their leadership attempts, so by taking these steps, the facilitator is doing two things: giving the hijacker opportunities to lead and showing how to do it well.

Creating the Right Conditions and Environment Increases Participation

The first few meetings may not be very productive, despite best planning and efforts, until the four main participant types are identified. These participants may make it difficult to manage the room and to accomplish any significant amount of productive work. This being said, there are ways in which the business analyst, acting in the role of a facilitator, can set up and structure a meeting so that people are encouraged both to attend and to contribute. There are a few key things any analyst can do to increase the likelihood of success in getting stakeholders, business users, and technology teams involved and actively participating. These things include: conducting routine informational activities, creating input funnels, and running input activities.

Informational Activities

There is not a human being alive who does not need to feel important in some fashion. This need is so strongly ingrained that it means a person's job and how well they do this job becomes a part of personal identity. Further, when something new comes along, and this something new is perceived to threaten this identity, the person needs to have an opportunity to provide input into the new "situation," to have concerns heard and questions answered. Projects that do not take these factors into consideration are doomed, even if those projects were to implement a solution made of gold because the business will revolt against both project and solution.

Successful projects must start with a high-level set of activities, which provides information to the executives and works to get those executives involved. Once this involvement has started, the project team will begin to disperse information to the business and customer communities in order to make them aware that changes are coming.

While informational activities at this point are not heavily intensive processes, these activities do enable people to prepare themselves mentally and emotionally for impending change. These informational activities must be able to provide basic information about what the business and its customers can expect, who will be impacted, and how. In addition, this early information should provide details about the expected participation from each impacted group, where they can find more information, and how to contact the project team with any questions, comments, or feedback.

Input Funnels

A well-planned project contains both outgoing and incoming communication channels. Those channels include combinations of informational and input activities (outgoing channel) and feedback funnels (incoming channel). While the outgoing channels disperse information from the project team, the incoming channels provide opportunities for the business and its customers to respond and provide their thoughts and inputs for the new solution. In this way, the business is provided with very specific and direct methods and opportunities to contribute throughout the project. These channels and funnels help the business and its customers to feel both heard and important, and ultimately increases their participation levels. However, it is not enough to hear what is being said, it is also critical that the inputs are then incorporated into the solution where and when appropriate.

Many project teams make two common mistakes when they plan change management strategies. Often, they will only consider the cost of the communication channels, or they only consider outgoing channels. When the project team only considers the cost of communication channels, this mistake is made purely as a cost reduction measure. When cost is the primary factor in selecting and implementing communication channels, the key message communicated to the business community is that their input is not valued. Unfortunately, these project teams limit the ability for two-way communication and reduce the ability for the business community to participate. In addition, the channels themselves are one-sided because they are intended to disperse information out from the project. When the project team mistakenly considers only outgoing channels, this mistake is made under the assumption that requirements elicitation will be the opportunity for stakeholders and users to provide input. Unfortunately, this is often a false assumption because many requirements are often generated by working with subject matter experts. All too often, those subject matter experts make assumptions based on their own personal experiences or opinions and without consultation with other business team members.

By waiting for the requirements activities to begin, it is far too late in the project to begin collaboration. This timing factor makes the buy-in process much harder and actually increases the likelihood of changes to scope. Additionally, business analysts must know and understand the role of a facilitator before any of the real activity can begin because it will be one of their primary responsibilities throughout the project. The role of the analyst is to facilitate collaboration between the business and the technology teams in order to generate the specific requirements necessary to build the solution that enables business strategy. This means that, in any given meeting or session they will conduct, the analyst is not an attendee and not a participant. The analyst is the facilitator, leader, and the driver of the session (even when the project manager or sponsor is in the requirements sessions). In this way, the analyst is wholly responsible for ensuring that the objectives are met, the work is achieved, and the needed results are delivered.

Facilitator's Role

A facilitator is any person who defines and controls the process of a public event, such as speeches, presentations, learning venues, conferences, and workshops. Within the project, it is the primary role of the business analyst to act as the facilitator during requirements sessions. It is critical for the analyst to direct the meeting, from the concept and the invitation to the action items and meeting minutes, and to manage the flow of information and contributions throughout the entire process. An unskilled facilitator will allow participants to control the meeting. Further, the unskilled facilitator will not establish adequate times to accomplish tasks and will need to hold more meetings to achieve the same results as a skilled facilitator.

A skilled facilitator will lead and drive the meeting to meet all of its objectives. This person will ensure that adequate follow-up actions or breakout sessions occur, and the result of each component is appropriately reported and logged. In addition, a skilled facilitator defines the process by determining the agenda (including breaks and seating), layout, venue, conference lines, virtual meeting sites, presentation format (such as slides, handouts, whiteboard), sending invites, assigning tasks, and eliciting participation from all members of the group or audience. The specific tasks a facilitator is responsible for include:

a. *Process Control*:   the facilitator controls the process by which the work is accomplished and the results are obtained. As the facilitator, the business analyst is responsible for ensuring that the requirements sessions follow a controlled flow, time is well managed, and the goals of the meeting are achieved.

b. *Neutral Attitude*:   the facilitator is not in a position to judge the validity or accuracy of information provided by the participants, nor to take sides in a difference of opinion, but rather the facilitator is responsible for ensuring that differences are escalated to those who do have the authority to validate information or make decisions about the best course of action. Does this mean that the analyst cannot ask questions? No, it does not mean this at all. It simply means that the analyst is responsible for ensuring that the sessions are led, and the participants actually contribute and accomplish the work or goals of the session.

However, the business analyst is still the business analyst and must adapt the role of the facilitator to suit the needs of the business. Ordinarily, the facilitator is neutral. The business analyst as the facilitator, on the other hand, will not seem neutral because they bring advice to the table and help to define solutions. This means that the analyst should be neutral but not passive. Neutral means not taking sides, but passive means not intervening or bringing advice to the table. Passivity is unrealistic, considering that business analysts are hired for their experience and skills. This alone suggests that the analyst has to bring something to the table to support the client. In this case, neutral means doing what is in the best interests of the business without favoring departments, egos, and personal preferences. It means not managing to the exception.

c. *Meeting Structure*:   the facilitator is responsible for setting up the physical and virtual locations for the meeting. The business analyst must fill this role of the facilitator by understanding and appreciating the power dynamics, the political structure, and the interpersonal relationships of the group. Far too many people, business analysts included, think that meeting structure is really all about booking a room and scheduling a conference call or web meeting. However, it is far more important than some simple housekeeping. Success in requirements elicitation requires that the business analyst is aware of group dynamics, interpersonal conflict, levels of buy-in, as well as physical and emotional comfort. Remember that people will not contribute, at least not very well, if they are not comfortable and have to worry about conflict, overheating, fatigue, hunger, thirst, or having to go to the bathroom at a critical point in the conversation.

d. *Meeting Setup (atmosphere and seating)*:   the facilitator is responsible for setting up and distributing the meeting agenda and invitations to all participants, and also for ensuring that the meeting space selected is appropriate for the size and comfort of the group. I once inadvertently held a meeting in the first room available. Unfortunately, there were fifteen people in a room built for only four! It was a short meeting and the group did not get a lot accomplished.

e. *Invites*:   the facilitator is responsible for ensuring that all people with a stake or need to be involved in the discussion are invited to participate in the meeting. The business analyst is probably going to be responsible for creating and distributing the meeting invitations. This means that the analyst has to understand how to write an effective invitation and e-mail, which will prompt the recipient to act.

   One of the biggest time consumers in projects is the time it takes to get responses from the business on meetings, e-mails, and requirements feedback. Many people do not seem to realize that it is not necessarily the recipient's fault. In fact, many people do not seem to realize that the way in which an e-mail is written can be the motivating factor in whether the e-mail is read and responded to in a timely manner. There is an exact structure (as described in Appendix A, Writing Effective E-mails) that an e-mail or invitation should utilize to be successful in eliciting a quick response from the reader.

f. *Agenda*:   the facilitator is responsible for ensuring that an accurate and appropriate agenda is prepared and distributed before the meeting so participants have the opportunity to prepare for it, or even to opt out if they feel they do not need to attend the meeting. If their input is required, then it is the responsibility of the business analyst—as the leader and driver of the requirements process—to ensure they are made aware of the importance of their input during the session and to reschedule if necessary.

g. *Defining Participation Levels*:   the facilitator is responsible for ensuring that all participants are aware of the level of participation that will be expected of the group, and, if there are any specific contributions required by particular groups or individuals, that they are made aware and are given adequate time to prepare. In this case, the business analyst as the facilitator must not only define the levels of participation from each stakeholder, user group, or team but also let everyone know what those levels are. The business analyst must set an expectation for the group and guide the process of the requirements elicitation from start to finish. It can be daunting and intimidating to start a new project, especially when the team is new. While the situation may be similar, there will always be some new aspects, perspectives, factors, and elements.

When people are put into a new situation, they are automatically on the defensive and emotional barriers are up. These barriers restrict the ability of the participants and the project team to process information rapidly. The familiarity, comfort, and confidence of knowing what is expected and when, will help to ease tensions and lower mental barriers. Establishing the expectations for participation levels throughout the process boosts confidence and enables everyone to process information.

It is important to remember that "buy-in" means "believe-in." There is a lot of energy and excitement in starting a new project. The best way to build buy-in from people is to get them excited, get them involved, and show them how to carry it forward. When people are informed that change is coming, it is new and exciting, yet scary at the same time. The business analyst must anticipate and overcome people's fears of being replaced or phased out or suddenly being seen as incompetent by collaborating with them.

Many times, the business analyst can identify a single person or a group of people who are obstinate and have blocked the way for change and the new solution because they do not believe in it. By working with the nonbelievers, understanding their needs and finding ways to meet those needs without changing the project course, the project will find a new champion. The loudest and most outspoken adversary can become the project's biggest champion. When this occurs, this person supports the initiative and it becomes a grassroots movement. The project is beyond buy-in when this happens because whether others like the champion no longer matters. What does matter is that people know how the champion behaves. When the champion is happy, that happiness is shared with everyone, and their lives become infinitely better. On the other hand, when the champion is angry, everyone is going to know about it, and the champion will prevent others from participating by seeking support for their divisive position.

Knowing and understanding the types of participants is crucial to being successful at this tipping point. It is equally important for the analyst to know and understand that the facilitator role is more than merely analyzing data and mediating between the business and technology teams. The full role of the business analyst is to set up a customer-centric experience on the project and to view each of these groups as part of the customer base. This fundamental change in attitude will ensure that both teams are encouraged to collaborate in an innovative space and in an environment where everyone's contributions are valued and important to the success of the project.

Understanding the role of the facilitator, as outlined here, is really only the start of the positive project experience. In order to be successful at encouraging buy-in, the business analyst must be a good ambassador, mediator, customer service representative, host, salesperson, marketing expert, and negotiator. The elements and combinations of each of these roles help to increase buy-in and to move both the business and technology teams past the roles and responsibilities (RACI) matrix into the role of an actively engaged participant.

REFERENCES

1. The Standish Group, 2011, *CHAOS Manifesto*.
2. Cook Enterprise Corporation, 2009, "Building Requirements Consensus".

SECTION II

REQUIREMENTS PLANNING AND MANAGEMENT

## 3

The Evolution of Requirements on a Project

Requirements evolution is really the shaping of the requirements through the life cycle depicted in Figure 3.1. This life cycle consists of a set of stages and tasks that generate specific artifacts and deliverables, which contribute to both the successive stages and the final set of validated and accepted requirements.

In general, requirements evolve out of scope to the high level, further evolve to the mid level, and finally down to the low level. This process is much the same for any other refining process that exists today, such as distilling liquids, sifting solids, and refining oil. By going through each of these processes, as illustrated in Figure 3.2, the larger and cruder elements are refined into more granular products with a variety of applications. The application itself varies, dependent on the type of refining and the minerals extracted.

The reason for an evolutionary process in requirements is simple: in software and systems development, the project team is transitioning from a vague concept to a fully formed and detailed solution. This transition requires an evolutionary process. Requirements start as a vague intangible concept and evolve to become a clearly articulated set of specifications. In order for this to happen, some of the commonly used industry tools, techniques, and templates have been adapted. They have been enhanced and quantified, given priority and context, and new tools and techniques have been added.

INHERENT PROJECT RISKS TO REQUIREMENTS

There are inherent flaws and risks to requirements, which come from both project inception and the individual resources that support this project during its

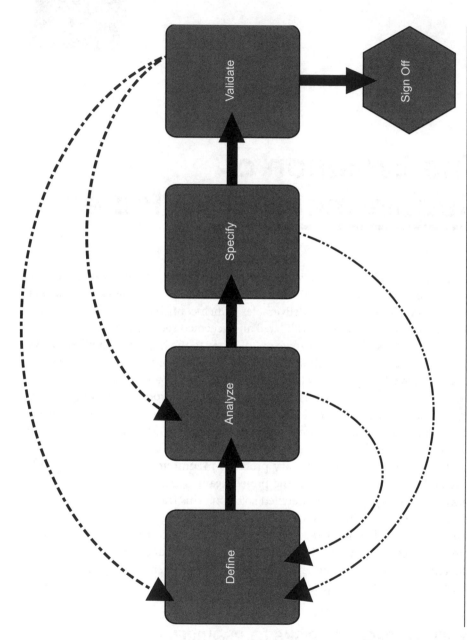

Figure 3.1 Requirements development life cycle

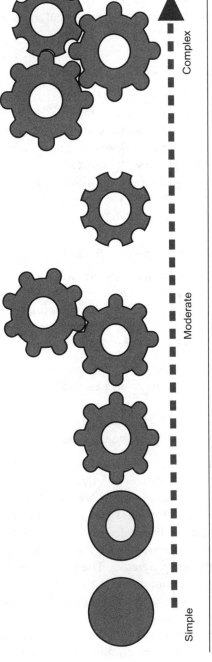

Figure 3.2   Structural development over time

life cycle. Make no mistake; both are actually risks. Each of these two elements of risk adds considerations for requirements activities. These must be managed appropriately and kept in check in order for the final solution to be well designed, built, and implemented.

Risks from Project Inception

The problems encountered during requirements activities are just as deterministic as the product defects that result from poor requirement quality. By the time requirements activities are underway, there have been so many other little things—which have often been overlooked, assumed, or done improperly—that poor requirements are a natural result. Unfortunately, much of the inherent risk comes from incomplete project inception, which leads to issues down the road. Risks from project inception include incomplete strategic planning of business architecture and mismanaging expectations.

Strategic Planning of Business Architecture

A big part of planning, which prevents runaway projects, is determining the details of the solution and context. Those are how the project team will deliver the best solution for the business problem, and how this solution fits into the surrounding business architecture. For many companies, this context has an impact on the outcomes of the project. These include:

- The alignment of the solution to strategic goals
- The decision about how to resolve a specific problem or to evolve the business
- Making the crucial build or buy decision
- Determining high-level resourcing decisions for the project

Strategy is really about figuring out how to connect all of the impacted systems and components, tools, and resources in a dynamic way to achieve both corporate and project goals. At the same time, it is about determining what will make all those parts move in unison towards those goals. Unfortunately, many projects include little consideration during project inception. For business architecture it is assumed that these considerations were either made by the business already or will be made as the project progresses. The problem is that this assumption is often incorrect. When the business makes the decision to initiate a project, the architecture and the full extent of the solution, within the context of that architecture, is often limited at best.

When the decisions are left to the project team, this expectation is not always communicated. On top of this, many project teams and analysts are taking the lead for solutions from the business. Unless resources on the project team ask specific questions, key information about business architecture may get over-looked. Finally, many businesses may look at both the problem and the solution with "tunnel vision." They may consider factors outside of their own purview as unnecessary and overlook critical elements of business architecture. This can have adverse impacts on the requirements development and deliverables. The key to solving this issue is to ask the right questions of the business about architecture. This is the crucial aspect that will enable the project to fill in all information gaps and generate a complete solution, which will fit seamlessly into the business architecture around it.

Managing Expectations

Far too often, project managers and business analysts do not set and manage realistic expectations with the business sponsors, stakeholders, and user community during project inception because those often impact scope and sales issues. Unfortunately, the lack of expectation setting and management can lead to the creation of an incomplete understanding of the solution and ultimately, to incomplete requirements.

The lack of expectation setting and management leads to incomplete solutions because this key component is actually an indicator of the health of the communication lines, which exist between the project and the business teams. Without communication, there is a lack of user involvement, the wrong things get built, the project has excessive changes and scope creep, requirements are poorly developed, and the whole thing is delivered beyond the schedule. The process of setting and managing expectations is more of an underpinning or a foundation upon which the project is built. With great management of expectations, the team works as a cohesive unit and is capable of recovering from a diversity of project issues and challenges. The key to setting and managing expectations is communication. Communication enables the team members, sponsors, and stakeholders to convey their expectations at the outset (setting expectations). And communication enables the team members to address changes to those expectations and negotiate those changes with the sponsors and stakeholders.

While expectations are set at the start of the project, they are managed throughout the life cycle. As such, there are many factors impacting them, and many nuances and intricacies involved in managing them. These factors include:

- Having open discussions at all stages and under all conditions and circumstances during the project
- Keeping communication lines open throughout the project life cycle
- Conducting communications and escalation planning
- Planning for communication in crisis situations
- Using the same language as the business when communicating with the business team

- Demonstrating consistency of messaging across all project team members
- Reinforcing the project mission throughout the life of the project
- Demonstrating cohesiveness of the project team

Together, these factors contribute to the creation of a solid architecture. This communication architecture enables incoming and outgoing communication across the project and supports the establishment and ongoing management of expectations.

Communication Architecture

Communication architecture is a formal framework for all project communications. Since effective communication is the foundation of a successful project, it cannot be left to chance or an ad-hoc activity. This architecture encompasses change strategy, communication infrastructure, outgoing channels, and input funnels.

- Change Strategy
  - Top-down, Bottom-up
  - Inform, Involve, Evolve, Maintain, Observe
- Communication Infrastructure
  - RACI
  - Communication Plans
  - Project Reports and Logs
- Channels
  - Website and Project E-mail Informational Activities
- Funnels
  - Website and Project E-mail
  - Point of Contact

Risks from Project Resources

Project resources bring their individual personalities, needs, and baggage to the project. All of these must be managed in order to support requirements development activities and to reduce the risks of inherent issues creeping in to the point that there are serious quality issues. These resources potentially bring one or more of the following to the project: ego, an inability to clear their own personal beliefs and biases, an inability to separate opinions and assumptions from fact, and scotoma (a blind spot, or an inability to perceive something within the field of vision).

There are many times when ego plays a significant role in the ability or perceived ability to complete a task. In the case of requirements, ego is a barrier to those business analysts who either come in to "save the day," or those who come in believing they are not good enough to complete the task. In either case, ego becomes a communication barrier and prevents the business analyst from being able to get the requirements done with any real degree of accuracy.

It is important that business analysts clear away both their own perspectives and those of others who will contribute to requirements. Unfortunately, many people have an inability to clear their personal beliefs and biases and get to the heart of the business need. This is especially obvious when subject matter experts are involved and make assumptions based on their own experiences.

In addition, many people have an inability to separate opinions and assumptions from fact. When it comes to requirements, business analysts can literally run around working on the wrong requirements and end up making change after change to the requirements.

Finally, the inability to perceive is called "scotoma." It is actually a medical term which refers to the naturally occurring blind spot which every person has. In requirements, it occurs when the analyst has been working too closely with the content and the subject matter to see the real issues within the documentation. The analysts who review their own work, and do not seek multiple peer reviews, will miss details because their brain fills in the gaps of what should be there when in fact, it is missing.

5 CRITICAL REQUIREMENTS STEPS THAT GET MISSED: WHAT BUSINESS ANALYSTS ARE NOT DOING (CONSISTENTLY)

The lack of professional formalization means that there is no single tried and true set of business analysis best practices. There are indeed some commonalities, but without a standardized set of best practices, there can be no real assurances that enough has been done to ensure that business analysts have captured the right requirements for the right products. This is exactly where the information technology industry gets statistics illustrating that only 20% of features are used all the time and a whopping 40%[1] are never used!

Over the years, I have worked with, mentored, trained, managed, and interviewed hundreds of business analysts. Nearly all of those analysts miss critical steps in requirements. Understand one thing: this does not make these people bad analysts, or even unqualified. They are missing these steps because business analysis is still a collective practice and not a formal profession with standardized tasks, metrics, and tools. Many of the analysts are simply borrowing tasks, tools, and techniques from other development areas.

So what tasks could your business analysts be doing that can change all this? These tasks are research, gap assessment (vs. gap analysis), ambiguity management, requirements validation (including facilitated sign off), and quantifying the effectiveness of requirements activities. More importantly, how can the project manager or the business teams determine whether business analysts are not doing these tasks? It is important to examine each of these to understand what they are, what they look like, and what the direct quantifiable results are. Then, and only then, will it become obvious whether these tasks are necessary and are actually being done.

Research

There are a lot of components which need to be understood in order to build accurate requirements, and only one is user input. Going to the users should be the *LAST* task a business analyst (BA) does in requirements elicitation, yet when interviewed, the single-most common answer to how requirements are determined is "I go to the user." The fact is that there is already a lot of detailed information contained within the project documentation, existing application, and environment documentation. The BA needs to study this and understand the business problem, goals and objectives of the project, scope, the environment the new application will reside in, and how it will interact with and impact other applications within this environment. By the time the user gets involved, the BA should already have a draft of context diagrams, workflow, requirements management framework, peripheral gap analysis, a high-level draft of requirements, and a plan of how they will accomplish the work on this particular project.

Gap Assessment (Versus Gap Analysis)

Gap analysis is a small sliver of the work comprising gap assessment. Where gap analysis studies individual gaps on a given project, gap assessment takes it further and manages gaps in the same way that issues would be managed, assesses risk and impacts, and draws links between gaps and the areas impacted by those gaps.

Ambiguity Management

Ambiguities are a common part of life. How many people in the nineties could program the clock on their VCR? Ever read the directions for putting together a new toy or piece of furniture? Have you ever had a conversation with someone and gotten the wrong message? All too often, people speak before listening and listen without hearing. In writing, the human brain completes thoughts that are not there. In general, people also forget to look at things from other perspectives and get feedback from others. In requirements, this creates ambiguities. Evidence suggests that ambiguities are the leading cause of low project success rates, missed functionality, and unused features. In a nutshell, ambiguities are risks!

The only way to ensure that ambiguities in requirements are exposed and addressed is to devise a solid process for ambiguity management, which is comprised of a set of clear steps dealing with each of the reasons that ambiguities exist. Further, ambiguities as risks must be managed in the same way risks are managed throughout the project to reduce their occurrence and mitigate their impacts and effects.

Requirements Validation

During the nearly one thousand interviews I have conducted, I always ask the candidate how they validate their requirements. Again, 99% say they "go back to the user" and are completely stumped when I ask them what they do when the user doesn't know. There are lots of proven tools and techniques available to support validation. The analyst usually just doesn't know how to apply them to achieve the best result. They cannot see the value of using them when they are not sure how the tools work and how they will impact the quality of their work.

Egos aside, candid conversations with business analysts tell me that almost everyone is struggling and learning by the seat of their pants. This is a direct result of the lack of practice formalization. Very few analysts will come out and say it. Every person wants to have a level of job satisfaction, to feel competent, and to be seen as competent by colleagues. This means that business analysts are not necessarily going to ask for help and advice on which tools and techniques should be applied in order to validate requirements.

Evidence of this problem can be found by looking at the numbers of projects with scope creep within a given organization, users and stakeholders who are complaining about missed functionality, and development time or break-and-fix cycles that exceed estimates by wide margins. If these patterns exist, the best advice is to work with the business analysts to educate them and to bring in a formal methodology that encompasses specific validation techniques. Any methodology without a specific set of validation steps is incomplete and not worth the money spent on it.

Facilitated Sign Off

Thorough requirements validation requires something that some business analysts are actually doing but not necessarily doing well: facilitated sign off. Countless business analysts (including the most senior) have asked me how to get stakeholders to read the requirements document. Despite all of the unknowns, this is one of the most significant challenges facing an analyst.

I have to share that I assume stakeholders will not read the requirements document, even though I give them time to do so. I also assume that those who do read it generally do not read it thoroughly enough to understand the details.

This is okay. I do not need them to. I do need the stakeholders to understand the functionality represented by the requirements. The best way for them to really understand the functionality is to participate in a facilitated walk-through of the functionality and sign off on it.

Think about it this way, if an average person who is not mechanically inclined wants to buy a car, do they need to know every little detail of how the car works in order to buy it and make effective use of it? No. The same is true for software. Business users need to know the features and main functions and not necessarily every tiny little detail about how the application delivers its results. They only care that it delivers results and when it does not, there is someone who can fix it.

Quantifying Effectiveness of Requirements Activities

The final step business analysts miss is the compilation of quantifiable metrics associated with requirements, which illustrate the effectiveness of the requirements activities. It is one thing to recognize that requirements need to change and improve and completely another to target exact areas for improvement and understand the degree of improvement needed. There is a great deal of controversy on requirements improvement and traceability, but there does not seem to be much discussion about how to measure and quantify those improvements.

In order to understand what aspects of requirements need to be improved, the organization must approach improvements in the same way they would approach any other process improvement project. They must determine the kinds of metrics that can be gathered for requirements; then they must analyze those metrics to determine the starting point (the benchmark). Setting a benchmark allows organizations to illustrate the current situation and to determine both the levels and the types of professional development the business analysts will need. Establishing future milestones provides organizations with the ability to perform a comparison at various points during the improvement process and supports the analysis of the effectiveness of the improvement efforts. In order to do this, it is important to understand the tools that will provide the metrics to be used for assessing requirements. Some requirements tools will come with built-in metrics for traceability, but a single tool, which will compile a full set of standardized metrics to support a true requirements improvement initiative, has yet to be developed.

By comparing the metrics of individual projects across the organization, specific opportunities for improvement will become apparent. In fact, this understanding of organizational requirements effectiveness will enable targeted areas of development for the business analyst team, improved collaboration between project teams, and support organizational agility.

All in all, missing any of these critical steps not only increases the risks the project will face but also will add to development and maintenance costs and decrease the overall return on investment (ROI). On top of this, the team will not have the detailed information required to support focused requirements remediation efforts. All of this translates into a reduced ability to support the core business of the organization, as well as an inability to remain innovative.

THE GOLDEN RULES OF REQUIREMENTS

In order for business analysts to achieve real success with requirements, they must follow a basic set of "Golden Rules." These simple rules are as follows:

1. Identify and define objectives
   - Objectives explain WHY the system is being created
   - Qualified objectives identify the desired goals, or ROI, and specify constraints
2. Verify the requirements against the objectives
   - Validates accurate scope for high-level requirements
   - Assures consistent focus for application rules
   - Provides critical management tools for scope change decisions
   - Repeats verification for every iteration of the requirements and design documents
3. Apply scenarios and use cases against the requirements
   - Mapping the requirements flow in a simple set of scenarios and use cases could expose gaps or ambiguities in requirements
     - A scenario represents the possible actions performed by the user, by asking: "what if the user does . . ."
     - A use case represents a task-oriented user view of the system and a full end-to-end unit of work, where the user could be a person or another system that interacts with this system but is outside the scope of this system
   - Applying scenarios and use cases assures valid usability and that requirements are detailed enough to handle all possible use cases and scenarios
4. Perform a consistency review
   - If one person wrote it with a specific intent, and another person reads it differently, it is ambiguous.

ATTRIBUTES OF GREAT REQUIREMENTS

While requirements may differ from analyst to analyst and project to project, there are specific key attributes, which demonstrate a high degree of requirement quality. As illustrated in Figure 3.3, these attributes are:

- Unambiguous—Understood by the reader as intended by the writer
- Deterministic—An outcome that can be predicted because all of its causes are either known or are the same as those of a previous event
- Concise—Uses exacting words to relay a very specific message
- Explicit—Uses specific, detailed descriptions to relay the exact message
- Consistently Worded—Utilizes consistent terminology and framework

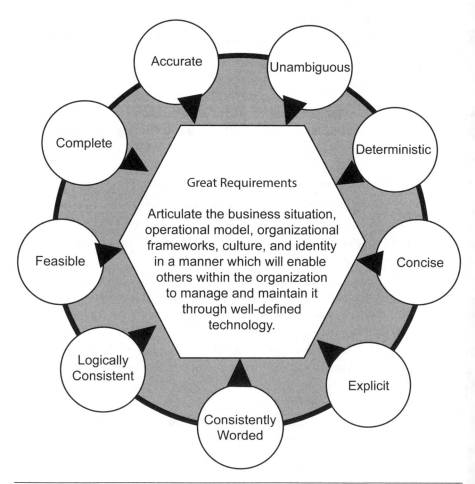

Figure 3.3 Attributes of great requirements

- Logically Consistent—Follows a logically consistent path from start to finish with no missing data or elements at any point throughout the process
- Feasible—Practical, that is doable, from business, technical, and testing perspectives
- Complete—Contains enough detail to convey what the new system must do under all circumstances
- Accurate—Identifies the *right* requirements to meet business goals, drivers, and needs

REFERENCE

1. Cook Enterprise Corporation, 2009, "Building Requirements Consensus," at http://www.building-requirements-consensus.com/.

## 4

Requirements Management and Development Strategy

A requirements management strategy is the plan for managing the requirements process from an administrative and operational perspective. This means advance planning of the management and administrative tasks for the requirements portion of the project, preparing the tools and templates to be applied in administrative tasks, performing the requirements evolution process, and managing all of these aspects in order to achieve precise and predictable results.

One of the critical things to be aware of is that requirements management, as it is currently considered and practiced among the general technology industry, is the control of the requirements outputs. This leads to the simple collection of requirements in a central place and the ability to trace them across the project life cycle. In fact, requirements management is the control of the process utilized to create the requirements and not the requirements themselves.

Management is the measurement, control, and monitoring of any given process which yields specific results. Management is utilized as a means of ensuring that the results are predictable by applying a stable process with carefully measured steps and stages. In requirements management, the difference is this: controlling the resulting documents limits the ability to predict the quality and to refine those results as needed; and controlling the process allows the identification of trends, issues, and risks, and exposes needed changes to achieve the desired outcomes.

As illustrated in Figure 4.1, the core of the requirements management strategy is a set of four elements: Plan, Prepare, Evolve, and Manage. Each of these elements provides a set of activities that must occur throughout the requirements

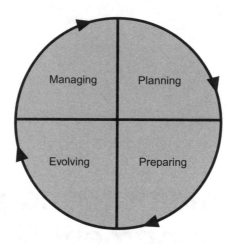

Figure 4.1 Elements of management strategy

phase of the project. Before putting pen to paper and documenting the requirements, the business analyst team must undertake the planning and preparation tasks. This ensures that requirements management, document management, process controls, and reporting are not ad-hoc activities as the business analysis team gets down to defining requirements and having to make frequent changes throughout the process of documentation. Instead, planning ensures that the full requirements process, including tools and management, are well planned. It also ensures that those specific tools are ready to be used and populated as the team progresses.

It is all too common for business analysts to find themselves in the position on a project where part, or almost all of the way through, they discover serious issues resulting from a lack of preplanning. These issues must be fixed—at significant cost and impact to the timeline of the project. The following story is an example of a real project in which this became apparent at the end:

Naming Convention Overflow

You have just joined a business process modeling effort for the final three months of a two-year project. Throughout the course of the project, the team diligently documented the workflow of five subsidiary companies, plus the parent company. After you have been working for two months, the project manager announces that she wants to extend your contract by another six months because she has just realized that the thousands of process flows, which have been mapped, have duplicate names and that this must be corrected before the flows can be catalogued into the process library held in the CARD Map application.

This example is not isolated. In fact, here is another example from another project with far more serious implications and issues:

> ### Requirements Management Mayhem
>
> You have just joined a project that has been ongoing for two years. The day before you joined, the team had finally implemented the first phase of the project, and things blew up. Not only had the system, which was built and implemented, crashed, but all of the other systems, with which it interacted, crashed as well. As a result, finance had to perform monthly billing manually for well over 60,000 customers. It is now up to the whole project team to figure out what went wrong and fix it.
>
> Reading the requirements document is pointless: it is over 200 pages of ambiguity, there is no traceability, there is no tool for requirements management, and no one on the team seems to know what has been built and implemented. In attempting to find answers, the business analyst team lead must spend countless hours and days picking through two years worth of team e-mails.

DEVELOPING A REQUIREMENTS MANAGEMENT STRATEGY

Every project is unique and must have its own requirements management strategy, although it is preferable that some of these strategic elements are created and managed from an operational perspective at the enterprise level. For example, tools should be determined and managed at the enterprise level and specific project records should be managed at the project level. This both ensures consistency of tools and usage and enables customization of the tools to meet individual project needs without reinventing the wheel every time. Where the organization does not subscribe to a specific requirements management toolset, the business analysis team will have to establish the tools they intend to utilize for the project. Either way, developing a requirements management strategy is critical to the success and streamlining of all management tasks later on.

In order to develop a requirements management strategy, the business analysis team must answer these basic questions:

- What tools are available to manage requirements?
- Do the existing tools meet the needs of this project?
- What customizations are needed to meet the needs of the project?
- How will requirements, gaps, and ambiguities be managed throughout the project?
- What other tools are needed for this project?
- Do these tools already exist?
- What is the quickest way to create tools, which are needed but do not yet exist?

- What naming conventions exist for the company?
- How will these naming conventions be applied to this project?
- What naming conventions need to be created prior to the project?
- How will the documents for the project be stored?
- Is there a separate project portal?
- Does the portal need to be customized?
- What do the deliverables and artifacts look like?
- Are the templates developed and ready to be populated?
- What are the key deliverables required for this project?
- What tasks and activities will add value to the requirements, given the time frame and project objectives?
- What tasks, within the requirements life cycle, can be applied within the particular project time frame?

Planning Requirements Management

Would a construction company build a house without a plan? Of course it wouldn't. Why, then, do so many business analysts start requirements activities without the proper tools in place, or even a solid plan for managing them? Requirements management is the pragmatic establishment of housekeeping items related to the administrative managing of requirements throughout the life cycle of the project. This activity must be planned in order to create a streamlined process, which is not developed on the fly, so the business analyst team can put their heads down and perform the requirements activities. Some of the primary considerations for planning requirements activities are who, what, where, when, and how (as depicted in Figure 4.2). It is by taking these factors into consideration that planning activities can be fully effective.

The specific planning tasks for the requirements activities begin with stakeholder identification, as described in Chapter 1, and development of the RACI matrix according to the guidelines discussed in Chapter 2. Next, the business analysis communication and escalation plan must be developed. Once these have been established, it will be important to determine how long it will take to complete the requirements tasks and to identify the approach.

Identifying the stakeholders and determining the roles and responsibilities in the RACI matrix have been clearly laid out in Chapter 2. This task is no minor feat and requires special considerations for success. It has been separated into its own chapter in order to cover the specific challenges and nuances in enough detail to prepare the business analyst for success. The next planning task is to develop the business analysis communication and escalation plan. While the project should have a project-level plan in place, it is imperative that a specific plan is established in order to manage communications between the business analysis team and the stakeholders. This plan is also discussed in detail

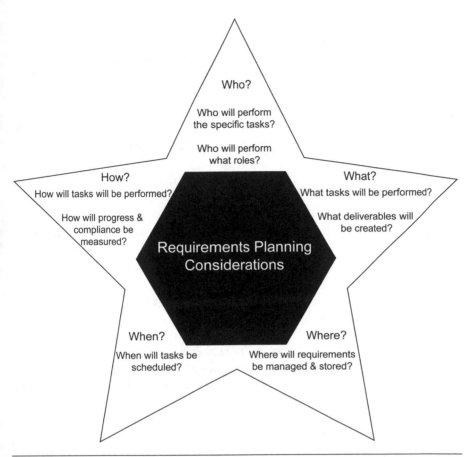

Figure 4.2   Requirements planning considerations

in Chapter 2. With these plans and matrices in place, the next task is to identify what work needs to be accomplished on the project. This requirements work breakdown will form the basis for the estimation activities.

In order to identify the requirements tasks, the analyst must follow the process for deriving the high-level requirements out of scope, as described in Chapter 5, and it can be based on the analyst's previous experience with the development of requirements for that area. By utilizing the estimation process that is outlined in Chapter 5, the analyst can determine how long it will take to complete the requirements development tasks.

Once this requirements breakdown has been completed, the work must be allocated across the business analysis team (assuming there is one). Obviously, where there is only a single analyst, it is this person who will accomplish the requirements tasks according to the developed plan. The next recommended task in planning requirements is to determine the approach, traceability tools, and process. The approach outlined in this book is designed to be applied across multiple methodologies by simply adapting the tasks and the deliverables to suit the needs and the context of the project. By describing the context for each of the inputs, tasks, deliverables, and artifacts, the business analyst can determine which of these will add value to the end result, depending on the particular project and its unique constraints. One of the significant factors in the selection of approach is the stakeholder needs analysis—understanding stakeholder expectations. In this way, the analyst can determine how to deliver within the parameters of those expectations.

The next recommended task in planning requirements is to determine the traceability tools and process. Traceability tools should be synonymous with requirements management tools; however, that is not always the case. Traceability tools tend to be focused on quality assurance. Requirements management tools, while still maturing, tend to be focused on collection. Ideally, the requirements management tool provides change control, version control, traceability, and benchmarking. Often, the selection of a specific project is outside the purview of the business analysis team, as the tool has been selected at the operational level. However, where there is no requirements management or traceability tool in place, it is incumbent upon the business analysis team to establish a common framework for the capture of traceability elements.

By planning the management tools and templates for the entire requirements phase, the team will achieve more consistent results and predictable quality, be able to create ongoing activity reports, and be more generally productive. Without planned management activities, managing requirements becomes a full time task, consuming valuable time from the business analysts. These same analysts could be spending time on requirements activities, instead of finding documents, shuffling folders, locating and fixing templates, redoing naming conventions, and picking through e-mails to find requirements and changes or corrections to requirements.

Preparing for Requirements Management

The next item the analyst must understand and plan out is how data, rules, requirements, and processes will be managed throughout the project. This will save a tremendous amount of time later and will enable the analyst to focus on the real tasks once the elicitation has begun. Preparing for requirements management is setting up the tools and templates that have been identified as necessary for the project. Tasks included in this are: defining and documenting naming conventions, determining file locations, customizing tools and portals for the project, and setting up templates for documentation.

In addition, the following key planning and preparation tasks must be completed as the entry criteria to the elicitation stage:

- Establishment or customization of the requirements management tool
- Establishment of the framework for the document repository (file structure, or portal solution)
- Establishment of document naming conventions, which align to internal standards and/or industry best practices
- Establishment or customization of the gap management tool
- Establishment or customization of the ambiguity management tool
- Reviewing or creation of the communication plan
- Breakdown of requirements work into function sets or feature groups
- Ability to ensure adequate resource coverage and time allotment for the work to be conducted
- Scheduling of the requirements tasks and major milestone meetings

Once this setup has been completed, a complete deliverable index must be made readily available to the business analyst team in a central repository. This provides quick reference (when people forget) and enables rapid ramp-up in the event that new team members are brought on. A final note: in the event that the team is suddenly no longer available to provide the information necessary to the new team, it becomes readily available so they can just walk in and pick up where the others left off. It will reduce the amount of hand-holding and tribal knowledge.

REQUIREMENTS MANAGEMENT ACTIVITIES

As illustrated in Figure 4.3, requirements management is the task of managing requirements throughout the life cycle of the project. They are managed in much the same way that assets and data are managed. There are numerous reasons to manage requirements in a like manner to assets and data. These are: frequent changes throughout the project, the need to map project deliverables back to business drivers, the need to ensure business problems are resolved, and the need to ensure that the project meets its targets. Ultimately, all of these add up to spending time and money wisely and making the business more effective at all aspects of its services—this is to say, increasing revenue without increasing costs.

Requirements are subject to change throughout the definition phase as well as throughout the project life cycle. Analysts must recognize that requirements change during two key phases: evolution of the requirements (from elicitation of concepts to specific defined requirements in the final document) and correction (after finalization and sign off has occurred). During evolution, the requirements are incomplete and evolving. They are not really changing, so much as taking shape. Once they have been finalized, requirements primarily change as a result of the need to correct them. They will need to be corrected if they are inaccurate, incomplete, or infeasible.

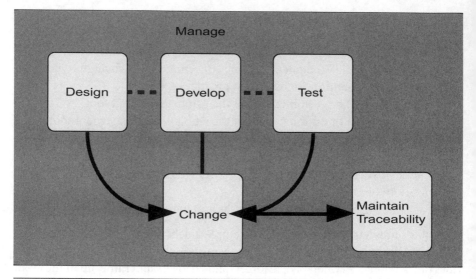

Figure 4.3 Requirements management

While many business analysts will argue that there are times when the requirements change as a result of the business "changing its mind," this is a far less likely scenario when the defined requirements are correct, complete, and accurate, and when those requirements are aligned to the business needs instead of the whims of individual stakeholders. This is where and why it is critical to avoid managing to the exception.

The process outlined in this book is not only a strategy for conducting the due diligence of requirements up front in the development life cycle while the cost is low but also a strategy for the evolution of the requirements to ensure that, once they have been finalized and signed off, they are less likely to be incorrect, inaccurate, incomplete, or infeasible. It is important to note that it is not simply what business analysts are doing in requirements definition, but when, why, how, and how well.

As previously mentioned, one of the important elements of planning business analysis activities is planning the approach. It is crucial to understand and to plan when key business analysis tasks will be performed, as well as when and how the levels of effort will change as the project progresses.

Requirements are managed in order to ensure that they evolve from concept to product, and—if they need to be corrected later on—that the business analysts will have the ability to make changes to all of the impacted requirements, deliverables, and artifacts quickly. This ensures consistent documentation and maintains knowledge points for all team members so that, at the end of the project, the correct product is created and delivered—despite any changes made throughout the project life cycle.

TOOLS AND TECHNIQUES

There are many tools that will enable effective requirements management. These tools range from simple spreadsheets to databases, to complex requirements, to project and program management suites. Whatever tool the analyst selects or has available, requirements management is an absolute *MUST*! If there is no tool available, the business analyst must create one (I recommend an Excel Spreadsheet in this instance).

Traceability

Traceability is the ability to trace requirements backward and forward (bidirectionally) through the development process, as a means to ensure coverage and that the end product meets the business objectives, drivers, and goals. This means that anyone on the project team should be able to trace from project scope item to requirement, to design and development item, and on to testing. Traceability is necessary to answer questions about what is being developed, what has been delivered, and whether it functions as expected or needed. Traceability can be as simple as creating a requirements index or catalogue that references scope items, requirements, ambiguity log items, design and development documentation, test procedures, test cases, and defect logs. All items in the traceability log, tool, or index must be referenced by name or other unique identifier.

The management of requirements through traceability enables the team to compile benchmarks and metrics for all the associated elements and requirements and to discover key issues within performance areas or processes. In addition, requirements management will provide a high-level comparison of the overall need and requested functionality against the delivered functionality. It also provides a purview of the issues that arose along the way. This specific log provides a crucial perspective on the project life cycle trends, localized risks, and critical areas for improvement. Managing traceability is a team effort. It requires input and collaboration from the business, business analyst, and design, development, and test teams to be truly effective.

Change Control

As previously mentioned, requirements either evolve throughout the requirements definition process or are changed after it has been completed. When requirements change after the definition process or requirements stage has been completed, the analyst must utilize an established change control process, such as the one depicted in Figure 4.4. This process is typically standardized and mandated by the organization. It may be initiated by the project manager after the analyst has notified them of the need to make changes to the requirements. It is, however, important for the analyst to gather as much information as possible about the changes, the impacts, and the associated costs of those changes, and then to provide this information to the project manager for escalation to the business stakeholders and project sponsors.

Changes to requirements must be released after running through a miniature requirements cycle, and should be documented as an addendum to the original requirements, as this will avoid any confusion among the project or business team members. In this addendum, the changes must be well documented, along with the rationale for those changes. When requirements change, there is a direct impact to the numbering convention that has been utilized. This impact occurs either when the convention has been applied too early in the requirements development process or when the requirements have been finalized and signed off. To manage changes to requirements, these conventions must be considered.

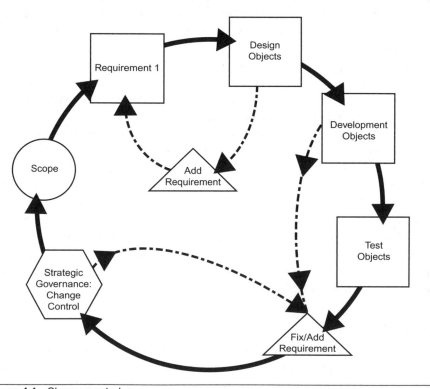

Figure 4.4   Change control

As such, specific guidance has been outlined, under the heading of naming and numbering conventions, later on in this chapter.

Ambiguity Management

Ambiguities are a common part of life. For example, the directions for putting together a new toy or piece of furniture are about as ambiguous as documents get. It is no wonder that so few people actually read them. All too often, people speak before listening and listen without hearing. In writing, the human brain completes gaps in thoughts (especially when the reader is also the writer), and in general, people forget to look at things from other perspectives and to get feedback from others in order to see from another perspective. In requirements, this creates ambiguities. It has been suggested that ambiguities in requirements are one of the leading causes of low project success rates, missed functionality and unused software features. In a nutshell, ambiguities are big risks!

The only way to ensure that ambiguities in requirements are exposed, and subsequently addressed, is to put a solid process for ambiguity management into place. This process must be comprised of a set of clear steps, which addresses each reason for ambiguities, as a means of identifying them during the requirements evolution process and preventing those ambiguities from making it into the final requirements document. Further, ambiguities must be managed in the same way that risks are managed throughout the project in order to reduce their occurrence and to mitigate their impacts and effects.

Ambiguity Log

An ambiguity log is a log or index for managing and tracking comments and questions about specific requirements as the business analysis team begins the ambiguity review process. Far too often, questions and concerns are sent to individual analysts via e-mail. The problem with this is that they can get lost in the shuffle, ignored or forgotten, misplaced during resource replacements, and metrics cannot be tracked against them to measure the quality of requirements.

All inputs to the ambiguity log include a unique ambiguity number, ambiguity name, name of the document containing the ambiguity, page and location within the document, name of the specific requirement containing the ambiguity, description of the ambiguity, as well as the type of ambiguity (fixes requirements, improves the domain knowledge, or will improve testing). The main purpose of the ambiguity log is twofold: to track and manage ambiguities in requirements so that they are addressed and corrected and to allow quantifiable metrics to be collected for an understanding of the effectiveness of requirements activities and the quality of requirements.

Contributors to the ambiguity log include: business analysts, designers, architects, project manager, developers, business users, stakeholders, and the test team. This ensures that: BEFORE the requirements are signed off, everyone has a chance to ask for and get clarity on specific requirements; the entire team fully understands them; and the requirements are polished to remove any trace of logical inconsistency, inconsistent wording, other inaccuracies, or vague information. While there are no true document dependencies on this log, validation of requirements cannot occur in an efficient and effective manner without it.

Sign Off

The ambiguity log is not signed off as a whole item until all of the open ambiguities have been addressed. Individual ambiguities are signed off by the person or resources who initiated them in order to ensure that they understand the response and feel as if their concerns have been addressed.

Requirements Management Tool

While requirements management tools are only beginning to gain credibility within the industry, it is important to understand how they fit into the architecture of business analysis. Requirements management tools provide storage and linkages between requirements, rules, and processes and typically connect with testing software to increase the ability and efficiency of traceability across the life cycle of the project.

In the absence of a formal application, any requirements management tool could be considered an established system for collecting requirements and establishing traceability across all related requirements components. Regardless of the tool or system being utilized, it will require customization for each project during the planning and preparation stage to ensure that appropriate metrics can be extracted once requirements activities have begun and for accurate measurement and monitoring of performance and progress.

Preparing the requirements management tool requires setting up the project workspace, granting access to the business analysis team, ensuring adequate storage capacity for all deliverables and artifacts, and, in some cases, establishing naming conventions for those deliverables and artifacts. It also requires ensuring that other teams will have the access and the deliverables they need for their work downstream.

Naming and Numbering Conventions

This book recommends three naming conventions: business process models, business rules, and requirements. These naming conventions can be utilized when the company does not have an existing naming convention for these document types in order to make the management of the documents and artifacts easier for the business analyst and to avoid unnecessary confusion with the business and technology teams as the documents evolve from draft to approved versions. The basic principles of the naming convention are:

- Name it once
- Make it easily searchable
- Make it easy for the reader to locate specific content
- Never reuse the name or number.

Numbering Business Process Models

The first naming convention deals with how to label and name business process models. In the case of process models, the naming convention begins with the document name. "P," before the process name and sub-name, denotes that the content is a business process document.

In the example process name in Table 4.1, "2010-03-22 P42 Sales: Calculate Retail Tax v1.3," the file name is comprised of: the date of creation; "P" for process and the digit representing the process number; the primary process name, "Sales;" the subprocess name, "Calculate Retail Tax;" and the version and revision "v1.3." The subprocess denotes that the process "Sales" contains other processes as part of the end-to-end sales workflow. If there were no subprocesses for the "Sales" process, the name would be: "2010-03-22 P42 Sales v1.3."

Process Control

It is best practice to ensure that all processes are listed in an itemized inventory, or process catalogue, to be utilized as a quick point of reference. In order to facilitate this inventory, the numbering must be assigned statically. The number must not be changed once assigned to the process, and it must not be duplicated in other processes within the same project. This means there will only ever be a single process, 42, for any given project, and this process subject will never change—despite changes to the steps, controls, actors, and systems.

For example, if process 42 for a shopping cart maps the end-to-end process for the calculation of provincial or state taxes for online retail purchases, then process 42 will always deal with the calculation of provincial or state taxes for online retail purchases and could never be changed to registering as a new user.

Table 4.1   Business process naming convention

2010-03-22 P42 Sales: Calculate Retail Tax v1.3					
Date	Document Type	Document Number	Process Name	Subprocess Name	Version Number
2010-03-22	P	42	Sales	Calculate Retail Tax	V1.3

Numbering Business Rules

The second naming convention deals with how to label and name your business rules. While this convention is similar to that for process numbering, the difference lies in the manner in which the document type has been denoted within the name itself.

Document Name

In the example business rule document name as seen in Table 4.2: "2010-03-22 B1 Webstore v1.3," the file name is comprised of the date, "B" for business rules, a numeric code for the rules document number, the primary feature or function name "Webstore," and the version and revision "v1.3". Depending on the number of business rules, the document will contain either all of the business rules for a single component of the overall project or all of the business rules identified for the entire project.

As with process documentation, business rule numbering must be assigned statically, and the number must not be changed once it has been assigned to the rule. The assigned numbers must not be duplicated for other rules, even if they are listed in other documents within the same project. This means that, if there are four business rules documents for a given project, there will only ever be a single rule 36 for this project, the rule will only exist in one of the rules documents, and this rule will never change through editing.

For example, if business rule 36 for a shopping cart states that provincial or state taxes for the purchase must be calculated on the total purchase amount before discounts are applied and that taxes must be calculated using the state/provincial tax rate for the customer's delivery address, then the business rule would always deal with calculating the sales tax based on the delivery address and could never be changed to "Sales discounts cannot be applied to sales lower than $5."

Each rule must be preceded by "B," which denotes that it is a business rule so that in reference, it will never be confused with requirements or process numbering referrals. For example, if a business rule 36 for a shopping cart states that provincial or state taxes for the purchase will be calculated on the total purchase

Table 4.2 Business rule naming convention

2010-03-22 B1 Webstore v1.3				
Date	Document Type	Document Number	Function/Feature Name	Version Number
2010-03-22	B	1	Webstore	V1.3

amount before discounts are applied using the state/provincial tax rate for the customer's delivery address, then the business rule would be written as:

B36.0 Calculate the total sale on the selected items in the web user's shopping cart.

B36.1 Calculate the sales tax based on the state/provincial tax rate for the state or province selected by the web user as part of the delivery address.

B36.2 Calculate the sales tax before any discounts are applied to the subtotal sale amount.

B36.3 Calculate the total sale amount by adding the subtotal, the delivery charge, and taxes, and then subtracting any applicable discounts.

If there is a requirement that references this particular business rule, the requirement would be written as:

1.0 Website must include shopping cart functionality for web users to purchase products and services online.

1.1 Web user must be able to select their state and/or province from a selector.

1.2 Display the "Amount Due" to the web user.

Applicable Business Rules: B36

Numbering Requirements

The third naming convention deals with how to label and name requirements. Requirements are primarily referenced by name, not number, within the documentation until just before the document is finalized for sign off. References may include numbers, but be aware that fixing this can become a time-consuming exercise when changes and numbering have been finalized.

Document Name

"RQ" before the requirement name denotes the document contains requirements. If there are excessive numbers of requirements, it is acceptable to list business and technical, or functional and nonfunctional, requirements in separate documents. In doing so, this creates one standard that denotes the content as: "BRQ," "TRQ," "FRQ," or "NFRQ." Ensure that each requirement and rule references every other document so that all documents are considered during design, development, and testing.

For the example in Table 4.3: "2010-03-22 RQ Website Re-architecture v1.3," the file name is comprised of the date, "RQ" for Requirements, the project name "Website Re-architecture," and the version and the revision "v1.3." Again, when it comes to numbering individual requirements, regardless of whether multiple documents are created to contain all of the requirements or are all listed in a

Table 4.3 Requirements naming convention

2010-03-22 RQ Website Re-architecture v1.3			
Date	**Document Type**	**Project Name**	**Version Number**
2010-03-22	RQ	Webstore	V1.3

single document, the numbering must be assigned statically. The number must not be changed once assigned to the requirement and must not be duplicated in other documents within the same project. For example, requirements would be written as:

1.0 Website must include shopping cart functionality for web users to purchase products and services online.
1.1 Web user must be able to select their state and/or province from a selector.
1.2 Display the "Amount Due" to the web user.

Applicable Business Rules: B36

2.0 Website must include account management functionality for web users to manage accounts online.
2.1 Web user must be able to Save, Edit, and Delete Account Information.
2.2 Display the "Account Information" to the web user.
2.3 Provide web user with the ability to Edit and Save or Cancel changes to account information.
2.4 Provide web user with the ability to Delete an account when account user is logged in.

Account Information is limited to:

- Name
- E-mail Address
- Phone Number
- Shipping Address
- Billing Address
- Credit Card Number
- Credit Card Expiration Date
- Credit Card Security Code
- Applicable Business Rules: B10, B29, B45

Impacts of Changes to Requirements

Where a requirement has changed wording or additional sub-elements added, the original requirement must be included in the addendum entry, followed by the bolded and capitalized text: "**CHANGED TO:**" and the new text for the requirement must immediately follow. Where new sub-elements are being added, the original requirement must be included in the addendum entry, followed by the original sub-elements and the bolded and capitalized text: "**ADDITIONAL ELEMENTS ADDED:**" and the new sub-elements must immediately follow, with consecutive numbering. In other words, if the last element was 2.4, the new element will be 2.5. Where new requirements are being added, numbers may be assigned as a continuation from the last numbered requirement in the requirements document. This means that if the last requirement in the original document was number 200, the next requirement will become number 201. It is recommended that requirements, added in an Addendum or as the result of a change control process, be specifically identified as such. NEVER RENUMBER THE REQUIREMENTS IN A SIGNED OFF DOCUMENT.

5

Establishing Metrics and Benchmarks

The purposes of establishing metrics and benchmarks within business analysis are: to provide a set of quantifiable measures that can be used to increase the accuracy of project estimation; assess return on investment for the business analysis activities; assess continuous improvements initiatives; improve tactical project governance; assess the performance of resources, projects, and techniques against the benchmarks; and to create tangible performance improvement scales and goals.

It is one thing to recognize that requirements need to change and improve, but then completely another to target exact areas for improvement and understand the degree of improvement needed in each area. There is significant controversy over requirements improvement and traceability, as well as over measuring the effectiveness of requirements and assessing the overall performance of business analysts. However, there does not seem to be much discussion about how to measure and quantify those improvements, how to measure their effectiveness, or even how to assess the performance of individual resources. In order to identify and fully understand the aspects of requirements needing to be improved, business analysts have to utilize the same approach they would for any other improvement project: determine the kinds of metrics that can be gathered and then analyze those metrics to determine and understand the starting point or the benchmark.

Setting a benchmark helps in several ways. First, the benchmark helps to illustrate the current situation. Next, it helps to red flag areas for improvements to techniques and methods. Further, it supports the determination of performance management efforts. The benchmark illustrates the current situation by setting the first set of quantifiable metrics associated with the activities. It is ground zero, against which all future activities will be measured. In addition, the benchmark helps to locate obvious red flag areas. Very often, people have a "gut feel" that something is wrong; however, it can be difficult to pinpoint exactly what it is or to identify the real source of the problem. By establishing a set of metrics and calculations, we can take an impartial look at the situation and understand exactly what is going on. This impartial look will focus efforts for improvements to techniques and methods, and enable the development of key performance indicators (KPIs) and a roadmap for progress. The benchmark also supports performance management by helping to identify the levels and types of professional development needed to make the necessary improvements. Further, the establishment of milestones enables the comparison of progress at various points during the improvement process, and determines the effectiveness of the efforts. These milestones, and the timing for reaching them, can be indicators of how well things are progressing.

In terms of requirements and business analysis, there are several attributes to be measured and subsequently compared, added, subtracted, multiplied and divided. The measurement of these attributes paints a picture of how well the requirements activities are being performed on any given project.

Any company or business analyst undertaking a process improvement effort should consider beginning with the volume of the deliverables completed on any given project. As a part of this volume of deliverables, there is a subset of attributes that can be measured. This subset includes the volume of requirements that were documented and the volume of ambiguities found (this will be discussed in great detail in Chapter 9, "Validation"). Later, during the testing stage, the volumes of failed test cases attributed directly to the quality of requirements can be tabulated and measured. Further, once the solution has been moved into production or has been deployed, the volume of defects can be measured. Finally, the last attribute that can be measured is the volume of requirements actually implemented. What is implemented represents a statement, in and of itself, on the effectiveness and quality of the requirements. Regardless of why something was not implemented, when the development process reaches the implementation stage, the final requirements (changed and approved included) should represent the accurate picture of everything that was developed and implemented. When this does not happen, it essentially means that the requirement could either not be developed or implemented for some reason. If a requirement cannot be developed or implemented, the requirements should be changed by utilizing the change control process. In this way, the requirements should always align with what is developed and implemented. If it does not, there is a problem somewhere in the process, even if that problem is simply an issue of compliance to the process.

The identified attributes, when combined, start to paint a picture of the quality of the requirements being produced and the activities employed to produce them. The quality of requirements is low when the ambiguity fails tests and the defect rates are high. Therefore, quality is easily derived by tabulating the defect, fail, and ambiguity rates as a single total. Further, since higher defect, ambiguity, and fail rates also impact the time it takes to complete requirements, it is important to calculate the time to fix each of these attributes. In addition to collecting the time to fix these attributes, it is important to calculate the time it takes to actually develop the requirements. It is equally important to understand that the time to develop requirements is compounded by the time to fix the issues, and that the quality of the requirements is decreased by the number of issues to be addressed.

As discussed, many organizations can identify the volumes of requirements written on each project. It is imperative, then, that requirements be properly documented and numbered. It is a hindrance to the requirements improvement process when requirements are buried in e-mails, executive summaries, and various sections of related documents. The volume of requirements becomes more precise when the business analysts have followed a standard documentation, numbering, and classification protocol. Quite simply, the volume of requirements is a count of the documented low-level requirements.

During a typical life cycle, the next quantifiable metric that can be compiled is the volume of requirements actually designed, built, and implemented by the design and development teams. Ideally, this information is available in the requirements management tool and traces back to the high-level requirements and project scope. If it does not trace back, or there is no management tool in place, it may take some wrangling and negotiating to survey the designers and developers to extract this information from them. Again, many organizations and teams are able to compile the volumes of passed and failed tests. While this will give the business analysts an approximate, overall sense of how well they did during requirements, it is simply not detailed enough to help to understand the trends in requirements and to identify the specific activities for improvement.

So what do all these pockets of metrics mean? How can business analysts compile, analyze, and compare them to understand how effective the organization's requirements practices are? To start with, the volume of requirements divided by the time it takes to complete each step can be calculated in order to understand how many requirements are completed in a given day. Compiling ambiguity metrics using a formal ambiguity log allows the business analyst to identify, understand, and monitor trends in specific types of requirements issues, which crop up and impact the overall quality of requirements. By adding this metric to the formula, the analysts and managers will be able to measure the full effectiveness of the organization's requirements techniques and activities.

INPUTS FOR METRICS AND BENCHMARKING

The inputs for metrics and benchmarking activities are:

- Number of requirements documented throughout the project
- Number of ambiguities discovered in ambiguity reviews
- Number of bugs identified in testing
- Number of defects identified after implementation
- Amount of time it takes to document requirements
- Amount of time it takes to fix discovered ambiguities
- Amount of time it takes to fix identified bugs
- Amount of time it takes to fix identified defects

OUTPUTS AS QUANTIFIABLE RESULTS

Quantitative analysis determines the amounts and proportions of the requirements of a specific project or organization's business analysis practice area. The results, which can be calculated with the identified metrics, are requirements effectiveness, quality, and analysis productivity. By measuring and calculating each of these results through quantitative analysis, it becomes easier to generate real and justifiable improvements.

Unknown Portfolio Value

A number of years ago, I had the opportunity to work for a large consulting firm to improve their business analysis practices. After establishing a framework for analysis, I started getting calls from account managers asking who was available for business analysis roles and whom would I recommend. I realized that I could not do this because I had no idea who was considered to be a business analyst and how well they performed, let alone if anyone was available on the bench.

I set about to "take stock" of the business analysts against the competency frameworks that I had created. This would give us an accurate picture of our business analysis capability. Ultimately, it was determined that the company had started with an understanding that it had some capability in this area, but it was not as predominant as development. By understanding the capability through carefully planned metrics and then utilizing those metrics to create a competency assessment, it was revealed that, while the company began with an estimated $500,000 per year of annual income attributed to business analysis, it landed at over $8 million within two years.

In that experience, I learned that this capability improvement would not have been possible without first understanding the real situation through quantitative analysis. In truth, it was more than just the development of a competency framework because that competency framework had to align to the performance of business analysis activities, such as requirements. It was through this framework and quantitative analysis that this competency framework was made possible. The framework itself asks more than "is a business analyst good at performing this task?" but also "*how well* does the analyst perform this task?" Further, it seeks to establish a set of measures to prove that each analyst has been evaluated in exactly the same manner, and, as such, the measure is verifiable and provable.

MEASURING REQUIREMENTS EFFECTIVENESS

The effectiveness of any process is measured by how much work is done within a given period of time. Within requirements, project resources and, specifically, business analysts have been reluctant to measure effectiveness because, once existing issues have been identified, the organization becomes obligated to fix them, and many teams and organizations generally do not know how to do this. In other words, organizations and resources have blinders on and are deflecting responsibility for requirements issues. However, by accepting accountability, breaking the barrier, and beginning to measure the effectiveness of requirements activities, the organization can start to identify patterns within the activities that lend to the creation of, or expose, underlying issues. Identification is the right place to start addressing and correcting the issues that lead to poor requirements.

Poor Requirements as a Technology Illness

Consider poor requirements as an illness. The obvious sign and symptom of this illness is that projects are challenged and fail (die). If the project were a person, that person would go to a doctor who would conduct tests to find the source of the illness. Only then could it be treated. The doctor would not venture to guess and then start medicating the patient without running some tests. If the diagnosis turned out to be wrong, the treatment would be ineffective. Worse, the treatment itself could further exacerbate the problem, and the patient could become more ill. It is only through the testing of the patient's vitals, blood work, and other imaging tests that the source of the illness can be found. These tests are conducted against the benchmark of previous mappings and illustrations that have been developed on the human body.

This example draws a parallel between the diagnosis and treatment of illness within the human body and the projects of business analysis. It is only through careful testing that we can determine the root cause of project failure, then work to improve that failure through careful and deliberate treatment. While organizations can count up the number of requirements and divide this number by the time it takes to define and document the requirements, this does not complete the picture. There are other activities that occur later on and new issues that crop up to bring the business analysis team back into requirements, which have to be measured as well.

Requirements Are Like Inventory

If a person worked in a store or a business, which sold physical products that had to be bagged and given or shipped to customers, and this person had to order more stock, how would they know what to order if they did not take inventory and closely monitor trends in sales? While it could be done, it would be a very expensive way to run the business. In fact, the store would probably end up with unsold products, overstocked perishable items, and a shortage of items needed for flows in sales trends or special events.

How then, can organizations, and even business analysts, expect to improve requirements without a yardstick against which to measure the activities? No one would ever know if the process has actually improved, or if this improvement was mere perception or correlation to other trends and events. The problem with this is that, once conditions change (new project, new team, new solution, etc.), the situation would resume: the same problems with requirements would resurface.

Requirements benchmarking provides organizations with the ability to create and manage a requirements scorecard by which they can assess, measure, and monitor all requirements activities. Having access to this information will enable more accurate program and project planning, resource allocation, the effectiveness of tools, and the knowledge of the resources who apply those tools.

Calculating the Requirements Effectiveness Index

The effectiveness of requirements is a measure of how well requirements activities are being performed by simply calculating how many requirements have been captured, over what period of time, and what other events (such as ambiguities and bugs) have added to the time it took to generate them. Table 5.1 illustrates the collection and calculation of the requirements effectiveness rating.

By translating this rating to a weighted metric on a scale of 1 (the worst) to 5 (the best), it will be easier to register a simple common index for five levels of effectiveness. These are:

1. *Needs urgent attention*—there are major issues with the effectiveness of the efforts being applied to perform requirements activities. These issues will most likely be found across all of the business analysis tools, techniques, and resources.
2. *Needs significant attention*—there are consistent issues with the effectiveness of the efforts being applied to perform requirements activities.

Table 5.1 Effectiveness of requirements efforts

Metric	Step 1	Step 2	Step 3	Step 4	Rating
RQX: Number of requirements		**CRQX:** Add these 4 numbers together	Multiply CRQX by 100 **(CRQX × 100 = RQFX)**	Divide **RQFX** by the Total Time **(RQFX/ Total Time = Requirements Effectiveness)**	
AMB: Number of ambiguities (assume 20% of requirements volume where this is not tracked)					
BUG: Number of issues found in Test					
DFT: How many defects were found after the product went live (into Production)?					
TRQX: How many days did it take to elicit, analyze and write the final requirements document, and get it approved?		**Total Time**: Add these 4 numbers together			
TAMB: How many days did it take to fix ambiguities?					
TBUG: How many days did it take to fix issues found in testing?					
TDFT: How many days did it take to fix defects found after it went live?					

These issues will most likely be found across some of the business analysis tools, techniques, and resources.

3. *Needs attention*—there are consistent issues with the effectiveness of the efforts being applied to perform requirements activities. These issues will most likely be found in several pockets across many of the business analysis tools, techniques, and resources.

4. *Needs minor fixes*—there are some minor issues with the effectiveness of the efforts being applied to perform requirements activities. These issues will most likely be found in pockets of some of the key areas of the business analysis tools, techniques, and resources.

5. *Outstanding*—The efforts being applied in requirements activities are well-managed. Consistent improvement methods should be applied to maintain this rating.

Further, calculating the requirements effectiveness index on a scale of 1 to 5 enables management to establish targets and reference points, against which the business analysis team can measure activities, and it enables a dashboard-like scorecard that the chief information officer can provide to the executive about improvements initiatives.

Calculating the Requirements Quality Index

It is not simply enough to determine how effective requirements activities are. It is equally important to calculate quality, since this is representative of the requirements themselves and not just how effective the activities to produce them are. It is possible to improve processes without affecting the outputs and the quality of those outputs. Table 5.2 illustrates how to benchmark and calculate the quality of requirements being produced. Quality has a direct impact on project outcomes in terms of bugs and defects.

Days without Accidents

In manufacturing, shop floors often have a safety board that proudly displays the count of how many days since the last accident. This count is not a measure of how fast and diligently the team worked, or how effective the line was at producing its product, or even how well that product was made. It is merely a count of how well the process was followed, and the level of safety achieved throughout. In order to assess the quality of the product, it is scrutinized by inspectors who ensure that it meets standards set by the company, the industry, and applicable government regulations. If it does not meet these standards, it is either scrapped or recycled back to the start of the process until it does meet them.

Table 5.2 Requirement quality rating

Metric	Step 1	Step 2	Step 3	Step 4	Rating
BUG: Number of issues found in Test		Add these 2 numbers together	Divide the result of **BUG + DFT** by the result of **RQX + AMB**	Multiply the previous result by 100. Then divide that number by the Total Time	
DFT: How many defects were found after the product went live (into Production)?					
RQX: Number of requirements		Add these 2 numbers together			
AMB: Number of ambiguities (assume 20% of requirements volume where this is not tracked)					

Quality is not necessarily tied to effectiveness. In a scenario, such as in this example, the team could have been very productive and yet not produced any significant output, the process could have run smoothly without incident, and the team could still have produced a product that did not meet standards.

Calculating the Requirements Productivity Index

Finally, it is important to assess the KPIs of teams through productivity. Productivity will directly enable a more accurate estimation of requirements activities across a project and will allow the project and the organization to determine how long these activities will take. Table 5.3 depicts how to calculate the productivity index.

It is important to note here that this KPI can also be used to assess the performance of the individual. This is not a negative thing. Just as people are graded in every other job function, or even as they were graded in school, this should not be viewed as a competitive measure of the individual against their peers. It should be viewed as the means for improving one's performance against their own past performance. It is important for business analysts to understand that a KPI is not a threat to their job. It is the path to an even better performance with which to feel great.

Table 5.3   Team productivity rating

Metric	Step 1	Step 2	Step 3	Step 4	Rating
RQX: Number of requirements		Add these 2 numbers together	Divide the result of **RQX + AMB** by the result of **TRQX + TAMB**	Multiply the previous result by 100. Then divide that number by the Total Time	
AMB: Number of ambiguities (assume 20% of requirements volume where this is not tracked)					
TRQX: How many days did it take to elicit, analyze and write the final requirements document, and get it approved?		Add these 2 numbers together			
TAMB: How many days did it take to fix ambiguities?					

First Key Performance Indicator Set Can Be Scary

Several years ago, I went to work on a project where the first scheduled implementation of the product had devastated the architecture and impacted technologies. A thorough root cause analysis revealed that no one on the business analysis team could answer the simple question "what went wrong?" Further, they could not answer "what was delivered, and how does this align to the requirements?"

It was a really scary prospect. In trying to sort out the problems and to resolve the issues, a set of rudimentary KPIs were created to let the team know how effective their requirements had been. At first, the team balked at this and justified their outcomes because they believed this was a reflection on their personal abilities. However, when the next phase was implemented, and the KPIs were again tabulated, it was revealed that the team had shown a significant improvement. That improvement was also reflected in the quality of the requirements, as bugs and defects were dramatically decreased.

Notice here that the business analysts went from defensive to accepting when they saw an improvement. What also happened was a psychological change. People who had previously felt ignored and disenfranchised and walked around with their shoulders down, suddenly walked taller and with their heads held high. There was a marked change in attitude from negative to optimistic.

Business Priority and Criticality

The assessment of business priority and criticality provides both valuable and measureable insight into some common elements of functional complexity. This information is crucial when faced with having to make decisions about re-scoping, change requests, and go/no-go opportunities. These decisions are made blindly, with little in the way of full understanding and tangible evidence to support them. Instead, they are typically made using "gut feel" and experience, as opposed to being a calculated decision based on solid and provable or established facts.

The International Institute of Business Analysis (IIBA) recommends prioritization according to the following factors: value provided to the business, associated risks to the business and technology architecture, the complexity and difficulty in implementation, estimated changes of success, compliance to various policies and regulations, how requirements are interrelated, stakeholder buy-in, and the sense of urgency. I would suggest that each of these items is actually in line with criticality and functional complexity.

For the purposes of this book, and the calculation of functional complexity that will be explored in the next topic area, business priority is the ability to establish an appropriate priority sequence that determines when something needs to be developed and implemented. True, many of these items impact when an item should be built, but in some cases they impact how they should be built or how they will impact the business. The issue here is that they also impact functional complexity and this, in turn, impacts timelines, budgets, resources, and the need for greater degrees of test coverage. This being said, priority assignment works best when it is used as a weighted matrix scored against the business's established criteria.

Business criticality, on the other hand, is an assessment of why it should be built. The basic criteria are: "Mandated," "Crucial," "Important," "Useful," and "Wish," from highest to lowest importance. In its place, MoSCoW (Must, Should, Could, Would), as recommended by the Business Analysis Body of Knowledge (BABOK), would suffice; however, as will become clear during the discussion on ambiguity, the term "should" has no place in requirements. By using this set of criteria, the business analyst is able to understand why key functions and features must be present, how to divide functionality among team members, and how to determine appropriate priority—which aligns objectives to scope—down to individual requirements. In this case, it is also suggested that assigning a weighted score to each of these attributes in a matrix is an effective method for obtaining scoring consistency across all teams and projects. The matrix in Table 5.4 provides an example of a simple weighted scoring method.

Functional Complexity

One of the biggest sticking points analysts often have is with the comprehension of functional complexity of both requirements and the overall system under development. This is because there are only a few structured and consistent approaches to this analysis, many of which focus heavily on elicitation with little attention, if any, to other areas such as analysis, documentation, and validation.

This book provides an overview of how to assess and understand functional complexity by defining criteria that increase or compound the complexity of both the business architecture and the new solution. Further, this approach assigns

Table 5.4 Business criticality

Weighted Code	Criteria
1–MANDATED	Will result in regulatory noncompliance and potential legal or financial penalties if not implemented
2–CRITICAL	Product will not meet customer needs if not implemented
3–IMPORTANT	May adversely affect customer or user satisfaction if not implemented
4–USEFUL	No significant customer or functional impact if not implemented
5–WISH	No impact but will increase customer perception of value if implemented

quantifiable and objective metrics to these criteria, for the ease of calculating a "high," "medium," or "low" result. By utilizing this method and calculating a simple result, the element of subjectivity, which may arise out of the analyst's lack of experience with a particular system or business architecture, is removed and a more rational and consistent assessment of complexity across multiple business analysts is made possible.

Where the BABOK recommends assessing the numbers of identified stakeholders, business areas impacted, systems impacted, technical resources needed, the level of risk by type, and the distinctiveness of the individual requirements, this approach recommends that the assessment inputs include the attributes of the existing business, data or enterprise architecture, the number of integration points with other systems, types of applications integrated or interfaced with, volumes of transactions, number of functions to be performed, number of tasks to be completed, and types of transactions performed. Other attributes, such as network features and security features (such as encryption and type of encryption) can also be captured, and specific domain-level attributes can be assessed— if they will add significant complexity to the new system.

Table 5.5 provides an example of the recommended functional complexity assessment. Table 5.6 identifies the ranges within each row and column to identify the best fit and assign a complexity rating to each row item. In this case, the matrix is calculated in Microsoft Excel, so the business analyst inputs the numbers for each row item in the appropriate column, and the spreadsheet will calculate the rest.

In this case, there is an additional item called "Audit Complexity," which also must be calculated—as seen in Table 5.7—and entered into the functional complexity matrix. This is because financial auditing brings its own blend of complexity to the mix and, if done incorrectly, could impose legal ramifications.

The purpose of assessing functional complexity is multifaceted: it enables more accurate estimation for resourcing costs and timing, it will enable analysts to make clear decisions about the types of deliverables they should be producing for each project, and it could impact the requirements themselves. Generally speaking, the more complex the business and enterprise architecture, the more complex the project, hence, the more documentation the analyst must produce at higher quality. In DO-178 (Document Order) software considerations, this would refer to the classification of levels or grades of software, from critical to nonessential, described in Chapter 14.

ESTIMATING REQUIREMENTS ACTIVITIES

There are several accepted and commonly used approaches for estimating technology projects as a whole. These approaches are: analogy-based, group,

Table 5.5 Functional complexity analysis

Function	Low 1	L-M 2	Moderate 3	M-H 4	High 5	Weighted Complexity Score 100	Max Weighted Item Score 100%	Final Weighted Complexity Score 100%
Business Criticality						0	10%	0.00
# Integration Points						0	2.50%	0.00
# Users						0	2.50%	0.00
# Processes						0	5%	0.00
# Transactions						0	5%	0.00
# Financial Calculations						0	15%	0.00
# Calculations						0	10%	0.00
Safety						0	10%	0.00
Security						0	10%	0.00
Audit						0	10%	0.00
Integrated App Types						0	10%	0.00
Transaction Types						0	10%	0.00
Response Analysis	0	0	0	0	0	0	100%	0.00
Complexity Rating								0

Table 5.6 Weighted complexity scoring range

Function	Low	L-M	Moderate	M-H	High
	1	2	3	4	5
Business Criticality	5	4	3	2	1
# Integration Points	0–5	6–19	20–30	31–49	50+
# Users	1–150	151–299	300–500	501–999	1000+
# Processes	1–50	51–199	200–300	301–499	500+
# Transactions	0–499k	500k–999k	1m	1m–50m	50m+
# Financial Calculations	1–50	51–199	200–300	301–499	500+
# Calculations	1–50	51–199	200–300	301–499	500+
Safety	1	2	3	4	5
Security	1	2	3	4	5
Audit	5	4	3	2	1
Integrated App Types	Word Processing	Performance	Reporting	Auditing	Financial
Transaction Types	Processing	Reporting	Exchanging Data	Transferring Data	Financial

Table 5.7 Audit complexity

Valid Codes	Criteria
1–EXTERNAL	Mandatory external audits and traceability required for regulatory purposes
2–ANALYTICS	Validates calculations and outputs and generates analytics using the outputs
3–INTERNAL CONTROLS	Validates calculations and outputs, generates reports, and controls the process
4–REPORTS	Validates calculations and outputs and generates management reports
5–SYSTEM	Simple calculation and outputs validation to verify and control process and reduce errors

parametric, work breakdown structure-based (bottom-up), size-based, mechanical, and judgmental; they are categorized as formal, expert, or combination types of estimation.

While each approach demonstrates a different ideology for estimation, all approaches and methods are inherently flawed and come with a host of criticisms. However, as with any method or approach for developing an understanding of any given "thing," the real flaw lies in implementation or application. The same is true for Agile: users learn about half of it, apply about a quarter of it, and complain that it is flawed.

The approach shared here is not intended to replace how all aspects of a project are estimated. It is merely intended to help refine how requirements activities are estimated. This estimation can then be utilized by other models for project estimating as appropriate.

There are considerations and complexities that make sense and are currently among the approaches to existing estimation approaches, methods, and specific techniques (such as constructive cost model, Function-Point and software lifecycle management). Estimating requirements is called out here because, in and of itself, it is not granular enough to provide an accurate picture. Let's throw away the box for a moment and find the most rational way to achieve the result needed. The best and most accurate predictor of future behavior is past performance. "The truth is that past performance is in fact the best predictor of future performance, not only with individual human beings but with teams, companies, technology, political bodies, and other time-bound entities."[1]

Ideally, projects would be estimated according to past history of developing similar blocks of functionality, and those would be compiled into an overall estimate of the project with a three-point approach (best, worst, and average case scenarios) built in, in order to account for the complexities of the unknown staffing model. However, one of the limitations of this approach is that many companies are not recording time spent and tasks in enough detail to create such an estimate.

Let's talk about estimation for what it is. Estimation is the ability to predict the amount of effort required to complete a specific project, based on the compilation of its underlying development tasks and activities, and then to assign a cost to this effort in order to understand how much the development work of the overall project will cost the business. With this information in hand, the business can then map this information against how much value it needs and expects to get out of the product generated by the project development work.

So, how can project teams generate an estimate of the work—if they are not looking back at how the work has been accomplished in the past, and how much effort each of those pieces took to develop? Many techniques are applied. By and large, many estimation techniques amount to a *scientific wild-ass guess* (SWAG) because they are not taking the historical facts of previous development into account but are using the gut feel of the expert (or group of experts) involved. The idea that each project is unique reigns when it comes to each new project, but the truth of it is that many companies are simply not tracking the time spent on the level of detail required to create a clear picture and estimate.

How Uniqueness Gets in the Way of Projects

Remember that CARD Map process project, where thousands of process flows had to be renamed and caused a six-month project extension (Chapter 4, "Requirements Management and Development Strategy")? Other than poor planning for document management, the biggest problem with the names was that the processes had been gathered across five subsidiaries of the parent company and across the parent company. While this alone would not be an issue, something more important occurred. Each of the companies, including the parent company, felt that their business was so unique that their processes had to be documented separately, which meant that the project was over two years in length and a trivial document management error caused delay. If in fact the processes had been unique, it is likely that the names would have been more unique and would not have had thousands of duplicates. As it turned out, the businesses discovered that the "uniqueness" of their business was not as unique as they had thought.

Consider this: both a utility company and an insurance company utilize similar processes for accounting, human resources, customer service, and so forth. Where the line of business is different, the processes are not because they are dictated by external regulatory bodies. In the end, when all processes had been mapped, this company discovered how many of them were so similar that they had wasted both time and money duplicating them.

Let us take a look at what can be measured: the functional complexity of individual features, length of time to generate requirements, the number of ambiguities, and the number of defects. Not only can these attributes be measured, but they can be compiled and compared against each other to create a solid estimate that goes beyond the typical SWAG estimation.

Why bother? It is important because one of the most common reasons for project overruns is poor project estimation. I've seen it with my own eyes. Why call out requirements and estimate requirements activities? Isn't estimating the overall project effort enough? Well no, because requirements are the foundation for the design, development, and testing efforts. Therefore, requirements have to be estimated separately in order to understand the volume and complexity of those requirements and the effort needed to turn those requirements into the final product.

The method proposed here is nothing new and is based on a combination of a few of the techniques already in use across many projects. However, these techniques are refined and coupled in a way that makes the outcomes valuable and puts those outcomes in the context of the overall project development effort. This method starts with development of the high-level features and functionality, indicated in the scope, and cultivating those into high-level requirements. This information is used to generate a business criticality assessment, as previously discussed, and then this same information is utilized to understand the functional complexity of each feature. Both business criticality and functional complexity are assessed for this estimation model, and the business criticality score rolls into the functional complexity assessment as a single attribute. Again, the functional complexity model presented here builds on the attributes suggested by the IIBA in the BABOK.

To create the actual estimation, the functional complexity assessment can be utilized in two ways: to create an overall estimate of the numbers of requirements for the whole project, as seen in Table 5.8, or to understand the numbers of requirements needed for each individual feature, as seen in Table 5.9. In either case, the recommendation for completion of the estimation is to consider WHO will be performing the requirements activities, as this will play heavily into the quality of the work, the productivity of the resources, and the effort needed to actually define, design, and develop the solution.

Not all business analysts are created equally, and consequently, consideration must be made for the competency, capability, and capacity of the business analysts to complete the requirements work. In my own observation and research,

Table 5.8   Sample complexity assessment

	# Requirements		
	Low	**Medium**	**High**
Simple	<5	6–16	17–27
Moderate	28–48	49–69	70–90
Complex	91–121	122–152	153–174
Advanced	175–205	206–236	>207
Criticality Padding	10	20	30

Table 5.9   Sample range of requirements volumes

	Estimated # Requirements		
Functionality	**Optimistic (L)**	**Average (M)**	**Pessimistic (H)**
Analytics	30	40	50
Appellate	10	15	20
Charges	5	5	10
Claims	35	50	65
CL Transfers	10	15	25
Determination	5	8	10
Generate Request for Information	5	8	10
Post Determination Claim Process	10	15	20
Protest	5	10	15
Reconciliation	25	30	40

Table 5.10 Sample requirements estimate

| Functionality | Estimated # Requirements | | | Estimated Time/Requirement (hrs) | | |
	Optimistic (L)	Average (M)	Pessimistic (H)	Optimistic (2)	Average (4)	Pessimistic (6)
Analytics	30	40	50	60	160	300
Appellate	10	15	20	20	60	120
Charges	5	5	10	10	20	60
Claims	35	50	65	70	200	390
CL Transfers	10	15	25	20	60	150
Determination	5	8	10	10	32	60
Generate Request for Information	5	8	10	10	32	60
Post Determination Claim Process	10	15	20	20	60	120
Protest	5	10	15	10	40	90
Reconciliation	25	30	40	50	120	240

a highly skilled analyst can complete upwards of two requirements per hour (from start of elicitation to sign off), an average analyst can complete about one requirement in four hours (again, from start to finish), and a less qualified analyst can complete approximately one requirement in six hours (again, from start to finish). This can be used as a general baseline; alternatively, individual companies and teams can measure their own productivity by using the formulas presented in this chapter.

Here, the three-point analysis comes in, both to estimate the overall requirements and to estimate the individual features. By using this baseline, an average effort estimate can be set. For now, let's use the numbers above as our model. Three-point analysis is the mapping out, or projection, of best, worst, and optimal cases and averaging the results of each to obtain a fair set of results. Table 5.10 illustrates an example of the estimation calculation.

Here, the best case is 2 requirements per hour, the worst case is 1 requirement per 6 hours, and the optimal case is 1 requirement every 4 hours. These would be averaged out to locate the most likely actual number of hours per requirement, and this information could then be used to calculate the amount of effort needed to generate the estimated number of requirements needed to create the solution.

REFERENCE

1. Steve Pavlina, 2010, "The Past DOES Equal the Future".

This book has free material available for download from the
Web Added Value™ resource center at *www.jrosspub.com*

SECTION III

ALL THINGS REQUIREMENTS

## 6

Elicitation

"Requirements gathering" is a common misnomer for the process of eliciting and documenting business and technical requirements. This term implies, incorrectly, that requirements are merely lying around the business waiting to be collected. However, in reality there is much researching, interviewing, analyzing, and validating to be done in order to generate a complete set of functional and nonfunctional requirements. In fact, the elicitation stage (as it is more aptly named) requires active research, facilitation, and leadership on the part of the business analyst to achieve the needed outcomes. This means that some requirements will be exposed by reading through architectural documentation and diagrams, and some of them will be exposed by interviewing the business user community and stakeholders. Both activities are tied together with the leadership skills the analyst must have in order to lead the elicitation effort and to garner both support and collaboration from the impacted groups.

Elicitation tasks and activities are designed to help the analyst work through a systematic process of discovery that fully illustrates the problem, the overall objectives, and the business interactions and processes as they currently exist. It also means defining the anticipated future state in these same terms. In other words, elicitation should clearly identify how the business looks and interacts in the current day and state, as well as how it is expected to look after the implementation of the developed solution. The elicitation stage is when business analysts undertake to define the requirements. Again, these are needed for design and development to occur, and for the creation of a specific system or application to address the business problems, goals, and drivers.

Within the context of a project, requirements provide the overall blueprint for the end product. They begin as high-level objectives, are transformed into scope, and evolve over the course of the requirements phase into low-level or detailed requirements for the particular product functionality. These requirements form the foundation for the architects and developers to design and build the new system or application. In addition, requirements provide a benchmark by which the end product can be tested for quality and its ability to meet or address the original objectives of the project.

Before analysts are in any position to really start requirements elicitation or meeting with the business community, it is imperative that they spend some time reading existing project operational documentation, such as the charter, plan, and scope. These will provide the initial information that will provide focus for the first round of elicitation activities. The information gleaned from these documents will enable analysts to make the most effective use of stakeholder time by preparing well-planned and timed questions right out of the gate. While reading the project documentation, it is critical to make note of any questions and of any risks, issues, or considerations that come to mind.

FROM BUSINESS OBJECTIVE AND PROBLEM, TO SCOPE AND REQUIREMENTS

It is important to recognize that requirements development is not a passive process. It is an active process for the capturing, understanding, derivation, exploration, analyzing, and testing of requirements.

One of the issues with writing requirements can be that many junior business analysts see too many options and can quickly become overwhelmed. With the advent of event-driven programming, what happens in the application is highly dependent on what the user selects or wants to do. This user-defined selection can cause any junior business analyst to feel lost in a maze. The truth is that, through requirements, the business analyst defines the events and options for the user to select. These options start with the objectives of the project. In essence, the highest level requirement can be said to be the answer to "what is this project trying to accomplish," or "why is the business doing this?" Traceability definitely starts here. At the end of the project, the team must be able to prove that they have accomplished the objective and show how it was accomplished. If this cannot be established, traceability will be the only method for locating where things went wrong and how.

Next, the business analysis team moves on to scope. The questions, "what is this project trying to accomplish" or "why is the business doing this," become "what does this project look like?" For example, if the objective is to improve transaction processing times by 25 percent for a claims processing system, the scope may include new user interfaces that are easier to use, automation of the data collection process, revision of the claims system to reduce processing steps, and automation of all manual approvals that may create a bottleneck for the processing of individual claims.

From this point, scope would transition to high-level requirements, by answering the same question ("what does this look like?") for each element within the identified scope. The requirements would formulate the blueprint for system functionality, which would basically make each of those items that were identified within scope appear in the final product, thus meeting the overall objectives.

INPUTS AND OUTPUTS OF ELICITATION

Ultimately, in order to develop a new technology system or process, requirements activities must be successful. Analysts must collect documentation from the project, architecture, and business in order to extract crucial details for the requirements. This collection and extraction of details is the real key to writing quality deliverables that are consumable for each audience group.

It is important to reiterate the differences between needs, wants, and expectations before the business analyst delves into requirements activities. This will provide clarity about the types of information that the analyst should be eliciting from the business throughout this process. As discussed in Chapter 1, a "need" is the problem to be solved, the required tangible results, or the strategic goal to be achieved. A "want" is a statement of an individual's personal desire. An "expectation" is a type of unofficial service level agreement for how the product will look, feel, and operate; how the service will be delivered; and how much, and how often, communication will occur throughout the project.

Best Practice Tip

Because of the particularly personal nature of "want," together with the fact that a "want" may have (almost) nothing to do with or be in conflict with business needs, it is important to focus requirements elicitation on the needs, instead of asking stakeholders and users what they want. Ask questions about the problem or the goal, not about desire. Ask questions such as:

- What is the problem or goal?
- How does this problem or goal impact the business?
- Who in the business is impacted by the problem?
- Are those impacts quantifiable?
- What other systems are involved?
- How did the problem start?
- What do they need to see change?
- How does an ideal solution operate?
- How will the business benefit from the ideal solution?
- What are the tangible and quantifiable results they need to see?
- What are the success criteria for correcting the problem or meeting the goal?

KNOWING WHERE TO FIND SOURCES FOR REQUIREMENTS

First and foremost, business analysts must be able to seek out and to identify common sources of information. They must be able to guide the business to provide this information so that they can efficiently begin the elicitation process. The following documents are considered inputs and information sources to the elicitation tasks and activities:

- Tribal knowledge (knowledge held by individuals who participate in the process or workflow at various points; this knowledge may be written down, or it may simply be remembered)
- Needs and stakeholder analysis
- Project scope
- Project charter
- Existing business rules
- Existing governance, policies, and regulations
- High-level requirements (if they exist)
- Existing business architecture documentation, which contains crucial information about:
  - Who (does what)
  - What (they do)
  - Where (they do it)
  - Which (tools do they use to do it)
- Existing enterprise architecture documentation, which contains crucial information about:
  - Systems specifications
  - Data needs, formats, and flows
  - Existing infrastructural specifications
  - Security details
  - Application details
  - Integration information

WHY EACH SOURCE IS VALUABLE IN ELICITATION

Each source of information will provide crucial details for the requirements themselves. However, it is important to understand the context and importance of each source in order to make the most of it. Knowing the value each source can add to the overall requirements documents is important.

Tribal Knowledge

Almost every company and project contains some degree of tribal knowledge, which must be captured in order to be successful. Tribal knowledge is the collective knowledge of the individuals working within the business and technical environment. This knowledge is gained from direct, on-the-job experience with the daily routines and functioning of the processes, as well as from other people and systems within this environment. Tribal knowledge, as an information source, is useful for identifying any processes that are not written down and business rules, tasks, and workarounds that are required for the system to function and make work get done.

Most tribal knowledge is unwritten and stored in the memories of individuals, or it is not formally documented and is stored in a widely-accessible knowledge base or repository. This information can be difficult to identify and understand because individual techniques can vary, some details may not be considered important and can be overlooked, unspoken assumptions can be made about why a particular task is done a certain way, or those performing the tasks do not want to share information perhaps in order to hold onto their jobs.

Project Scope

The project scoping document provides the parameters for the project by outlining the specific problems, business goals, and drivers to be addressed by the products of the project as well as the core functional areas that have been identified to address those specific problems, business goals, and drivers. In addition, the project scope identifies what will be worked on by the project team and, equally important, what will *not* be addressed by the project, as well as the assumptions and constraints of the project. In essence, the project scope is the document that establishes clear boundaries for the end product. It sets a clear picture for the project team to address a specific set of problems, issues, or functionality in order to maintain focus and keep the team on track.

The audience for the project scope includes business executives, sponsors, stakeholders, and the project team in order to maintain deliverable focus. However, it is also utilized by the business analysts to create a starting point for requirements and requirements traceability. This document is produced by the project manager (and, in some cases, the project working sponsor) in collaboration with the business stakeholders to establish a clear set of boundaries for the work to be completed. These boundaries are intended to focus the project effort on a targeted area and to reduce the amount of scope creep, which may occur during the project, while at the same time minimizing the amount of intervention and decision making by the sponsors, who may wish to include key areas that lie outside of the scope.

The scope document helps to reduce scope creep and sponsor intervention by providing the parameters and the "line in the sand" for the project. In effect, it is the early identification of potential areas of scope creep and planning for how those areas will be handled as they arise on the project. The project manager, the sponsor, and the stakeholders meet to determine the functional areas to be covered by the project and to clarify those areas that will not be covered. This scope information is stored in the scope document. During this meeting, the assumptions and constraints are also captured and included.

Assumptions are beliefs held by the business that impact their decision to include or to exclude functional areas from the project. These assumptions may later prove to be invalid, and, as such, the scope may change through the change control process. Constraints are factors that directly bind the project within certain parameters. Again, these constraints may change as the business evolves or other factors change. These changes may impact the scope of the project and, as such, are managed through the change control process.

Scope, assumptions, and constraints directly impact requirements and are, therefore, crucial for the business analyst in requirements planning. This scope document actually forms a big part of the solution definition to help the project team understand the business objectives for the project. Within the context of requirements elicitation, the project scope forms the basis of features and functionality for analysts to direct their requirements tasks. The business analyst can use this to set the framework for discussions with the business, as well as to identify who will need to participate in those discussions. Requirements must be decomposed out of the scope elements to identify the means for creating each functional element listed within the scope. All traceability starts with scope. In doing so, the analyst can prove that the deliverables align to the stated business objectives, goals, and drivers of the project.

Project Charter

The project charter is an agreement or contract between the business and the project team to deliver the items defined in the scoping document. It contains an overview of the resources (by role) who will work on and oversee the project and details what their responsibilities will be toward the end solution. It further details the roles, number of resources needed per role, project reporting structure, and how the project team accounts back to business stakeholders and the business at large. The primary audience of the charter is intended to be the project team and the business (executives, sponsors, stakeholders) and is meant to ensure that everyone associated with the project has a clear understanding of the business objectives and expectations for the outcomes, roles, and responsibilities on the project.

The project charter is produced by the project manager or sponsor (in some cases) in collaboration with the business stakeholders, who plan the main organizational structure of the project. It is produced after the project plan has been developed and the work and roles have been identified. While it may be in place before specific resource allocations have been made, it will be updated with the specific names of those resources once allocation has occurred.

Within the context of requirements elicitation, the project charter provides guidance to the analysts for leadership and accountability for the deliverables and work products under their purview. It further enables the planning of requirements and business analysis activities by providing the framework for the expectations of the business in terms of status reporting, escalation routes, reporting structures, and the core operating model of the project. While the charter may not directly impact the requirements or the work being done, it will directly impact the planning and management of this work. In this way, it will ensure the success of the requirements activities and the business analysis team.

> *"High achievement always takes place in the*
> *framework of high expectation."*[1]

In requirements and projects, the project charter provides the framework for high expectation. However, it is only a part of this framework. The project plan, project scope, knowledge of the tools and techniques, and skill and discernment in applying them make up the rest of this expectation. It is only in the context of the project charter that these other elements can support the achievement of the business objectives.

Project Plan

The project plan provides a detailed work breakdown structure for the project life cycle. It contains the list of project tasks, the time allocated to each task, the overall schedule, and the resources assigned to each task. This plan is intended to provide a detailed work plan, which will guide the project team to achieve the direct results mandated by the scope and charter documents. This document, produced by the project manager, allows them to coordinate the activities, to ensure effective task coverage, and to manage the project resources, budget, and schedule for the successful delivery of the project outcomes. As such, the plan includes the tasks, estimated man-hours to complete each task, the task deliverables, and the resources assigned to each task. The project plan is most often represented to the team and the stakeholders in a Gantt chart.

Gantt charts illustrate the tasks to be completed in the project, across the timeline. Each task is shown in blocks of time relative to the overall schedule, and identifies the resources responsible for performing them. In addition, it illustrates how each of the tasks relates to other tasks on the project (pre-requisites and dependencies).

The project status reports are generated against the plan illustrated in the Gantt chart, in order to demonstrate the progress being made by the team. These status reports are utilized to communicate this progress back to the sponsors and stakeholders.

The project manager develops the project plan, in collaboration with senior project resources, by understanding the needs of the business, the objectives of the project, and the work to be done. They first build out the work breakdown structure and then estimate the time to complete each identified task. Once this has been completed, the project manager can begin to schedule the workload across the calendar and estimate the overall plan for the accomplishment of this work. Finally, he/she assigns those tasks to resources by role and plans for the number of resources in each area.

Within the context of requirements elicitation, the project plan provides the timelines and budget guidelines for specific activities in order to be able to predict the anticipated completion and implementation dates as a means to ensure a directed and strategic approach to every task. It is crucial for success that *every* business analyst on the team has access to this document, as it will enable the analyst to make crucial decisions about what, and how much time, key tasks have to be completed. In essence, this is a precursor for the planning of the requirements tasks to be completed. By utilizing the framework provided within the project plan, coupled with their knowledge of the context, purpose, and outcomes of each business analysis task, business analysts are in a prime position to be successful in planning the activities that will be performed in the achievement of the project deliverables and outcomes. Without this information, the analyst is simply not in a position to plan the work to be done and would have to work to perform every task within the realm of requirements, regardless of the time allotted and the deliverable context. This is because the analyst would simply have no idea what tasks belong within the context of the specific project being worked on.

> *"Failure to plan on your part does not constitute*
> *an emergency on my part."—Unknown*

The truth is that the project plan does more than enable the planning of requirements and other business analysis tasks. It provides focus and a sense of inclusion and partnership within the team. It drives home the idea that the project is a well-coordinated effort to help the business achieve its goals. Every person wants to be on the winning team. But it takes leadership, trust, and membership to have a team. It is the team who will achieve the goals, and the team who will be successful when this plan and guidance is shared.

High-Level Requirements

The high-level requirements document details the first round of increasing detail and granularity for requirements, as the analyst begins to drill into each item within the scoping document. Again, this is to understand exactly what functionality, security, processes, and impacts are necessary to make each individual item within scope a reality within the end product. High-level requirements are primarily consumed by the analysts, the business, and the project team and are a foundation for the lower-level, more granular details that will evolve through analysis activities. This document is used by the business analyst to decompose the contents into greater detail. It is used by the business team to understand how the solution will meet the need. Finally, it is used by the project team to design, develop, and test the solution.

Business Architecture Documentation

Business architecture is the collection of information that describes who does what, when it is done, where it is done, which information is consumed, and what the outputs are. In the Chapter 1 discussion on business architecture, these documents were identified as a key source of workflow details (what, how, which data), stakeholders, and impacted groups (who).

Enterprise Architecture Documentation

Enterprise architecture is a generic term for the documents and diagrams that contain detailed specifications, as well as information, about existing systems, networks, security protocol, data, and applications within the technical environment. The purpose of this documentation is to provide the information essential to product life cycle management—through activities such as support, maintenance, upgrades, and systems enhancements within the environment from a "big picture" perspective—in order to ensure that the new solution fits into the existing architecture and meets the strategic objectives of the business. These documents will include network diagrams, architecture diagrams, specific system details, and configuration details.

WHAT INFORMATION IS COLLECTED DURING ELICITATION?

The information gathered, both from individual sources and from collections of documentation, amounts to details about the goals of the business, problems to be solved, and impacts of those problems on the business and its ability to conduct its work and transactions in an effective and affordable (sustainable) way. In addition, these sources provide descriptions about the results that are needed, as well as the assumptions, constraints, risks, gaps, and opportunities that exist.

During the elicitation stage, the analyst must establish the plan for obtaining key information from the inputs. By understanding what can be extracted from each source, and what each source is, the business analyst can move forward with a systematic process for extracting this information. Again, the inputs from which this key information will be extracted are tribal knowledge, project scope, charter, plan, high-level requirements, and business and enterprise architecture.

Tribal knowledge is important because, when systems do not work as expected, the employees are often forced to manipulate key functions in order to create workarounds and complete work by utilizing the system. Therefore, tribal knowledge usually contains details about how the process should run, as well as why and how the existing system does not run the way it should. In addition, tribal knowledge contains the "way things get done," which may include personal preferences and quirks about how the process is performed by a specific group or an individual employee. This information may not have been documented as a part of the official process or implementation; however, it is a part of how that process was adopted by the team or its members to "make it their own."

Our Methodology Is Broken

Several years ago, a consulting firm was approached about helping a retailer fix its project management office methodology and to standardize requirements. During the initial audit, management expressed concern over how the project methodology, which had been implemented the year before, had not been adopted.

Upon further analysis, it was discovered that many of the employees and resources did not even know there was a methodology. Those who did know about it had no idea what it was or how to apply it. The consulting firm that had developed it for them only planned for a single week of training: if employee schedules conflicted with this, and they were unable to attend, there was no other opportunity to be trained.

While many employees in this scenario went about life as usual because they had not been trained on the new methodology, there were still those who did adopt it. These people provided ad-hoc information and advice to others on their projects, and the methodology took on a life of its own. Because of this, management believed it was broken. The collection of tribal knowledge enabled the new consulting firm to recommend a solution to bridge the gap instead of replacing the methodology. Without this information, the company may have wasted the hundreds or thousands of dollars they had spent on it.

The project scoping document outlines the primary areas of functionality that will have to be included in the requirements. It is important to reference these areas in order to prevent scope creep. This provides focus for the require-ments extracted during the elicitation process. In addition, the project charter is important in elicitation because it will enable the analyst to determine who to reach out to, in order to locate the inputs or to invite them to joint application development (JAD) sessions. This information will enable the business analyst to ensure that all impacted groups have the opportunity to provide input. Further, the project planning document will provide the time parameters for scheduling elicitation activities. This will enable the analyst to establish the schedule for these activities and set the level of urgency for responses from the stakeholders. The high-level requirements provide a more detailed set of functions that will be decomposed during elicitation. The high-level requirements help to define areas where the analyst must research more fully and generate more details for the design and development teams. These will allow the analyst to identify informa-tion within the architecture documents that is either necessary or will add value.

Again, business architecture is the primary source of workflow details, stake-holders, and impacted groups. In the context of elicitation, many of these details will be the source of both requirements and related considerations. In other words, this documentation will provide specific details that will either influence or become part of requirements, which are related to the existing business frame-works (business rules, impacted processes, influencing policies, and regulations). Within the context of elicitation, enterprise architecture provides the analyst with specific requirements that enable the new products to interact and exchange data with each other, to monitor the technical environment as a holistic system, to manage end-to-end work flow across multiple systems, and to support each other in a more seamless (almost symbiotic) relationship.

THE RISKS OF EXCLUDING BUSINESS ANALYSTS IN IMPLEMENTING COMMERCIAL-OFF-THE-SHELF SOLUTIONS

One of the key areas where businesses and analysts can lose their footing, is on a project implementing a commercial-off-the-shelf (COTS) solution. It is still important to capture requirements for the solution. COTS software is supposed to be cheaper and easier to implement, right? WRONG! Too often, businesses make the assumption that they can simply unpack the box and install it on pre-existing systems because that is what people do at home. However, the costs, risks, and complexities of an enterprise network make this a vastly different scenario from downloading software to a personal system.

Without an analyst, businesses could be missing the big picture up front.

Many companies believe that they can complete the research and product selection without the input of a business analyst simply because they can easily evaluate the up-front costs. Unfortunately, they could be missing the bigger picture and select COTS products based on the cost per license, features, and interactions with the environment—all under the assumption it can be installed as is. Believing this, companies will often operate under the false assumption that they do not have to document any requirements for COTS product implementations.

The only costs that companies are really saving,
is the cost to build from scratch.

The fact is, companies also have to consider specific questions about the overall costs and benefits of implementing a COTS solution in the environment. This means business analysts must not only be involved, they must also capture requirements for customization and implementation.

Requirements for COTS implementations: Without adequate requirements, projects are missing the details that will make their COTS implementation a success in the long run. Requirements for code extensions, impacts to the environment, configuration management, product life cycle, program management, features, and the implementation must all be documented for successful COTS implementation.

Extending the code: Most COTS solutions can, and should, be adapted to the enterprise architecture and business needs. It is important for the business analyst to capture the requirements, which can extend to code, and COTS solutions cannot be simply unwrapped and installed. These extensions will account for integration points between the new and the existing systems.

Maintenance: The next factor in the implementation of requirements for a COTS solution is its maintenance and support within the environment. Not only will there be additional support which must be accounted for, but the product will require an owner and, most likely, will become part of an existing program. All of these will dictate additional specific requirements, which will need to be documented.

Impacts associated with upgrades: Not only do many companies forget to plan for the benefits realization of implementing a COTS solution, but far too many companies do not plan for upgrades to them. They omit these because it is considered the responsibility of the vendor to provide the business with the scheduled upgrades. Some considerations to make in documenting the requirements for COTS products are:

- Does the product fully support initial and evolving requirements?
- Does it fully support fixed/unchangeable operational requirements and procedures?
- What are the quality requirements for reliability, performance, usability, and so forth?

HOW IS THIS INFORMATION USED DURING ELICITATION?

The basic purpose of the elicitation inputs is to enable the planning of joint application sessions, which serve as a guide for the research activities. Essentially, the inputs will provide the framework for the elicitation process and give the process a starting point. This alone makes it more effective. The project plan, scope, and charter documents provide a basis for the planning of the requirements activities. Tribal knowledge, high-level requirements, and business and enterprise architecture provide the foundational set of information to feed requirements.

The business analyst drafts a plan and rough schedule for the requirements activities based on the project level documents. This plan is verified against the requirements foundation documents in order to ensure that every area is covered and that enough time has been allocated for its capture during elicitation. Once the planning and schedule has been set, the analyst can begin to organize research and interviews for the business team. In addition, the analyst can start to draft a framework for the requirements document.

WHAT ARTIFACTS AND DELIVERABLES WILL BE CREATED IN ELICITATION?

The requirements research and elicitation stage produces several deliverables and artifacts, which will be utilized later in the requirements life cycle to drill down into greater detail and provide the lower level and more granular requirements. These documents include:

- Current State Documentation
- Rough Future State Documentation
- Mid-Level Requirements

In addition, where business architecture documentation is either light or nonexistent, the following deliverables may have to be generated in order to create a full and complete solution.

- Business Process Models
- Business Rules

Current State Definition

The current state documentation is designed to illustrate the existing technical issues, business problems, and systems before the new system(s) or process(es) has been implemented. This documentation can include flow charts, process maps, activity and context diagrams, marketing diagrams, use cases, and architectural schemata. The purpose of the current state is to define and establish a common understanding of the business drivers for the project so that all team members, business stakeholders, users, and executives are on the same page. This common understanding enables the business team, in collaboration with the project team, to better define a solution and plan activities that will lead them to the desired outcome.

Current State Inputs

Due to the nature of current state documentation, there is a diversity of inputs which go into the development of these deliverables. These inputs to the current state include: problem identification, existing business rules, process flows, enterprise architecture, process descriptions, work flows, and existing context diagrams. Inputs for current state can also include: interviews with stakeholders about issues with the current processes, the way it should work, how current processing does not meet compliance, and how cumbersome or confusing the overall workflow can be. They also include information from the help desk on known issues and help tickets.

Current State Outputs

The picture that is created by the current state is like a puzzle. This puzzle is comprised of the outputs created during the task. In essence, each of the documents forms a single piece of the overall puzzle and, by viewing these pieces collectively and within the context of each other, the business and the project team is able to understand the complete picture of the current state.

The outputs from the current state definition include: documentation that compiles problem statements, risks and impacts from problems and issues, relevant existing business rules, relevant existing enterprise architectural diagrams, process descriptions, work flows, and existing context diagrams. To be clear, the inclusion of some of these documents as outputs does not necessarily mean that the business analyst will be responsible for creating the documentation. In some cases (e.g., enterprise architecture), the analyst is merely the person who compiles the documents into a single source in order to reference them in the current state document.

Current State Scope and Dependencies

The scope of the current state includes the existing processes, workflows, systems, and problems associated with each of these outputs. All other stages, tasks, and deliverables are completely dependent upon the current state definition because the end solution must be able to fit into the existing environment and resolve the full problem to support the business. To this end, it is critical that the current state be complete and accurate for the project to be successful.

Tools and Techniques for Defining the Current State

Due to the diversity of the documentation collected during current state definition, it is imperative that the tools and techniques utilized are equally diverse. It is critical that there be a clear picture of the problem and the current business and technical architecture at the end of this task. In order to define the current state, the business analyst must utilize both interactive facilitated sessions and research to compile any existing documentation. The business analyst will compile many of the facts into a single point of reference document, which will serve as a focal point for the collection of other related information. This point of reference will reference other related documents in order to identify the problem and how it relates to the business and technical environment around it.

The current state is created and stored in the document repository with all other current state deliverables. By placing all of these deliverables into a single folder in this repository, the business analyst is enabling the management and maintenance of the current state. In the end, this will make it easier to locate and utilize that documentation throughout the remainder of the project. Where the inputs and other collections of documents are absent, the business analyst must either create those deliverables or request that other appropriate project resources create and provide them. Those architects would create the enterprise architecture diagrams and provide them to the business analysis team to complete the current state documentation.

Current State Audience and Sign Off

The audience for the current state is the business and project teams. Again, this documentation is used to illustrate a full and complete picture of the issues to be resolved, the interactions with other systems and processes, as well as the business drivers behind the project. It creates a common understanding of the starting point for the new systems, applications, and processes. The business and the technology teams must sign off and validate that the current state documentation is complete, consistent, and accurate. The business analyst is responsible for ensuring that they are complete.

High- to Mid-Level Requirements Evolution (Refinement)

The next stage of requirements is to develop the so-called mid-level requirements. These are the same high-level requirements, which have already been created, with increasing detail and granularity. The mid-level requirements result from the analyst continuing to drill down into each item within the high-level requirements document in order to define detailed functionality, security, processes, and impacts. These detailed attributes are necessary to author complete requirements. Complete requirements are those that help each individual system feature to function seamlessly within the end product.

It is important to remember that requirements do not transition from 30,000 feet to zero in a single pass, and that the process of evolution is actually necessary to generating requirements that are complete, consistent, and accurate. There is a significant degree of analyzing, processing, rationalization, justification, and validation that occurs throughout the development process. This increasing level of detail is necessary for the designers and developers to understand the full processing and functionality of the new system, together with how it interacts with dependencies and upstream systems within the environment.

Why Requirements Must Evolve

The process for writing a book is simple. Come up with an idea. Conduct research. Create an outline to organize the flow of information. Write a draft. That's right, a *draft*. Not the final version, which will wow everyone with your intellectual brilliance, but a draft. And it is not just a draft. It is the first draft, and the first of many, to be exact.

Take this book, for example. I started writing these stories in a very personal way, as though I was sitting and having a conversation with the reader. After the first draft, I had to remove all personal references. For the second draft, I had to search for and remove all sentence fragments. In requirements, these would be incomplete logic. This book would be hard to read and understand if I did not. For the third draft, I had to ensure that I had covered all of my topics so that a complete picture was created for the reader. In requirements, such information gaps would mean the reader would have to assume or ignore the missing functionality.

Mid-Level Requirements Scope and Dependencies

The process of evolution is really the beginning of the formal requirements document (the first draft), so the scope of this deliverable includes detailed functionality of the new technology or infrastructure and references to business rules and processes. This document may, or may not, go into technical requirements details that are based on the analyst's up-to-the-minute knowledge, level of analysis, completed processing, and the availability of support required by the technical design, development, and testing teams to complete the first draft of the requirements.

Mid-Level Requirements Inputs

In order to further refine high-level requirements into mid-level requirements, business analysts must review their notes and all work completed to date. To be successful, they must also have access to the business team and stakeholders to clarify any points as they work through the refinement process. Specifically, the inputs to the mid-level requirements are the high-level requirements, the business rules, the business processes and workflow, the known technical requirements, and the functional and non-functional requirements. Nothing can really be set aside at this point, as those documents and sources may contain key information or details that will support the further refinement of the requirements.

Mid-Level Requirements Outputs

The primary output of the mid-level requirements is the first draft of the requirements document. It is referred to as mid-level in this case just to eliminate any confusion about the process of evolution of the requirements. It is a rough draft of the detailed requirements to date. As when writing a book, it is *not* the completed document. There will be many more passes to edit the content and to ensure that every detail is complete, consistent, and accurate.

These requirements are not numbered; rather, each is marked with a placeholder, "R." However, the general formatting has been established, and the order of the functionality is in place. It is recommended that requirements are numbered according to the numbering conventions of this text, and, once numbers have been assigned, they should *never* change. Revisions to the requirements documents after numbering has been assigned will follow the convention prescribed under changes and change control. Doing so will avoid confusion between the various document versions that may be circulating among the project and business teams and keeps everyone on the same page.

Audience and Documentation Sign Off

The audience of the mid-level requirements primarily includes the business analysis, architecture, development, and testing teams. While there is no formal sign off for this level of documentation, the design, development, and test teams must understand and informally accept the mid-level requirements. This informal "sign off" represents a checkpoint. This checkpoint is used to ensure that the components are feasible, the teams are all on the same page, and the requirements are developed with input from other teams. This means that other teams contribute by determining whether the functionality can be delivered within the context of the current environment and time frame with the available resources, and whether the requirements are both appropriate and testable.

Policy Renders Future Dating Functions Untestable

A number of years ago, a project to implement a new driver insurance penalty program was in mid-flight when the business analysis team lead was replaced. The concept of the program was to impose penalties on drivers for demonstrating risky driving behaviors, such as speeding and driving while intoxicated. Those penalties would be imposed over the course of three years, so in addition to the initial fine and the increase in their insurance rates, these drivers would also receive an annual penalty fee for three years. This meant that the program application had to generate invoices over those three years for each impacted driver.

However, in discussions with the testing team about the multi-year functionality, it came out that this functionality could not be tested. Further discussions revealed that the testing environment could only test functionality based on the current date because it was against policy to push the dates forward in the testing environment to ensure that the functionality would work.

In this situation, it was only the discussions with the test team that revealed this limitation on testing. This limitation impacted the requirements and changed the way the business analysis team handled the "future" functionality.

High- to mid-level requirements are derived as the analyst begins to categorize high-level requirements and align the business rules. The requirements are further defined as the analyst begins to map out scenarios utilizing mind-mapping, cause and effect tables, or simple process flows for each requirement. This mapping will enable greater detail and reveal areas where further definition is required. Table 6.1 illustrates the differences between high-level and mid-level requirements.

The objective of this task is not to complete the requirements, but to get them to the point that they are ready for the analysis process, where further investigation through gap analysis and more detailed end-to-end scenario planning will occur. With this objective in mind, it is important to remember that this task still requires some organization of the requirements draft in order to ensure that the management tasks are up-to-date.

This means that there will still be some minor housekeeping to keep management on track and to prevent a compounded backlog of management tasks to complete at the end. To keep the management tasks on track, the requirements at this stage must always trace back to the business goals, drivers, and objectives, as illustrated in Figure 6.1. This is achieved by ensuring that, as individual requirements are documented, the index is updated with the category, function, and feature details that describe how the item in scope is going to be implemented.

Best Practices Housekeeping

Requirements are not numbered until just before being published at the completion of the specification stage. This is to prevent excessive and time-consuming changes to references in the finalization process.

Requirements are referenced primarily by name, not by number, within the documentation. While references may include numbers, business analysts should be aware that fixing these when changes occur can become a time-consuming exercise once they have been finalized.

NEVER use a page number when referencing requirements from other requirements or parts of the document, as this is subject to frequent change and can confuse the reader. Instead, reference the feature or function and allow the reader to locate the specific requirement based on this information.

Table 6.1 High- to mid-level requirements mapping

High-Level Requirement	Mid-Level Requirement
The Administrator must have the ability to Add, Change or Inactivate a CSR's profile.	Resource Analyst and Administrators must be able to create a CSR profile that contains the following information

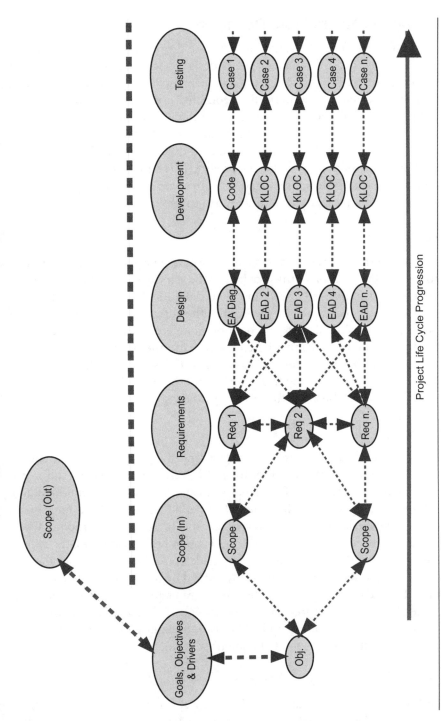

Figure 6.1 Requirements traceability

Outlining the Future State Definition

Where the current state is designed to illustrate the picture of the business situation as it exists today, the future state is designed to illustrate the planned or desired outcome after the new solution has been implemented. Both current and future states are mosaics comprised of collected documents, which formulate a single picture. This documentation can include flow charts, process maps, activity and context diagrams, marketing diagrams, use cases, and architectural schemata. The purpose of the future state is to define and establish a common destination, or set of objectives, for the project. This ensures that all team members, business stakeholders, users, and executives are on the same page and are better able to plan necessary activities toward the desired outcome.

Future State Inputs

The important thing to remember is that the future state definition is focused on the to-be. It is the solution to the problem or the vehicle to create the picture that the business has in mind. As such, inputs to the future state include: interviews with stakeholders about process ownership; the current state; a compilation of the way processes should work or could be more effective; specific documents related to regulations that must be complied with; the business rules; and the governance framework to determine how the overall workflow will be controlled throughout the new processing framework. These inputs will be utilized to create the full picture of the business future after the new solution is live.

Future State Outputs

The future state documentation represents an integral piece of the requirements puzzle because it provides context for the individual requirements and functional elements and for how those functional elements fit into the overall solution. Therefore, the outputs from the future state definition include: the future state point of reference document; the process controls (or gates); the process ownership matrices; the anticipated workflow; transaction processing times; the revised business rules; and the improvements to be made. As for the current state, the outputs of the future state are not necessarily created by the business analyst. Again, documents—such as enterprise architecture diagrams and data models—will likely be created by the architecture teams. The business analyst will be responsible for business and process modeling and will only be accountable for the collection of the future state into a single point of reference document.

Documentation Scope and Dependencies

As for the current state, the analyst will create a single document that references the other collective information sources composing the full future state mosaic.

To this end, the scope of the future state includes: workflows; process maps; process narratives; updated activity diagrams and business rules; and architecture diagrams, which illustrate the anticipated or desired future state. The analysis and validation stages are dependent upon the future state, in that low-level requirements, use cases, and gap analyses are all based on this document set.

No Planned Future

Remember that new driver insurance program? One of the biggest problems was that, once the first phase was implemented, it broke everything. In-depth root-cause analysis showed there was no future state documentation in place. This meant that no two teams had the same picture of the final solution or of how this solution would fit into the business. In fact, the development team (who, in this case, were also the architects) did not mention to the business analysts that the new code was being developed right into the existing program, the existing program was to be decommissioned, and (as if this was not enough) this program's code was segregated and divided between four new servers just before development began.

The business analysts needed to know the information about how and where the code was being developed. Without the future state documentation to set expectations, the solution developed did not match the requirements at all. Ultimately, all of the teams had worked in isolation, essentially developing disparate designs and requirements, and the implemented solution did not work.

Tools and Techniques for Defining the Future State

Again, the diversity of the documentation that formulates the future state definition dictates that the tools and techniques utilized are just as varied. The objective is to define a clear picture of the solution within the context of the future business and enterprise architecture. To define the future state, the business analyst must utilize techniques similar to those that define the current state. Facilitated sessions with the business team will be the primary technique.

During definition of the current state, the business analyst also utilizes research to collect any existing documentation. In this case, however, all of the documents must be generated from scratch, as they depict the to-be. They may reference the existing state sources to support the development of the new to-be picture, but the documents themselves are designed to define a solution that has not yet been built or implemented. As such, the existing documents will serve only to identify integration points, applications, enterprise architecture, required transactional processes, mandatory business rules, and overall data flows.

The business analyst will compile the to-be solution elements into a single future state document. This will serve as a focal point for solution requirements and business and enterprise architecture. Again, this document will reference the other deliverables and artifacts in order to identify the solution and how this solution fits into the context of the business and technical environment around it. The future state document is created and stored in the project repository with all other collective future state deliverables and artifacts. The purpose of the single repository is to enable management and maintenance of the documentation within the context of the project.

It is the responsibility of the business analyst to create the future state documents, or to coordinate their creation with the other appropriate project resources, and provide them to the project team. The architects are responsible for creating the enterprise architecture diagrams, and the data architect is responsible for creating the data models and providing those diagrams and models to the business analysis team, who completes the future state documentation.

Future State Audience and Sign Off

The audience for the future state documentation is both the project and the business teams. In effect, this documentation acts as an extension of the scope and charter documents because it sets the expectation with the business for the outcome of the project. This documentation is used to illustrate a full and complete picture of the implemented solution and the to-be state, the interactions with other systems and processes, as well as the business drivers behind the project. It creates a common understanding of the starting points for the project and for the new solution. The business must sign off and validate that the vision illustrated by the future state documentation is complete and accurate. The business analyst is responsible for ensuring this future state is logically complete and consistent.

Best Practices

The future state documentation provides a more detailed picture of the anticipated project outcome and further cements the expectations with the business for what is being developed and what will be delivered at the end of the project. It is imperative for the success of the project that the business and technology teams are involved in this process in order to ensure buy-in, sign off, and accuracy of the solution.

Business Process Modeling

Business process modeling (BPM) is the task of creating the diagrams that illustrate the step-by-step flow of work and processes, which are required to initiate, perform, and complete a specific transaction or set of tasks. These diagrams are useful for understanding the full end-to-end process that occurs in accomplishing a given task or set of tasks. For the most part, business process models form a large part of the business architecture documentation. As discussed in the business architecture section, this is required for the business analyst to generate requirements for a solution within the context of the business and its operational framework.

In spite of the importance of this documentation as an input requirement to the business analysis process and activities, there are many projects that are initiated without having any of this in place. When this happens, it becomes the responsibility of the business analyst to compile and compose these deliverables in order to have the necessary inputs for generating a full and complete solution and set of requirements.

Business process models are sets of flow charts and process maps, which represent both human and system interactions for each step. These models illustrate the inputs, outputs, and human and technical interactions. These technical interactions can include data flows, transaction processing, data storage, and the flow of work that is completed at each step of the process, as well as any decision points and process controls required to validate the results of individual steps of the process.

Business Process Modeling Inputs

The inputs for BPM are details about how tasks are performed by each job function or system throughout the entire process. Inputs include:

- *Actors or Performers*—The job function or system that performs, or contributes to performance of, the task.
- *Process Steps*—The specific steps involved in accomplishing and performing the overall process.
- *Inputs*—The data or information that comes in from other systems upstream to be utilized by this process.
- *Outputs*—The data or information generated by this process for other processes.
- *Dependencies*—What other processes, documentation, or systems require the outputs from this process in order to run, process, or be completed?
- *Control Gates*—Points in the process that validate the process and ensure it is performed correctly and will produce accurate results, and points during the process that will halt the process when it fails or does not meet specific parameters.
- *External Processes*—Other processes that either lead to this specific process or into which this process will directly lead.

Best Practices

A good tip, when collecting information to create the business process flows, is to think in terms of the five "W's." These are who, what, where, when, and why. However, in this case, it is also important to remember to ask how. By remembering these types of questions, the analyst is sure to be able to elicit and document complete processes. Again, these processes will enable a complete view of both the way things are today (current state) and how they will be with the new solution in place.

Business Process Modeling Outputs

The typical deliverables and artifacts produced by BPM activities include swim lane and activity diagrams and flow charts. Again, the primary purpose of these models is to provide a detailed view of the end-to-end work flow. This view is essential to elicitation and validation of requirements, to provide a visual aid to the business that illustrates current and future states, to support the elicitation and validation of business rules, and to support the ambiguity review process. By utilizing these models, the business analyst is able to document requirements for every single step in the process. In addition, the analyst is able to think about how the process should be governed and managed in a more effective and efficient manner, which facilitates recommending changes to the business stakeholders and process owners. The ambiguity review process enables the business analyst to gain buy-in from the nontechnical business team by providing a visual representation of the features of the new system or application.

Business Process Modeling Documentation Scope and Dependencies

The scope of this business process modeling task is to interview the business stakeholders and users in JAD sessions. These sessions are utilized to acquire the detailed inputs to the BPM, which can be utilized to produce a detailed diagram of the entire process from end-to-end. To this end, the dependencies of the BPM task, with its deliverables and work products, are the requirements, business rules, design, architecture, development activities, and test plans. Each of these dependent activities will consume some segment of the deliverables by creating a context for the solution's work.

Tools and Techniques for Business Process Modeling

The ideal tools and techniques for conducting BPM are white board sessions, JAD sessions, interviews, brainstorming, mind-mapping, and other forms of facilitated working sessions. In order to make the most use of the time allocated for these sessions, it is also strongly recommended that the business analyst utilize the techniques outlined in the Guidelines for Conducting Effective Meetings discussed in Chapter 7.

Utilizing these techniques is especially important because BPM requires substantial involvement with the business in order to fully understand and document the workflow and existing processes. Business analysts must ensure that they get the full cooperation of the business. In addition, these techniques will foster necessary goodwill between the analyst and business teams. This goodwill and trust engages the business and keeps them involved throughout the process.

To begin the mapping process, the business analyst will organize the mapping session with the business. The business is responsible for bringing any documentation related to their processes and how those processes are managed. This information includes key decisions made along the way, and who contributes (by role) to this process. During the mapping session, the business analyst begins by identifying the inputs to the process (what information or data is fed into it). Next, the analyst must identify how the process begins (which may be the data feed itself). From there, the analyst must ask the business to walk through the process sequentially (step one, two, three, etc.).

For each step, the analyst must identify the data inputs and outputs, who performs the step, whether any decisions are made at this step, where this step leads to, and, finally, how and where the output data is used. If there is a decision, it must result in either a yes or a no, and the analyst must further identify what happens in both cases. Since there will always be an answer from the decision point, which pulls the process from the main path, it is important for the business analyst to identify whether and how the process can be restored to the main path. If this is missed, or the business has not identified it, the analyst must work with the business to resolve this logical inconsistency in the process. By mapping this resolution, the requirements will be complete and the development team will be able to create the appropriate code to avoid bugs and defects in the application.

Once the process has been drafted, the business must have the opportunity to verify that the information is complete and accurate. For new processes, this may mean that the business approves new steps and accepts ownership for these steps. After the drafts have been edited and the feedback from the business has been incorporated, the process flows are finalized. In the finalization process, the maps version control is set, the names and file locations are entered into the index, and the maps are uploaded into the document repository.

There are a variety of new and interesting process mapping tools in the marketplace today. While this may be dictated by the company, it is imperative that the business analyst understands the basics of mapping, with or without an automated tool, as it is the underlying skills in mapping that ensures the consistent success of the analyst in process modeling. This being said, any process modeling tool that is utilized in the diagramming and documentation of the process should allow the analyst to create a visual end-to-end workflow. This should be illustrated with standard flowchart "symbols," activity diagram images, and clip art as well as swim lane, activity, flow chart, and context diagram styles. The most common and industry-accepted style for BPM is BPM notation.

Business Process Modeling Audience and Documentation Sign Off

The primary audience for this task and its deliverables and work products (artifacts), is the business analyst team, the design and development team, the test team, the stakeholders, the sponsors, and the business users. The business will utilize these documents to ensure that the appropriate workflow has been captured and will be translated into requirements for the new system. The analyst team will utilize these process models to generate detailed requirements for the identified workflow. The remainder of the project team (architects, developers, and testers), will utilize this documentation to ensure appropriate designs and consistent development of the "right" solution and to generate the test scenarios and cases. The business must sign off and validate that the process models are complete, consistent and accurate. Finally, the analyst is responsible for ensuring that the content of the models is logically complete and the processes do not compete with one another (where one process cancels another out).

Business Rules Definition

Business rules are the key policies and regulations that govern conducting certain aspects of business. These policies and regulations are derived from both positive and negative business experiences, industry standards, market research, government legislation, as well as other systems and factors of the technology environment. As with process models, rules actually form a part of the business architecture. Again, however, many projects are initiated without consistent rules documentation in place, and the responsibility rests on the shoulders of the business analyst to compile and compose these documents.

The documentation is intended to outline and list all the rules which impact a project, in a central repository, in order that they can be incorporated during design and development, and ultimately control the functionality of the final solution. It is imperative that business rules are documented for every project, and that every rule must be incorporated into the new system, application, or process in order to be compliant to the governing body, which has outlined the policies and regulations. By publishing the business rules in a separate project document, the analyst enables reusability of the rules and provides a single standardized point of reference. Providing the point of reference enables a greater degree of mutual understanding of the rules across the board and removes the potential for multiple instances of divergent interpretations that lead to confusion and conflict.

Business Rule Inputs

Remember that business rules are those rules that support process governance and control by ensuring that key criteria are met, regulatory compliance is met, and company policies are adhered to. To this end, the primary inputs to the definition process and deliverables are: organizational, departmental, divisional, and corporate policies; state and federal legislation; industry standards and norms; and protocol imposed by private and professional certifying bodies.

Business Rule Outputs

While many analysts often embed the business rules into the requirements, the primary output of the rules definition process is the business rules documentation. This must be separate from both processes and requirements because these rules could be applied across multiple systems and solutions, and could therefore be utilized by multiple projects and requirements. In effect, rules supersede requirements.

The more consistent the application of business rules across multiple systems, solutions, and projects, the greater the degree of transactional accuracy and consistency that will be achieved by the business. Figure 6.2 illustrates the relationship between requirements, rules, and processes. A business rule might look like:

> *Passenger groups with over 15 people must make reservations by calling the customer service center. They must not make reservations using the public online reservation system.*

Business Rule Scope and Dependencies

The scope of the business rules deliverables is limited to the rules of the system, processes, or applications that will be directly impacted by, or will have a direct impact on, the project. The overall processing and transactions performed by the new solution are wholly dependent on the business rules documentation. It is critical that this is complete and accurate in order to build an effective product, which meets the business needs.

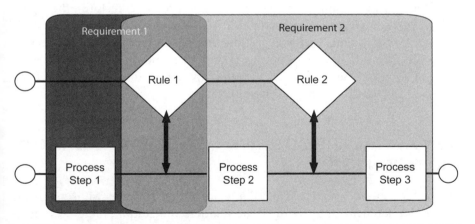

Figure 6.2 Relationship between rules processes and requirements

Business Rule Audience and Sign Off

The audience of the rules documentation is the business, analysts, and design, development, and testing teams. The business, however, is responsible for sign off and validation that the rules are complete, consistent, and accurate. The analyst is responsible for ensuring that they are logically complete and do not compete (where one rule cancels another out).

WHO WILL USE THE ARTIFACTS AND DELIVERABLES FROM ELICITATION?

As mentioned in each of the individual artifact and deliverable discussions above, the basic usage and audience for all artifacts is primarily the business analysis team, and the primary audience for all deliverables is the downstream design, development, and test teams. This is where many technology resources tend to become confused. These resources tend to get confused because the deliverables are signed off by the business. However, the business is not the consumer of the documents. These documents are, in fact, utilized by the other parts of the project team to complete the work of designing, building, and testing the solution. Therefore, these documents must be written for these audiences, not the business team.

In addition, another common misunderstanding is that only the business signs off. However, in this context, the business can only sign off on the features and functionality, and they can only do this when the analysts can demonstrate how this meets the need, resolves the problem, or creates the desired result. It is the architecture, development, and test teams who must sign off on the feasibility of the system (within the context of the enterprise architecture), the logical consistency, completeness, and testability. This juxtaposition creates the situation where analysts mistakenly expect the business to read every single technical requirement, in all its dry, boring, and mind-numbing detail. However, by changing the conversation and resetting the expectation, this task becomes fairly matter-of-fact for the average business person.

HOW ARE THE ARTIFACTS AND DELIVERABLES CREATED IN ELICITATION USED?

The artifacts and deliverables from the requirements activities will support the design, development, and testing of the solution. In addition, these documents will support implementation, training efforts, future upgrades and enhancements, product life cycle management, configuration management, scheduling and release activities, and potential future business decisions for the development and deployment of other solutions within the same environment.

With such widespread and far-reaching impacts, it is crucial that these documents are complete and unambiguous. They are, in effect, the corporate inheritance, left behind after project teams, sponsors, and users have moved on. Those who follow in the footsteps of the project team, or any of its single members, must be able to pick up the documentation and take over as quickly as possible. This means not having to pore over years of e-mails and file folders for the meaningful snippets and contributions of previous members.

TASKS AND ACTIVITIES OF ELICITING REQUIREMENTS

Techniques for Eliciting Requirements

Elicitation is a compound set of tasks, including research and collaboration with the business and technical teams, geared toward accurately capturing and generating requirements. The two strongest techniques for the elicitation of requirements are, therefore, research and facilitation. In this case, the term facilitation is used as a generic term to describe the collaboration with these other teams. This collaboration occurs in groups of varying size or in one-on-one interviews. The important thing to remember here is that the analyst performs the role of a facilitator. As discussed in Chapter 2, the role of the facilitator is to define and control the process.

It is important to understand that the full elicitation process utilizes both research and JAD to create the outputs. The real activities of this process are developing these outputs and preparing them for the analysis process. While it is not necessary to complete every output, the analyst must first know and understand the context and value-add of each output in order to make decisions about how to customize them or whether to do them at all. For example, when a project is implementing a COTS solution, it may not be necessary to create mid-level requirements. In fact, the elicitation of COTS requirements will focus on the customizations of the product and the integration points for the enterprise architecture.

Regardless of how the outputs are adapted and which ones are ultimately developed, tribal knowledge is a key factor in the elicitation of requirements for all solutions. This is because tribal knowledge is the cornerstone of the business identity. It is how the employees relate to the company, which translates into how those employees deal with customers and perform their everyday tasks.

How Tribal Knowledge Is Collected

As previously mentioned, tribal knowledge is different from all other sources of information because this information is either unwritten or not widely shared among the business team. This means that—while all other sources of information can be utilized for research, and the results of this research can be validated in meetings with the stakeholders and business community—tribal knowledge must primarily be elicited through facilitated sessions.

The JAD session within the elicitation process has been designed specifically for the business analyst to collect this tribal knowledge. The analyst must meet with and interview the stakeholders and users in order to properly capture this tribal knowledge. It is important to meet with the stakeholders or technology team about the research being conducted because, with diverse standards and document styles, it can be useful for these resources to help interpret the documents and other inputs.

Facilitation

There are several types of facilitation an analyst can utilize when conducting interviews in order to reach a specific outcome within a specified period of time. Each provides the analyst with an effective framework for conducting the session and directing the input and contributions of the participants toward a predetermined outcome. These types of facilitation are as follows:

Interviewing—a small or, typically, one-on-one meeting in which the business analyst poses specific questions to the business stakeholders or users in order to elicit specific information.

Brainstorming—a group activity in which the business team collectively contributes ideas to the discussion. Those ideas are documented, categorized, and prioritized by the group.

Presenting—one or more individuals exhibits or communicates specific messages to an audience. This exhibition can be either interactive or lecture style.

Mediation—two parties meet with a neutral third party to support a decision-making process. This is primarily utilized when there is a high level of interpersonal conflict.

Conciliation—two parties work with a neutral third party as a go-between to support the decision-making process. This is primarily utilized when there is a high level of interpersonal conflict and the two parties cannot or will not sit in the same room together.

Negotiation—two parties work to resolve a dispute or come to a decision through mutual representation. In this case, each party is represented by a third party that has a vested interest in the outcome.

The selection of the facilitation type will depend on a variety of factors, including size of the group, the work to be accomplished, the time period allocated for accomplishing the work, and the group dynamics. While the role of the facilitator may indeed be to define and control the process, the role of the business analyst in facilitation is to use the selected technique to accomplish a defined set of work and achieve specific results. This means that, as discussed in chapter 2, the business analyst must find ways to work with and engage all of the stakeholders. The following list outlines the situations in which each of the above types of facilitation could be used effectively:

- Interviewing
  - Team is functioning cohesively.
  - Zero level of conflict.
  - All team members have buy-in and agree on the solution.
  - Scheduling conflicts limit the number of group facilitation events.
  - Long timelines for achieving the work.
  - One-off questions specific to an individual.
- Brainstorming
  - Team is functioning cohesively.
  - Zero conflict.
  - All team members have buy-in and agree on the solution.
  - Tight timelines to produce collaborative results.
- Presenting
  - Team is functioning cohesively.
  - Zero conflict.
  - All team members have buy-in and agree on the solution.
  - Longer timelines allow for presentations before collaborated sessions.
  - Presenting results of work or reviews back to the business.
- Mediation
  - High levels of interpersonal conflict.
  - Individual team members do not agree on the solution or do not have buy-in.
- Conciliation
  - Moderate conflict.
  - Primarily business and project team having issues determining the best-fit solution.
- Negotiation
  - Business departments and/or various sub-teams do not agree on the functionality to be included.
  - High inter-team conflict.
  - Power dynamics at work.

Guidelines for Conducting Effective Meetings

It's time to start meeting with stakeholders to elicit requirements. It is important to recognize and understand that it takes more than opening a meeting invite in the calendar, dropping some names in, and sending it off.

> ### With Everything Else I Have to Do this Week, Why Should I Meet With You?
>
> Have you ever gotten a meeting invite with no content, and you have no idea what the meeting is about? What do you do if you get two of those for the same time slot? Worse, have you ever gone to a meeting and thought "why am I even here?" Have you been to meetings where more socializing than work gets accomplished?

The reason for planning and conducting effective meetings is to establish a set time with other team members in order to get collaborative work done. These helpful guidelines will get requirements elicitation meetings going smoothly and enable the business analysts to achieve more productive work. In addition, this set of guidelines demonstrates how to respect everyone's time and recognizes that stakeholders, business analysts, and project team members have many demands on their time during the average work day. It takes careful and deliberate time management to make progress.

The general rules are to make the purpose clear, set the tone, be precise, tell the meeting attendees why the meeting is needed, and set the expected participation levels and outcomes. So let's take this a step further. How the invitation e-mails are written and worded to the business matters—it is everything. People have to make snap judgments about which meeting to attend when there are conflicts and schedule overlaps, so include a well-worded subject line *and* an agenda.

Research

The elicitation stage begins with research. This will consist of brief interviews; studying the project scope, charter, and plan; as well as studying any existing business architecture documentation describing the current business rules and workflow, and enterprise architecture documentation providing insight into the existing technical environment. The culmination of this information will provide the analyst a better view of the project, the business objectives, the framework in which the end product will reside, and finally, the impacts that interactions with other systems in the environment will have.

To make sense of this barrage of varied documentation, the analyst will create the current state definition, consisting of business process models (or workflow, context, or activity diagrams) and the high-level requirements document. The high-level requirements will consist of requirements that are taken from the items in the project scope document and categorized into functional feature sets (such as Catalog or Shopping Cart). In order to complete this view, the analyst will conduct the research prescribed above, as well as document the business rules by gleaning them from research and elicitation activities. To be proficient at conducting these tasks, the analyst will need to be well-versed in organizational behavior, underlying business operations, team development, change management, communication techniques, document management, and research techniques. An analyst must exhibit personal traits as an assertive team player, an innovative individual, and a confident leader. The competency areas required for research and elicitation are approximately 30% business knowledge, 45% people and soft skills, and only 25% technical knowledge.

Research and elicitation is concluded when the business analysis team has created a draft of the requirements to work with. These do not have to be complete in order for the analysts to proceed to the analysis stage, as these requirements will be fleshed out and become more fully developed through this stage.

Best Practices Elicitation

The key to being successful with the elicitation and research activities is to follow a few simple rules:

1. Be diligent and thorough in the research conducted before approaching stakeholders
   a. Conduct as much research into the project, environment, and impacted systems as possible, practical, and appropriate.
2. When approaching stakeholders, demonstrate that their time and their contributions are valued
   a. Utilize and stick to an agenda.
   b. Block adequate time to achieve the meeting goals. (I never book less than two-hour sessions at the start so that real work can be achieved.)
   c. Acknowledge all ideas that are brought forward and address them.
   d. Prepare for the meeting with questions and defined goals.
   e. Take detailed notes during the meeting.
3. Follow-up with stakeholders after the meeting to provide documented results and minutes
4. Remember that *all* stakeholders need to feel they have been heard and their contribution is valuable (even if what they are asking for is out of scope or not realistic)
   a. Take time to get personally acquainted with the stakeholders—especially those who are the most vocal about opposition to aspects of the project.
   b. Build a personal rapport with stakeholders.
   c. Find out what these stakeholders' needs are so that the business analysis team can collaborate with them on the project, and, even more important, so that they will collaborate with the project team.

Remember "A Server Named Bob" from Chapter 1? In this situation, what the user asked for was completely unrealistic and definitely not in scope. The team members worked with him on every occasion to ensure that they responded to his requests and to let him know that they simply could not give him what he wanted. After the first request, they explained that over 3000 other employees also logged into this server every day and would not appreciate logging into "server Bob." The point is that his request, despite being both unrealistic and completely out of scope, was acknowledged and responded to every single time.

Everyone Has a Hot Button

On the same Windows XP migration project discussed in Chapter 1 (server Bob), there was a fellow who worked in the mail room delivering mail to one of the corporate divisions. He was adamant about not giving up Corel WordPerfect for Office XP. In fact, every time the team uninstalled WordPerfect and installed Office XP, he would hack into the system and restore WordPerfect. After several attempts to reason with him, work with him, and even to coerce him into leaving the system alone and just working with it, the team discovered that there were a couple of things going on.

First, the team discovered that he had really wanted to be a part of the information technology group working in a graphic design capacity. Unfortunately, he simply did not have the academic qualifications for the role he really wanted. The one thing he did get to create, which gave him some feeling of being a graphic designer, was a divisional fundraising cookbook. After several discussions with him, he finally sent the team a copy of the annual cookbook he was working on.

The team called him after their review of the file and told him what great work he had done on the cookbook. Then, after complimenting his work, they told him it really did not belong in WordPerfect any more than in Microsoft Office. They advised him that his cookbook should be designed and laid out in PageMaker. He breathed a heavy sigh of relief and exclaimed that he had been asking for it for years but no one would let him have it. Once he knew the team was going to work with him to get the proper tools, he collaborated fully and stopped restoring WordPerfect to his system.

In this case, the project team needed to know why the user was so determined to keep the application in order to work with him and engage him. By taking the time to understand the user's specific (and very personal) needs, and then to appreciate the work that the user had been doing, the team earned his trust and gained his collaboration.

Joint Application Development Sessions

A JAD session is a particular type of facilitated session. While utilizing many of the common techniques of other types of facilitation, it has a specific set of parameters for participants. The participants of JAD sessions are primarily:

- Executive Sponsor: The executive sponsor charters the project, is the system owner, or acts on the owner's behalf. This person must be senior in the organization and have the adequate level of authority to make critical decisions and provide appropriate direction, strategy, guidance, and planning.

- Subject Matter Experts: The subject matter experts are business users, technical team members, and other functional experts who contribute key information for requirements, workflow, and technical architecture.
- Facilitator/Session Leader: The facilitator, as previously discussed, defines and controls the session. They are responsible for keeping the session on time with the meeting agenda, for tabling discussions, and for achieving results.
- Scribe: The scribe records the detailed proceedings of the meeting and publishes the meeting minutes. Meeting minutes should include action items, breakout sessions, decisions made, and a list of all participants. The scribe does not contribute any information to the meeting.
- Observers: Observers are usually members of the business or application development teams who have been assigned to the project. They observe the proceedings and do not contribute any information.

The key advantage of using the JAD session is that it can decrease the time and costs associated with requirements elicitation. This being said, one of the misconceptions about the JAD session is that the analyst is able to elicit, analyze, and validate requirements during the session. However, analysis and validation, as discussed and outlined in subsequent chapters, involves more than going back to the user.

REFERENCE

1. Kettering, Charles F. (1876–1958), 1934, as quoted in *Scientific American*.

## 7

Analysis

Analysis is the key stage where the business analyst derives a more detailed set of requirements by analyzing and decomposing the information that has been collected and compiled. Analysis is comprised of tasks and activities, which are designed to help the business analyst answer these basic questions:

- How can the solution be created?
- What is the work to be performed?
- How will the solution perform the required work?
- Who will utilize the solution?
- How will it interact with other systems or applications (upstream or downstream)?
- What data and information will it consume from other systems (upstream)?
- What are those systems?
- What data and information will it produce for other systems (downstream)?
- What are those systems?
- How will it impact and interact with the overall technical and business environments?

According to Dictionary.com, the term "analyze" means to "separate (a material or abstract entity) into constituent parts or elements" in order to "determine the elements or essential features" and to "examine critically, so as to bring out the essential elements," and finally, "to examine carefully and in detail so as to identify causes, key factors, possible results . . ."[1] In effect, analysis is the set of tasks and techniques used to identify the differences between two states, to magnify the gaps in processes, to pinpoint root causes and effects, and to resolve logical inconsistencies in order to fix the problems or generate the solutions needed by the business.

Throughout the analysis stage, the business analyst is primarily investigating, evaluating, and scrutinizing the information extracted from the input sources and documentation as part of the evolution process. In doing so, the analyst must model the information, conduct a gap analysis, and organize and prioritize the requirements. The Business Analysis Body of Knowledge, published by the International Institute of Business Analysis, outlines a specific order for these analysis tasks. It is, however, more important to understand the context for doing each task (why and the value derived), and to understand the appropriate order for doing each task (as opposed to a regimented order).

The process outlined here begins the evolution of requirements through modeling and gap analysis before organization and prioritization can occur. This order of events minimizes the changes that will be made to the outputs of these activities as the requirements are developed and managed. It is important to note that there will be crucial information for requirements, which will only become apparent as the elements and details from those inputs are being modeled and analyzed. This crucial information may impact both the priority and the organization of the requirements. The effort here is to minimize the number of iterations of individual tasks while increasing the effectiveness of the tasks themselves.

The purpose of organizing requirements is to create a cohesive flow to the documentation so that it is readily consumable by the architecture, development, and test teams. This being said, the purpose of prioritizing requirements is to define their order of importance. As prioritization is discussed, it will become apparent why this is helpful to projects. Because of the exposure of new information as requirements analysis proceeds, both prioritization and organization will be discussed in detail in the next chapter on documenting the requirements.

Modeling requirements takes many shapes and forms, from user stories to unified modeling language (UML), to business process models, to scenarios. Even cause and effect tables (also known as decision tables) are examples of requirements modeling. Whatever method is chosen to model the requirements, it is best to select more than a single method so that different models can present the requirements from various perspectives and expose any logical inconsistencies, errors, and omissions. One of the best techniques for exposing omissions and logical inconsistencies is to apply the concepts of cause and effect (decision) tables and mind-mapping to conduct gap analysis. These techniques will enable the business analyst to map out more complete scenarios utilizing the detailed current and future state documents, which were previously derived from the business architecture and project planning documentation. Specifically, this will expose incomplete or inconsistent logic, missing business rules, missing process controls, missed requirements (gaps), as well as external and internal risks. Inconsistencies and incompleteness in logic are exposed when the analyst maps out a full scenario (including preconditions, events, and results) and identifies any of the following situations:

- Missing preconditions
- Missing events that trigger results based on the combinations of actions and preconditions
- Missing results
- Missing combinations of preconditions, events, and results

Missing business rules are exposed when the analyst identifies missing preconditions and events, and explores these with the business in order to discover the ways in which key scenarios and combinations of scenarios are handled by the business or current systems. Missing process controls are identified when the analyst maps out the scenarios and identifies a lack of, or a discrepancy in, controls for those processes. For example, a loan may be processed, but no audits or approvals are necessary at any stage to govern the process and ensure compliance and accuracy. Finally, missing requirements are exposed each time the analyst identifies another missed item (such as a rule, control, or logical inconsistency), as there will be requirements associated to each of these elements. In addition, missing requirements are identified when the analyst completes the logical scenario by understanding and exploring how various combinations of preconditions and events will be handled, and what the results of those situations will be.

False Negatives and Positives

One of the important things to note is that logically incomplete requirements can lead to situations where the application registers either a false positive or a false negative. This occurs when multiple scenarios are combined and not thoroughly mapped. Unfortunately, this may mask an issue within the code. It masks the issue, meaning the result may show up as positive, when it should be negative.

INPUTS AND OUTPUTS FOR ANALYSIS

To start the analysis stage, the analyst will need to have completed the following key research and elicitation tasks, as these will provide the source information to be analyzed during the analysis tasks:

- Business process models (finalized, if they did not previously exist in the business architecture documentation)

- Current state documentation
- Future state document draft
- Requirements document draft
- Business rules document draft

HOW IS THIS INFORMATION USED DURING ANALYSIS?

The information obtained from the input documents and elicitation sources will be analyzed by utilizing multiple tools and techniques. Remember that analyzing is the process, techniques, or set of tasks that are applied to accomplish three basic things: to break the information down into separate features (feature derivation), to identify or expose essential elements, and to identify root "causes, key factors, possible results . . ."[2] To this end, each of the documents identified as inputs will provide specific information that will enable the accomplishment of the three basic objectives.

Business Process Models

Business process models help to define the end-to-end process and workflow. In addition, they outline and identify integration points, data storage, process controls, and governance. The workflow supersedes the roles and responsibilities that illustrate how specific work is accomplished, which roles are involved in its achievement, and how this work is controlled, measured, and managed. To this end, business process models provide key information for requirements. This information identifies missed requirements, identifies gaps in the information, and ensures that unseen, commonly unwritten requirements are identified and documented.

Within the analysis stage, business process models enable the decomposition of the mid-level requirements. These documents serve as a cross-reference, or provide supporting information, which helps the analyst identify missed requirements or greater detail for those requirements that have already been documented. In addition, the review and cross-reference of business process models enable the analyst to ensure that the requirements produced are logically complete because they provide an end-to-end view of the workflow to be done. Again, this workflow crosses roles, other processes, and system integration points.

Current State Definition

The current state is designed to illustrate the existing technical issues, business problems, and architecture before the new system(s) or process(es) has been implemented. Within the context of the analysis stage, the current state offers the business analyst a detailed view of the problems and the existing business and enterprise architecture, which enables the analyst to conduct the gap analysis. The gap analysis will enable the business analyst to identify other potential problem areas and determine how the business will get from point A to point B by utilizing the solution to be developed by the project. Essentially, the current state becomes a baseline or starting point for road-mapping and planning for the project.

Future State Definition Outline

The future state is designed to illustrate the planned or desired outcome after the new system(s) or process(es) has been implemented. Within the analysis stage, the future state offers a view of the destination point and of the end solution as it will be, once it has been implemented. This view enables the analyst to conduct the gap analysis. The gap analysis will enable the business analyst to identify the features and functionality that will bridge the identified gaps effectively. Essentially, the future state documentation becomes the solution baseline for requirements, design, development, and testing. This does not mean that this document is utilized to develop the architectural designs, to develop the code, or to define test cases; rather, it provides a big picture focus to support each of these activities. This overall view provides the analyst with the ability to create requirements that align to the solution.

Business Architecture

Within the context of the analysis stage, the business architecture provides the analyst with an overview of the business, the current state, and its impacts and influencing factors. By referring back to this information throughout the analysis stage, the analyst is able to verify and validate some of the pertinent elements of the solution, which are related to the details contained within these artifacts. However, it should be cautioned that this is not the only point of verification and validation. A more formal process, using clearly defined and articulated steps, will provide the final verification and validation of the requirements. This documentation is merely a source for tracing back in order to ensure that all impacts and influencing factors have been accounted for within the requirements.

Enterprise Architecture

Enterprise architecture is the task of mapping and planning the information technology infrastructure that activates the company's operating model. In other words, enterprise architecture is the practice of translating the operating model into technology that will ensure that the elements of the operating model work together. But it is more than this. Enterprise architecture is also the practice of integrating the technology into the operating model and infusing this model with new strategies, which will give the company a competitive edge.

To this end, the tasks of enterprise architecture are to map the information architecture and the technology architecture (systems, hardware, security, networks, collaborations, and systems management) integrated into the company's information technology environment. Information architecture is comprised of the key data, integrations, and applications utilized by the company in the performance of its work routines. As such, data models and flows are the responsibility of either the enterprise architect or the data architect to build and verify. The technology architecture includes the systems (data, application, and integration technologies), hardware, security protocol, networks, and the collaborations between all of these elements. The business analyst does not perform enterprise architecture duties, tasks, or activities, but may contribute to them, and definitely capitalizes on and leverages them. On a project, the enterprise and data architects analyze and build the diagrams that illustrate the integration of the new technology and data into the overall enterprise architecture. This is done to ensure that the system is well-integrated and will collaborate with other technologies in the accomplishment of the company's goals and to enhance the operating model to include the new technology.

Costly Commercial-Off-the-Shelf Integration

Many years ago, an insurance company had an application which served as a broker portal for their associated independent insurance brokers. As it turned out, the portal was purchased by the senior vice president of finance with virtually no planning or due diligence for managing it. There was no vendor management established, there were no service level agreements in place, and, more critically, there had been no enterprise architecture planning before installing the product into the environment. As a result, the product did not fit into the environment, and the data had to be manually exported daily and reimported to the application, once other systems had manipulated it. In effect, there simply was no data flow between this system and the other well-established systems within the technology environment.

In this situation, while the application did reside within the architecture, it was not truly a part of it, as it was unable to interact with the remainder of the information technology and data architecture. Within the analysis stage, the enterprise architecture documentation will enable the analyst to answer key questions about integration points and other influencing factors related to the systems within the environment, which may or may not have or be impacted, and how this new system or application will interact with the other systems in the environment. This technical view is critical to creating functional requirements and conducting gap analysis for understanding the fully implemented solution in relation to the environment in which it will reside.

While the business analyst does not have to understand every granular detail of the enterprise architecture, it is important to be able to interact with the architects and developers to extract the key information they will utilize to generate relevant requirements. This need to extract key information means that the business analyst must have an understanding of the big picture and how the solution will fit into the environment. It does not mean that the business analyst needs to understand the architecture well enough to develop and code the new solution alone.

WHAT ARTIFACTS ARE CREATED DURING ANALYSIS?

The analysis stage produces several documents and artifacts that are primarily intended to answer open questions about the product and refine the requirements down to lower levels of detail and granularity. These documents and artifacts include:

- Scenarios
- Gap analysis
- Cause and effect tables
- Activity diagrams
- Use case outlines

Each of these documents and artifacts are created in order to expose and explore detailed elements, which will be specified in the requirements, and to identify the corresponding causes and other relevant factors.

Scenario Definition

The scenario is a type of story or visual flow that illustrates how the new product will be used under specific circumstances to perform particular work. It identifies the input, processing, and output tasks to be performed along the way that will achieve the work. In essence, a scenario is an activity diagram, a use case, a UML diagram, or even a cause and effect table. Scenarios are best applied for ensuring the completeness and logical consistency of the requirements because they enable the step-by-step mapping of the workflow. By mapping the same and similar work across multiple scenarios, any missed steps and incomplete logic is exposed.

Within the context of analysis, scenarios support the development of logically complete requirements by providing the analyst with another view of the system. In addition, scenario definition allows the business analyst to anticipate and expose weaknesses and inflexibilities in business processes and systems, in much the same way that a SWOT analysis (strengths, weaknesses, opportunities, and threats) does for business operations.

Gap Analysis

Gap analysis is a method for analyzing something and identifying differences between multiple states (in this case, current and future states). Gap analysis is utilized as a means of creating the plan to move from the present situation to the ideal situation, as identified by the business. Within the analysis stage, gap analysis is an important tool for identifying the gaps in requirements by locating logical inconsistencies. This will be further discussed in the section on the tasks and techniques for analysis.

Cause and Effect Tables

A cause and effect table, also known as a decision table, maps the various scenarios against potential outcomes. In this case, scenarios are combinations of preconditions, trigger events (causes), and the potential outcomes (effects) mapped in a table. By using the table format as illustrated in Table 7.1, the analyst is able to see the various combinations of preconditions, trigger events, and potential results of each combination.

WHO WILL USE THE ARTIFACTS AND DELIVERABLES?

The primary outputs from the analysis stage are the gap analysis, requirement details, and refined future state documentation. This will be utilized by the analysts as artifacts and inputs for authoring the low-level requirements. In addition, these documents and artifacts will be used to identify and present risks and issues to the business in such a way that the business has enough information to make clear and rapid decisions about how to address and mitigate the associated risks. The recommended format for the gap analysis, in this case, is to include a risk/impact table within the document itself and categorize the gaps as a means of establishing a level of impact and a priority order for fixing them.

Table 7.1   Cause and effect table inputs

Scenarios	Preconditions	Causes	Effects	Postconditions
Describe a single scenario (use case) in this row	What information or conditions must be in place before starting this scenario?	What triggers or events occur during this process?	What is the result of this combination of preconditions and causes?	What are the postconditions for this scenario?

HOW WILL THE ARTIFACTS AND DELIVERABLES BE USED?

The deliverables and artifacts from the analysis stage will enable the documentation of clear, complete, and logically consistent requirements. They will cement and reinforce the individual requirements and provide the underlying rationale and details for key functionality. The primary outputs of the analysis tasks are scenarios, drafted requirements, gap analysis, and the finalized future state. These documents will be used to complete the detailed requirements documents. The analyst will also utilize this documentation to verify and validate the requirements when generating the next draft.

Tasks and Activities of Analysis

The analysis stage begins with scenario planning, mind-mapping, gap analysis, and problem solving. First, scenario planning will enable the analyst to develop requirements that are based on how the system or application will be utilized in various intended functions. Second, mind-mapping will provide a quick visual aid for the analyst to capture snippets of related information, entities, functionality, and so forth, upon which to build as they proceed through analysis and ensure all details are captured. Gap analysis will consist of reviewing the current and future state documentation, and may reference back to existing business documentation, describing the current business rules and workflow, and existing documentation about the technical environment. Using this data and information, the analyst will begin to identify gaps between the current and future states.

In order to identify gaps between the current and future states, the analyst will review the function sets or feature groups of the mid-level requirements and begin to create scenarios to map out the step-by-step interactions between the various users and features of the new system or application. This set of scenarios may consist of activity, or context diagrams, and cause and effect, or decision, tables. In order to complete analysis tasks, the analyst will conduct the gap analysis and scenario planning. The gaps identified will be entered into the gap analysis logs and templates and then translated into new requirements as appropriate.

Techniques for Analyzing Requirements

The purpose of analysis is to generate a detailed set of requirements in order to achieve the results needed by the business. This mandates meeting the basic objectives of analysis itself (to expose and explore individual elements and to identify relevant factors). The specific techniques for analyzing requirements and source information are gap analysis, scenarios, and cause and effect tables. Each of these techniques generates the artifacts and deliverables previously listed.

Again, deliverables and artifacts from these activities are: scenarios, gap analysis, cause and effect tables, activity diagrams, and use case outlines.

Gap Analysis

Gap analysis is essentially the task of comparing the current state ("where we are now") to the future state ("where we are going"). Unfortunately, the current idea of gap analysis is not sufficient, in that it does not recognize gaps as risks and sets no strategies for managing them. The current form of gap analysis also does not categorize, or manage and interpret, the types of gaps based upon the level of influence on the project or the architecture. In truth, gap identification and analysis can happen at many points during the project and in varying relationships to the project. The key is to understand how those gaps influence and impact the project and the needed results.

The Auto Mechanic and the Analyst

I actually learned about conducting real gap analysis from my stepfather, Glenn. He is an auto mechanic and, as a child, I spent many weekends at his shop watching him figure out what was wrong with a car based on what it was doing and how it was performing. While this has come in handy when helping my friends with car problems, it has also had an unexpected benefit. It gave me the insight I needed in order to break down a problem by simply understanding the chain of events within a given process. It was, in effect, gap analysis.

Inputs and Outputs of Gap Analysis

The inputs to gap analysis include the architecture documentation, the current and future states, the requirements, and the business rules. The primary output to any type of gap analysis is the gap analysis document. The whole purpose of the gap analysis document is to create a central point for items, which are exposed as necessary to complete the end product—items that will significantly impact the outcome of the project and impact the overall business environment. It provides a central set of documents to act as a guideline for the analyst, when refining requirements, and detailed information with which the business can make critical decisions impacting either the project or the business itself.

Again, the gap analysis document contains an individual gap and its associated risks and details within a single document. For the best impact, it should contain the following elements:

- Project identification
- Author of the gap analysis document
- Gap type (routine, realignment, or peripheral)

- The process, system name, or reference to the gap's location
- Gap description
- Impacts to the existing project
- Whether the gap is in scope or out of scope
- Risks and impacts table

It is important to note that the audience of the gap documentation is both the business and the analysis team. Each of these teams will utilize and consume this document for different reasons. While the business will utilize the gap analysis to understand the issues exposed by the project team, the analysts will utilize it to create more accurate and refined requirements. To this end, low-level requirements and project change requests are the primary dependencies, although the identified gaps can also give rise to other business cases and provide justification for changes to the current projects or programs.

Performing Gap Analysis

Gap analysis is a technique that can be utilized in three primary scenarios: analyzing and understanding the differences between current and future states (defining the path: routine gap analysis), realigning projects that are not delivering the functionality required to meet business objectives and understanding where and why the project went off track (reassessing and getting back on the path: realignment gap analysis), and exposing preexisting gaps that are not directly being addressed by the current project (peripheral gap analysis).

Routine Gap Analysis

Routine gap analysis involves identifying and exploring the differences between the current and future states as a routine part of the current project. This means that the analyst investigates the current situation (problems, factors, etc.), or point A, and compares this situation to the objective situation, point B. This information is then utilized to design the path to get from point A to point B. Typically, this also means defining the integration points of building an interface between two applications, or understanding important factors when transitioning from one system to another.

Realignment Gap Analysis

Realigning a project that is offtrack is similar to routine gap analysis; however, the analyst must now map three states instead of two—current and future (points A and B). The analyst must now also map the problem state, point C. In addition, to prevent future projects from repeating this break and going offtrack, the analyst will need to understand how the development progressed from the current state to the problem state. Finally, the analyst will also need to understand how to redirect the project in order to get to the future state.

One of the things that the analyst and the business must now consider is whether the desired future state must be altered based on what can actually be delivered from the problem state. If people were on a road trip and got lost partway to the destination, would they keep driving, or stop and figure out where they were and how to get back on track? They would, most certainly, not jump to the conclusion that the road trip (or project, in this case) must be restarted in order to correct the course.

Peripheral Gap Analysis

Since most projects are started to address a business problem or to improve the way a business operates, the analyst will periodically find gaps on the peripheries of the project being worked on. These are gaps that cannot be addressed by the current project because they are out of scope. In these situations, the best approach is to perform gap analysis as a means of providing advice to the business, for future changes to scope or projects, to correct the gap. This advice must include the discovery of an issue, identification of the associated risks, and impacts. Ideally, the analyst uses this advice to inform the business and request a decision about how the team should proceed. Often, the resulting business decision will be based upon the impacts to the project and the associated costs of the resolution. Where the business determines that it is best not to take action, the gap and its associated risks and impacts must still be documented, so the business may take action at some point in the future.

In order to be performed effectively, gap analysis should include a step-by-step walkthrough of the work and data flows to ensure the complete and accurate capture of integration points. In addition, gap analysis steps should include mind-mapping and facilitated brainstorming sessions with architects, developers, and business intelligence resources as a means to exposing logical gaps. Gap analysis must be documented as clearly and concisely as possible. To this end, each gap analysis document should identify a single gap, including details about where the gap is (i.e., the specific process name), what happens, why it is a gap, and what the recommended solutions are.

It is also important for the analyst to anticipate and answer the next set of questions the business stakeholders are going to ask. What does this impact? What are the risks? What is the probability the risks will occur? What are the impacts if they do? Anticipating and answering these questions is especially important when gaps are discovered on the periphery of the project because it provides the business with the opportunity to mitigate the risks associated with those gaps on a priority basis. It is especially important to answer these questions when a project is offtrack and not delivering the functionality that will address the business problem and meet the objectives. This information will be critical for stakeholders to make informed decisions and mitigate the risk of continuing down the wrong development path.

It is equally important for the organization to learn and evolve. Therefore, this information must be documented in the *lessons learned* log. The worst thing any company can do is to document the lessons learned, file them, and never incorporate them into future projects. There is also no hard and fast rule that states a business must wait for the next project in order to implement those lessons. Simple items within the lessons learned log could potentially add tremendous value on the project where they were learned. Those lessons could include a recommended action plan, the status of actionable items, when those are due, and who the items have been assigned to. This can be a major advantage of an iterative (Agile) approach over a waterfall (traditional) approach (as discussed in Section 4) to the project, in that shorter iterations make it easier to incorporate lessons learned into the next sprints.

Best Practices Gap Analysis

Gaps are risks to the project and should be recognized and managed as such. Best practices would be to create a gap log in order to manage gaps identified on the project. This log should include the following elements:

- Gap name
- Gap type (routine, realignment, or peripheral)
- Risks associated with the gap (what could happen if this gap is not addressed)
- Impacts of the risks (how the business/project could be impacted if the risk actually occurs)
- Whether it was addressed by the project and how (i.e., improved requirements or assigned to business for future action)
- Whether it is in scope for the project

This log should be closed at the end of every project, as every item must either be dealt with directly by the project or assigned to a business owner—who will become responsible for the subsequent resolution—through the project issues log.

Scenarios

Scenarios are stories about the solution and how the users will interact with this system in order to perform the work required. Scenarios can take many forms, including activity diagrams, use cases, and cause and effect tables. Together with business process flows and the future state documentation, the scenarios paint a full and complete picture of how the system will perform the overall workflow, transaction processing, and user interactions at the functional level.

Activity Diagrams

Activity diagrams are merely another form of scenario mapping and process modeling. As in Figure 7.1, these diagrams resemble flow charts, which illustrate

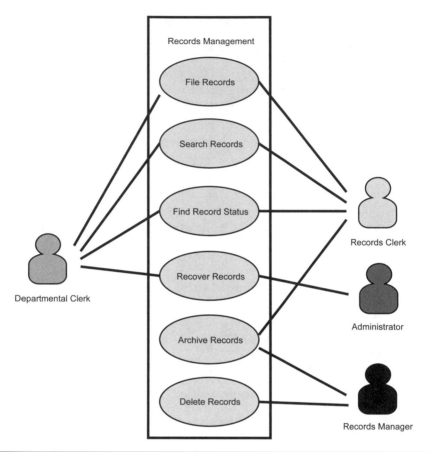

Figure 7.1 Sample activity diagram

the step-by-step processes and the flow of control throughout a given transaction. It includes key decision points, as well as both human and technical tasks and activities required to complete the overall transaction processing.

Document Structure and Management for Activity Diagrams

Activity diagrams are structured diagrams, which are managed in the same way that the business process model documents are. That is to say, each activity diagram is more effective when it is documented in its own individual document and all diagrams are catalogued in an activity diagram index.

Naming Conventions for Activity Diagrams

While there are no specific naming conventions laid out for activity diagrams, it is best practice—from a document management standpoint—to lay out the naming conventions at the start of the project and ensure that all analysts on the team follow this convention when generating the activity diagrams. For ease and consistency, it is recommended to create a naming convention similar to the established conventions for rules, processes, and requirements, as this will make it easier on all team members when they are attempting to locate specific activity diagrams.

Activity Diagram Inputs

Activity diagrams are intended to depict the actions and triggers of the workflow. They are the visual representation of an individual's interaction with the system when performing key work. To this end, the inputs for activity diagrams are the business process models, business rules, and data flow (which has been developed by the data architect). The culmination of this information will enable the business analyst to produce the necessary activity diagrams. The inputs include:

- *Actors*—The job function or system that performs, or contributes to performance of, the task
- *Activities*—The specific tasks to be performed
- *Related activities*—The specific steps involved in accomplishing and performing the individual task or activity
- *Inputs*—The data or information, which comes in from other systems upstream, to be utilized by this process
- *Outputs*—The data or information generated by this task, which will be utilized by other tasks (downstream)
- *Dependencies*—Other tasks, processes, or systems that require the outputs from this activity in order to be initiated and successfully completed
- *Decisions*—The key decisions made in this task that determine its outcomes and successful completion
- *Extension points*—Other tasks that data from this activity will lead directly into.

Activity Diagram Outputs

The activity diagrams represent a visual reference for the workflow of individual activities in the overall process. Therefore, the outputs from the activity diagrams include the diagrams themselves. These may include the task inputs and outputs that will be required for the activity to be completed successfully.

Scope and Dependencies of Activity Diagrams

The scope of an activity diagram is to cover the end-to-end workflow of a single activity or task to be performed by the solution. Typically, the "activity" is the user interaction with the system when performing a specific task. In the performance of this task, the user selects an option, which in turn triggers a series of events; thus, the system performs the selected task. The specification and validation stages are dependent upon the activity diagram documentation, in that low-level requirements are both verified and validated against this document set.

Tools and Techniques for Defining the Activity Diagram

The tools and techniques utilized to create the activity diagrams are primarily utilized for diagramming (mapping or modeling) purposes. The objective is to define a clear picture of the solution at all critical levels of detail in order to ensure that the developed and delivered product is indeed the required and specified product. To produce the activity diagrams, the business analyst utilizes techniques similar to those for producing the business process models. The primary technique will be facilitated sessions with the business team.

To begin the diagramming process, the business analyst will review the business process models and determine the key activities that need to be diagrammed in greater detail. The required process-related documentation includes key decisions made along the way, the primary data elements, and who contributes (by role) to this process.

The most widely used technique for diagramming activity diagrams is the UML. The UML is a standardized modeling language derived for object-oriented programming. This language includes a set of graphical notation techniques, which are applied to create visual models. These techniques provide a method for visualizing a system's architectural framework. In addition to the standard elements for activity diagrams, these models include such elements as:

- Database schemas
- Logical components
- Business processes
- Reusable software components
- Programming language statements.

During diagramming, the business analyst begins by identifying the inputs to the task (what information or data is fed into this activity). Then, the analyst must identify how the task is initiated or triggered (sometimes this is the data feed itself). From there, the analyst must walk through the task in step-by-step sequence (step one, two, three, etc.).

For each step, the analyst must identify the data inputs and outputs, who performs the step, whether there are any decisions to be made at this step, where this step leads, and finally, how and where the output data is utilized. If there is a decision, it must result in either a yes or a no. In this case, the analyst must further identify what happens when the answer to this decision is either yes or no. Since there will always be a positive or negative answer from the decision point, it is important to map the steps from this decision to the end of the task. In the case where this result pulls the processing flow of the task from the main path, it is important the business analyst identify whether and how this flow can be restored to the main path or how the process will be terminated or extended. If this is omitted or not identified, the analyst must work with the business to resolve the logical inconsistency.

Once the activity diagram has been drafted, the business must have the opportunity to verify that the information is complete, logical, and accurate. This means that the business must approve new steps within the task to verify feasibility and acceptability, and then accept ownership for these steps. After the drafts have been edited and the business feedback has been incorporated, the activity diagrams are finalized. In this process, the diagram version control is set, the names and file locations are entered into an activity diagram index file, and the maps are uploaded into the document repository.

Who Signs Off on the Activity Diagrams?

While there is no formal sign off, the business must verify that the activity diagrams are accurate, and the business analyst must verify that they are complete and consistent. The architecture and development teams must verify that the activity diagrams are feasible for the prescribed user interaction with the system or application. Within the analysis stage, activity diagrams enable the analyst to refine a detailed view of the new system, and the tasks performed by this system, in order to identify and explore business rules, analyze the requirements, and then ensure that those requirements account for the detailed end-to-end transaction processing.

Use Case Definition Outlines

Use cases are merely another form of scenarios. Use cases are often represented in the activity diagram format, but could also represent the end-to-end view of the user interaction by using a narrative that describes each step of a transaction. They provide a detailed view of the transaction, which enables the business and architecture team to fully understand the inputs, outputs, alternate flows, and extension points.

Document Structure and Management for Use Cases

Use cases are structured and managed in the same way as the business rules, in that each use case is more effective when it is contained within its own individual document, and when all of the use cases are listed in an index. For manageability, this can be the same index as the activity diagram index (in which case, it should simply be called the deliverable index). When writing use cases, analysts must also be sure to reference the applicable requirements at the start of the document. This will ensure clarity and allow for the designers, business, developers, and testers to easily find the cross-referenced material.

Use case inputs can include any data or information that is required for transaction processing, including user or system responses and upstream data obtained from another system or application. Since use cases are documents that tell a very detailed story about the interaction between the user and the system, they are best derived from the requirements and other source information.

Naming Conventions

While there are no specific naming conventions laid out for use cases, it is good document management practice to lay out conventions at the start of the project and ensure that all analysts on the team follow these conventions. For consistency, it is recommended to create a naming convention that reflects those of the rules, processes, and requirements, as this will make it easier for all team members when they are attempting to locate specific use case documents (this creates predictability).

Use Case Inputs

Use cases are intended to describe the workflow of specific transactions of the solution. They are the representation of an individual interaction with the system during a single transaction. To this end, the inputs for use cases are the business process models, business rules, and data flow. Compiling information from these sources will enable the business analyst to produce the use cases. Inputs include:

- *Actors*—The job function or system that performs, or contributes to performance of, the task
- *Processes*—The specific transactions to be performed
- *Related processes*—The specific steps involved in accomplishing and performing the individual transactions
- *Inputs*—The data or information, coming from other systems upstream, to be utilized by this process
- *Outputs*—The data or information, generated by this transaction, which will be utilized by other tasks
- *Dependencies*—The other tasks, processes, or systems that require this transaction's outputs to be initiated and successfully completed
- *Decisions*—The key decisions that will be made in this transaction in order to determine its outcomes and successful completion

- *Preconditions*—The specific criteria or conditions that must be in place before the transaction can begin and run
- *Main flow*—The flow of this transaction from start to finish
- *Alternate flow*—The flow the transaction will follow at various points in the transaction processing, which will pull the transaction away from the main flow onto alternate paths
- *Postconditions*—The specific criteria or conditions that result from the transaction processing
- *Extension points*—Other tasks that data from this transaction will lead directly into.

Use Case Outputs

The use cases represent the positive (main path) and negative (alternate path) steps in the normal flow of the transaction as it is performed by the system. Therefore, the outputs from this process are the use cases themselves.

Use Case Scope and Dependencies

The scope of the use case is to cover the end-to-end flow of a single transaction to be performed by the system. The transaction is a single user interaction performed within the system. The performance of this transaction specifies preconditions, triggers, and postconditions. While there is a widespread school of thought, asserting that use cases are utilized as a technique for eliciting requirements, they are actually best applied once the business analyst has a better idea about the requirement structure and is working to analyze and write the requirements. Use cases provide a new view of the requirements, which enables more complete and consistent authoring of the final document.

The analysis, specification, and validation stages are dependent upon the use cases in which low-level requirements are polished, verified, and validated against this document set. Use cases are intended for the business analysis team to first dissect and explore the source information. Later, they can ensure the completeness and accuracy of the requirements in validation. These cases are also utilized by the analysis team to present the requirements and the solution to the business, illustrating the end-to-end process and obtaining sign off on the requirements. Finally, use cases are utilized by the architecture and development teams to ensure that all of the functionality has been captured in the requirements, design, and development of the product.

Tools and Techniques for Defining the Use Cases

The tools and techniques that create the use cases are primarily utilized for diagramming or documentation purposes. These techniques are reflective of the style that has been chosen for the use cases. Remember that the objective of use cases is to define a clear picture of the individual transactions from a user interaction perspective. To this end, business analysts may either choose to utilize activity diagrams for depicting the use cases, or they may opt to utilize a version of pseudo-code to describe the step-by-step transaction. To begin the use case development process, the business analyst reviews the business process models and other inputs to determine the transactions that need to be mapped in greater detail. The business analyst then maps the transaction in the sequence of events along the main path. Once the main path has been drafted, the analyst can identify the points along this main path where alternate paths will pull the transaction from this main flow. Finally, the analyst can identify the extension points and outputs from the transaction.

When the draft has been completed, the business analyst must verify that the information is complete, logical, and accurate. In many projects, the use cases are the ideal documents for the business to review and approve, as they will provide a more appropriate level of understanding for the average business person. This is because these documents are not as technical as requirements and will support a greater comprehension of how the solution will work. In other words, they provide context to the requirements. After the drafts have been edited and the team feedback has been incorporated, the use cases are finalized. In this process, the use case version control is set, the names and file locations are entered into an index file, and the maps are uploaded into the document repository.

Who Signs Off on the Use Cases?

The business must validate that the use cases are complete, consistent, and accurate. The architecture and development teams must informally sign off on the use cases to verify that this is fact how the users will interact with the system or application. The business analyst is responsible for ensuring that it is logically complete. Sign off on requirements is partially dependent upon having this documentation completed because of its value in conveying the functionality to the business. This is because users from the business team will either have little interest, time, or ability to understand the seemingly dry and detailed technical requirements document.

Cause and Effect Tables

Cause and effect tables are simple matrices that are utilized to quickly illustrate the linkages between the preconditions, triggers (causes), outputs, and postconditions (effects). These tables are highly effective for mapping out large numbers of use cases, which ensures that all scenarios have been considered and accounted for. Table 7.2 illustrates a simple example of a cause and effect table based on the criteria depicted in Table 7.3.

Table 7.2   Sample cause and effect table

State	Filed (in doc mgmt system)	Not Filed (not in doc mgmt system)	Status	Priority
Existing	X		Active (used & edited)	Medium
Existing		X	Active	Medium
Existing	X		Active Historical (used but not edited)	Medium
Existing		X	Active Historical	Medium
Existing	X		Obsolete Historical (not used or edited)	Low
Existing		X	Obsolete Historical	Low
Nonexisting		X	Active	High
Nonexisting		X	Active Historical	High
Nonexisting		X	Obsolete Historical	OUT OF SCOPE
Future	X		Active	OUT OF SCOPE
Future	X		Active Historical	OUT OF SCOPE
Future	X		Obsolete Historical	OUT OF SCOPE

Table 7.3   Sample criteria for cause and effect table

Cause	Effect 1	Effect 2 ...	... Effect 20	Priority/Scope (Optional)
User Input	What is the first thing that happens when the user inputs data?	What is the next thing that happens when the user inputs data?	What is the next thing that happens when the user inputs data?	What is the priority rating of this item? How will it impact the project?
Requirement	What are the states or outcomes of my requirement?	What are the states or outcomes of my requirement?	What are the states or outcomes of my requirement?	Is this item listed here to demonstrate consideration, but not in scope?

The primary purpose of the cause and effect table is to provide a quick cross-reference of the IPO (input, process, output) process in order to ensure completeness and that *ALL* scenarios have been considered. This is especially important when examining requirements for logical completeness. It is easy to understand what the system must do when all criteria or conditions are met, but what about when only some, or none, are met? How should the system respond or react?

Cause and effect tables are an important technique for the development of requirements. They are useful across multiple stages of the requirements development process, including analysis, specification, and validation. Within the context of the analysis stage, cause and effect tables provide a quick look at the processes, without focusing on the requirements during the initial passes. Within specification, these tables allow the business analyst to formulate more complete requirements while writing them. Finally, within validation, these tables enable other business analysts on the team to validate the work of others during peer review.

Document Structure and Management

The cause and effect table is purely a matrix. The structure is to list all of the elements, column by column, from the left side of the matrix. Each row in the matrix represents a single scenario; each column represents a single element. Since the cause and effect table is an artifact that is not distributed outside of the business analysis team, and it is primarily used for the purposes of validating logical consistency, it is not necessarily a formal document. As such, it is only important to manage these documents when the scenarios are highly complex. This will prevent the team from having to start from scratch every time they wish to use this technique, and it will allow a revisit in order to verify the thought processes.

Naming Conventions

While there are no specific naming conventions laid out for cause and effect tables, it is best practice—from a document management standpoint—to plan the naming conventions at the start of the task and ensure that all analysts on the team follow those conventions when producing the cause and effect tables. Of course, this is under the assumption that these documents are not going to be scrapped after the completion of the activity.

Cause and Effect Table Inputs

Inputs include all preexisting states (such as on or off, open or closed, approved or not approved) and inputs, all actions the system or user of the system will trigger by interacting with the system, and all outputs and postconditions.

- *Scenarios*—the specific use cases for the transactions or activities to be mapped
- *Preconditions*—the specific criteria or conditions that must be in place before the transaction can begin and run
- *Inputs*—the data or information coming from other systems (upstream) to be utilized by this process

- *Triggers (causes)*—the specific system events that occur during processing
- *Outputs*—the data or information generated by this task that will be utilized by other tasks (downstream)
- *Postconditions (effects)*—the specific criteria or conditions that result from the transaction processing

Cause and Effect Table Outputs

The primary outputs of cause and effect tables are artifacts, or work products, for the analysis team. These can be a simple spreadsheet or a whiteboard session among the analysts, depending upon the complexity of the system. Remember that the cause and effect table is only an artifact the business analyst creates in order to validate the completeness and logical consistency of the requirements. Therefore, in any state of completion, this document is not intended to be consumed by any other team members and does not have to be filed and managed.

Cause and Effect Tables Scope and Dependencies

The scope of this document includes individual scenarios and the elements for each scenario. While there is no direct consumer of the cause and effect tables outside of the analysis team, this technique does result in more complete and consistent requirements. As such, other deliverables from analysis, specification, and validation are dependent upon the cause and effect tables. Once quality requirements have been developed, other deliverables in the project life cycle—such as enterprise architecture, source code, and test plans—are dependent upon the degree of analysis and validation that results from applying this specific technique.

Tools and Techniques for Creating the Cause and Effect Table

The business analyst must compile as many of the elements for each scenario as possible. In other words, the preconditions, inputs, triggers, outputs, and postconditions for each function or feature of the system must be collected. These are plotted in the shell, column by column, from the left side of the matrix. For ease of use, each of the elements should be grouped together (regardless of how many elements exist within a category). This means: if there are three preconditions, four inputs, and twelve triggers, then each of these is plotted in sequence (column by column). All preconditions would appear first, then all inputs, and finally all triggers.

Next, the business analyst maps individual scenarios across the matrix. Each row in the matrix represents a single scenario, and each column represents a single element. Every scenario must have a minimum of one precondition, one input, one trigger, one output, and one postcondition—even if those are zero or null. To map a scenario across the matrix, the analyst identifies all possible combinations of the elements. If, as in this example, the scenario has three preconditions, four inputs, and twelve triggers, the analyst must plot fourteen scenario combinations to account for all preconditions and inputs, and then uses those to build out the combinations of preconditions, inputs, and triggers.

Upon completion of mapping of the triggers against all possible combinations of preconditions and inputs, the analyst should have mapped 170 scenarios (luckily, it does not take long to do). There are so many possible combinations of elements because, for each single element, there is a combination that compounds the volumes of scenarios. In addition, each element must have an additional scenario to account for a null across everything except the outputs and the postconditions.

Once the tables are completed, the business analyst can review the requirements that have been documented to date to validate whether all possible scenarios have been accounted for. The key here is to validate that all possible resulting outputs and postconditions have been mapped to combinations of preconditions, inputs, and triggers. Further, the analyst must ensure that all possible combinations of preconditions, inputs, and triggers are mapped to postconditions and outputs.

Who Signs Off on the Cause and Effect Tables?

While there is no formal sign off for cause and effect tables, it is incumbent upon business analysts to verify the completeness of the mapping. It is crucial that these tables be complete and all scenarios accounted for in order to ensure that they will be useful during the requirements validation stage.

EXIT CRITERIA FOR ANALYSIS

The analysis stage is the phase wherein the analysis team applies a set of tasks to identify and expose elements and to uncover important factors that will enable them to create a full and complete set of requirements. This means that the bulk of activities within this stage will actually result in artifacts that will be consumed in the writing process of the specification stage. To know whether the analysis team is ready to leave this stage and to move to specification, the analysts should have mapped scenarios, cause and effect tables, and gap analyses that cover every aspect of the new solution in sufficient detail to be able to author complete and detailed requirements in the next stage.

Best Practices For Analysis

Analysis is both a starting point for defining more granular requirements and a starting point for validation. It is the starting point for validation in that, within analysis, high-level requirements and current and future states are examined from multiple angles in order to derive the next level of detail. In addition, the very techniques utilized for deriving this next level of requirements detail contributes to validation later on. However, performing some of these tasks during the analysis stage will help to create a clearer picture of the requirements and will ensure a greater degree of accuracy and completeness before the analysts get to the validation stage.

REFERENCES

1. Random House Dictionary 2013, Random House Inc.
2. Ibid.

## 8

Specification

The specification stage is where the refined low-level requirements are formally drafted within the document (also known as the business requirements document, or BRD) for the validation process. While this document contains a set of further refined requirements, it must be noted that this is not the final version. It may only be the first set of requirements in document form. Previous versions of requirements may have been written in a simple spreadsheet or a requirements management tool. In addition, while this version must be written in document form, numbers are not assigned until after they have been reviewed by the teams, and after the requirements have been verified.

WRITING TESTABLE REQUIREMENTS

One of the most common questions asked in testing is, "do we test what was built, or what was written in the requirements?" The answer is quite simple. The product built must align with the requirements. Therefore, testing of the product must occur against the requirements. To accomplish this, the requirements must be written in such a way as to be testable. In order for the analysis team to write testable requirements, it is imperative for everyone involved in the project to understand how requirements will be consumed, and for whom they are written. While the business stakeholders will verify and approve the document, and they will later see the results of those requirements at work in the new solution, they are not the primary audience for the requirements documentation. In fact, the primary audience for this document are the architects, the developers, and the testers.

This means that requirements must be written for the appropriate audience in order for them to utilize the information to create the architecture design, to develop the solution, and to test this solution. One of the drawbacks to many requirements is that they are commonly written in one of three primary styles: Shakespearean, pseudo-technical jargon, or colloquial English. Unfortunately, none of these styles is appropriate for writing requirements because it cannot be easily tested. The examples in Table 8.1 illustrate each style.

The Shakespearean style uses flowery language to describe the requirements. As shown in the table, use of the term "moreover" is, not only unnecessary, but compounds the ambiguity of the whole requirement. Pseudo-technical jargon brings in design elements of the solution. In the example given within the table, the requirement cites "a drop-down list of themes already created." In this case, the "drop-down list" is only a part of the problem because the requirement also cites that this list was "already created." Each of these indicates design elements that should have been left to the architects and did not add any value or clarity to the requirements. The colloquial English style uses the ordinary language people use in everyday conversation and in e-mails. In the colloquial English example, the requirement states that "Every painting always belongs to only one theme." This is not testable because it uses terms like "every," "always," and "only," which are not definitive and measurable.

Testable requirements are those that can be measured, are definitive, and have clear parameters for the functionality to be performed. Untestable requirements tend to be ambiguous in nature and leave unanswered questions for other team members to fill in with assumptions. The problem is that the architects, developers, and testers may all be making different assumptions about how to fill in those ambiguities. The differences and discrepancies in these assumptions will directly result in defects within the solution.

As discussed in Chapter 3, great requirements are unambiguous, deterministic, concise, explicit, consistently worded, logically consistent, feasible, complete,

Table 8.1 Examples of common requirement styles

Common Requirement Style	Sample Requirement
'Shakespearean'	An administrator should be able to perform all the search queries as a normal user. Moreover, he should be able to edit any of the information sections (like paintings, artists, themes, galleries, countries) and is responsible for updating and maintaining information links.
Pseudo-Techno English	The system has a drop-down list of themes already created for an administrator to choose from while adding a new painting information.
Colloquial English	Every painting always belongs to only one "Theme" for example such as modern art or nature, etc.

and accurate. In short, each requirement must be written in such a way that the reader knows exactly what the writer intended to say without the need for interpretation. Why? Think of it this way: can a computer interpret what is being said without being given clear instructions on how to do it and what each possible outcome should be? No, of course not. So think of the architects, developers, and testers in the same way as a computer. Could a computer interpret the terms "few," "several," or "many?" Could it interpret the phrases "under most circumstances" or "usually?" No. People designing, developing, and testing the system must interpret these terms and phrases, and their personal interpretations may not match those of the others on the team. They most certainly may not align to the expectations and needs of the business. So, knowing what great requirements should look like (and, equally important, why they should look this way), helps us understand how to write them so that they are, in fact, great requirements.

INPUTS/OUTPUTS OF SPECIFICATION

Having the deliverables and artifacts from analysis (the resulting scenarios, cause and effect tables, gap analysis, and high-level requirements) is critical to starting the specification stage because they will form the source information for this stage. Each information source will be utilized to author the low-level requirements document for review and approvals based on the details that were identified, exposed, and explored during analysis.

WHAT ARTIFACTS AND DELIVERABLES ARE CREATED IN SPECIFICATION?

The specification stage produces important detailed deliverables and artifacts. These include:

- Low-level requirements
- Finalized business rules documentation
- Refined use cases

Requirements Document

The requirements document (the BRD) represents the next phase of requirements activity. Again, these low-level requirements map back to the high-level requirements and to scope. However, the low-level requirements have a level of detail and granularity not seen in the scope or even the high-level ones. These details are a direct result of the analysis activities that identified and exposed elements of both scope and high-level requirements. This final draft of the requirements document is verified and validated through the validation stage. This stage ensures that the architecture, development, and test teams will have enough detail to perform their tasks and to generate the prescribed solution.

Who Signs Off on Low-Level Requirements

The business, architecture, development, and test teams must all understand and sign off on the requirements document. This is to ensure that the functionality can be delivered, within the context of the current enterprise architecture and timeframe, with the available resources. It also ensures that all of the requirements are testable. This being said, remember that the real audience for the requirements document is the architecture, development, and test teams. While the business must sign off and validate that the overall functionality is complete, consistent, and accurate, they do not necessarily need to know every single dry technical detail in the document.

Even if individual business team members are technically inclined, they simply do not have the time to get caught up in the details. In general, the business is more concerned with the answers to the following questions:

- How does it work?
- What are the features?
- What information does it need?
- How will the business use it?
- What results does it give the business?
- How will the business manage it?
- How does it connect with other systems to make it easier for the business?
- Can the project team ensure that the results are accurate and valid?
- What happens if it breaks down?
- How will the business support it?

By focusing on providing these details to the business, the sign off process will be generally more effective and productive.

Finalized Business Rules

Business rules represent the key policies and regulations governing certain aspects of the business. At some point in the life cycle process, these rules need to be considered final so that the team can work with them and move forward with the requirements activities. This does not mean that these rules will not change. It simply means that these business rules must be baselined at an appropriate point so that work on the requirements can proceed. Rules must be managed in the same way that other changes to the requirements and processes must be managed. Change control and document management standards will be utilized to determine how and when to amend the rules, and will further determine how those changes will be documented.

Business Rules Refinement

In order to refine the business rules, the analyst must utilize some of the same techniques they would utilize to analyze and refine the requirements. Specifically, the business analyst can map scenarios, conduct gap analysis, and interview the business stakeholders and users. By using these same techniques to refine the business rules, the analyst will arrive at an accurate and more complete set of rules. Ensuring the completeness and accuracy of these outputs is critical to the requirements development process.

Use Case Definition/Refinement

Use cases are step-by-step scenarios that describe each step in a single user transaction. Within the context of specification, use cases are refined into full and detailed narratives or diagrams, and can be validated by utilizing cause and effect tables.

WHO WILL USE THE ARTIFACTS AND DELIVERABLES FROM SPECIFICATION?

The primary audience for the requirements documentation is the architecture, development, and test teams. Remember that, while the business must verify the functionality and sign off on it, the project teams actually consume this documentation in order to design, develop, and test the final solution. Therefore, it is critical that the documentation produced during this stage be consumable by these teams to complete their tasks. In other words, these project teams must be able to read, comprehend, and transform the information contained within the deliverables into structured architecture designs, source and executable code, and into test plans, cases, and scripts.

How the Artifacts and Deliverables From Specification
Can Be Utilized—contributed by James Canter

"Typically, analysis of requirements artifacts by test analysts to design full coverage test cases takes less time than system and low-level software design and implementation. This puts design and development team members in a position to leverage requirements ambiguity discovered by testers. In one study,[1] the practice of publishing and distributing requirements ambiguity clarifications contributed to a 75% reduction in developer scrap and rework. Effective coverage of targeted system behavior by test design means that experienced test analysts must readily identify logical pathways in system processing to ensure that correct branching is made observable by tests, which correlate system inputs with desired, observable effects.

The identification of specific behaviors must be readily apparent in requirements, so that test analysts can trace specific test cases to them, in order to understand whether test design is complete. The discipline of tracing tests to required behaviors tends to uncover missing pathways. These gaps tend to be predominated by ineffective articulation of exception paths, though they can occur in fundamental scenarios.

Where narrative requirements are employed, test analysts are forced to name the use cases being implemented, trace use cases to various passages in the requirements, and then trace their test case to one or more use case names.

Hence, the closer the business analysis team can get to a use case format, the quicker testers can get through test design, and the more apparent, reviewable, and reportable test coverage becomes. As stated, this positions architects and developers to more effectively leverage discovery in the test design phase. Reduced time-to-market, higher product quality, and lower costs are rooted in clear, concise, unambiguous, and deterministic requirements."[2]

TASKS AND ACTIVITIES OF THE SPECIFICATION STAGE

The specification stage is about writing the requirements and revising the future state, business rules, and use cases. This means that the analyst creates drafts of the final documents and begins to author each of the functional descriptions associated with the solution. The question concerning how deeply to dive into requirements before the project enters the design phase nags at business analysts the world over and is the subject of much debate with their developer colleagues. The problem is that people do not generally understand that requirements are not merely the result of those analysts making notes during short sporadic meetings with stakeholders and user groups.

Requirements are a collaborative effort between business analysts, architects, and developers throughout the project. High-level requirements start with scope and drill down to the next level of detail. Business analysts tend to make the mistake of attempting to get as much written down on paper as they can and try to write really detailed requirements up front. This just is not possible or realistic, considering the level of knowledge and input provided at this early stage. In order to add more detail to the mid-level requirements, the analyst will review the function sets, or feature groups and scenarios, contained within the outputs that were produced within the analysis. This detail is drafted into the requirements document in groups of functionality. While the analyst is writing the requirements and rules, it is imperative to understand and review the ambiguity list as this will lend to the documentation of clear and consistent outputs that are free from ambiguity.

In order to be proficient at performing these tasks, analysts will need to be well-versed in business and technical writing, problem solving, and underlying business operations, and must have some technical and domain knowledge. They must exhibit personal traits as independent analytical thinkers, and detail-oriented and innovative individuals. The competency areas required for specifications are approximately 40% business knowledge, 40% technical knowledge, and about 20% people and soft skills.

Business Rules

The business rules documentation is utilized within the specification stage to review and analyze the requirements. In doing so, the business analyst is able to ensure a more complete set of requirements, based upon the policies and regulations of the business. In this way, the requirements are not only complete and logically consistent but are also in compliance with any mandated governance and controls.

Low-Level Requirements Document

Now let's get to the heart of it all: writing requirements. In order to write effective requirements, which deliver a clear and concise message to the architecture, development, and testing teams, the analyst must consider not only the organization of the requirements document, traceability back to scope, and high-level objectives but must also consider the word choice and structure of each of the individual requirements.

> Word Choice: *"Words mean more than is set down on paper. It takes the human voice to infuse them with deeper meaning."*[3]—*Maya Angelou*

Using the wrong words in requirements leaves the door open for this "deeper meaning" to creep in. Unfortunately, in requirements this generates ambiguity and interpretation by the reader. The objective of requirements is to convey a specific and exacting message to the reader so that the solution meets the business need. Thus, requirements are more effective when the wording abides by the rules and avoids the following pitfalls:

1. **Ambiguous Statements**
   a. *Ambiguous Boundaries and Measures*
      Ambiguous boundaries and measures appear when the requirement is written in a way that does not clearly specify numeric values or

list every item in a grouping or listing. In other words, the requirement is not measureable or quantifiable. Table 8.2 illustrates the terms and phrases which cause ambiguous boundaries, and Table 8.3 depicts sample requirement across development stages.

b. *Ambiguous Logical Operators (Or, And, Nor)*

It can be confusing to create a requirement that compounds criteria or allows various combinations of criteria before performing an action. Table 8.4 depicts examples of requirements using ambiguous boundaries. Table 8.5 illustrates examples of requirements using good and poor combinations of logical operators.

Table 8.2 Examples of ambiguous boundaries and measures

about	a couple of	a few
including	many	more
most	multiple	several
some	such as	up to

Table 8.3 Sample requirement across development stages

Requirement Development (Evolutionary) Stage	Example
Objective	To replace the legacy administrator console within the company's call center.
Scope	The new administrator console will allow both administrators and supervisors to manage employee profiles.
High-Level Requirement	The Administrator must have the ability to add, change, or inactivate a CSR's profile.
Mid-Level Requirement	The Resource Analyst and Administrators must be able to create a CSR profile that contains the following information.
Low-Level Requirement	Resource Analyst and Administrators must be able to create a CSR profile that contains the following information: • Name • Contact Info • Workforce Management #–(system generated) • Exelon Employee # • Supervisor Name • Full/part time • Address

Notice the capitals on the "and" between criteria set in the good example. This structure clearly defines that there is a combination of criteria that must be applied before performing the action.

However, in the poor example, it is not clear whether the person must have a bank account and a debit card, a bank account and a credit card, or simply a credit card to continue processing.

c. *Ambiguous References*

Ambiguous references point to one item in relation to something else. This is a common issue in requirements. The terms in Table 8.6 are considered ambiguous referential terms.

Avoid using such terms as "the following" in the requirements document; clearly specify where something is located or will be located. In addition, it is important to avoid using terms that refer to the main person, process, or system within the requirement. Table 8.7 demonstrates good and poor examples.

d. *Ambiguous precedence relationships*

This occurs when the task order is unclear, and the reader would be unable to determine the sequence of events and tasks. Table 8.8 shows examples of using ambiguous precedence.

Table 8.4   Examples of requirements using ambiguous boundaries

Poor Example	The user shall be presented with *multiple* screens to enter personal information.
Good Example	The user must be able to enter the following personal information into the system . . .

Table 8.5   Examples of requirements using ambiguous logical operators

Poor Example	If the user has a bank account *and* has a debit card that is active, or a credit card that is active . . .
Good Example	If the user is logged in *AND* has reservations, then do the following . . .

Table 8.6   Examples of ambiguous references

above	among	below
beside	between	etc.
it	such	the first
the last	the next	the other
the previous	them	these
they	this	those

Table 8.7 Examples of requirements using ambiguous references

Poor Example	A user should have the option to select one or more paintings and put them in a folder called "Favorites" that is generated by the application the first time it is started.
Good Example	Users must have the ability to select and designate multiple paintings as 'Favorites'.

Table 8.8 Examples of requirements using ambiguous precedence

Poor Example	The system should give the user the opportunity to exchange working shifts with another employee if approved, and if the shifts are the same and if both employees have the same status.
Good Example	The user must be able to exchange shifts with another employee when: 1. Both employees are either full time or both employees are part time *AND* 2. Both shifts equal the same number of total working hours *AND* 3. When the exchange has been approved by a supervisor.

e. *Ambiguous Adjectives*

Adjectives are used to describe nouns and pronouns. In writing, adjectives are used to embellish thoughts or enhance reader understanding. However, in requirements, adjectives can confuse the reader because they are not specific enough to define the detailed specifications the design team needs to create a consistent technical document, which defines the system that will meet the business need or solve the problem. These problem adjectives are illustrated in Table 8.9, and Table 8.10 shows the usage of these terms in requirements.

Table 8.9 Examples of ambiguous adjectives

all	any	appropriate
custom	efficient	every
few	frequent	improved
infrequent	intuitive	invalid
many	most	normal
ordinary	rare	same
seamless	several	similar
some	standard	the complete
the entire	transparent	typical
usual	valid	

Table 8.10 Examples of requirements using ambiguous adjectives

Poor Example	The user shall input a valid code into the system.
Good Example	The user must have the ability to input a time code into the system before exchanging work shifts. Valid codes are: x, y, z.

f. *Ambiguous Adverbs*

Adverbs are a common stumbling block for requirements authors. It is important to remember not to write in the same way that people speak in conversation—or any other situation for that matter. Writing for requirements is fundamentally different from writing an e-mail, a paper, or a story. Whereas adverbs are part of the descriptive makeup of a story, which makes it interesting, requirements need to be specific, clear, and detailed, and they need to be concise and exact. Typical adverbs, which have no place in requirements embellishment, are shown in Table 8.11. Table 8.12 provides an example of requirements using ambiguous adverbs.

g. *Ambiguous Synonyms*

Using a vague term to replace a specific name is an ambiguous synonym. This is a common mistake when the author creates longer sentences in requirements and has already used the specific item name. Wording and phrases to watch for are shown in Table 8.13.

A general rule to follow is: if there is a need to use the name more than once, then the requirement is vague and needs to be reworded.

Table 8.11 Examples of ambiguous adverbs

accordingly	almost	approximately
by and large	commonly	customarily
efficiently	frequently	generally
hardly ever	in general	infrequently
intuitively	just about	more often than not
more or less	mostly	nearly
normally	not quite	often
on the odd occasion	ordinarily	rarely
roughly	seamlessly	seldom
similarly	sometime	somewhat
transparently	typically	usually
virtually		

Table 8.12 Examples of requirements using ambiguous adverbs

Poor Example	The user shall be able to extract reports from the system frequently. They would usually get these reports automatically sent to them.
Good Example	The system will provide the ability for the user to build a customized report which will be run and extracted at user-defined intervals.

Table 8.13 Examples of ambiguous synonyms

the application	the component	the data
the database	the field	the file
the frame	the information	the message
the module	the page	the rule
the screen	the status	the system
the table	the value	the window

Examples of requirements using ambiguous synonyms are shown in Table 8.14.

h. *Ambiguous Verbs*

Verbs can be a significant source of confusion in requirements. The idea is that each step of every task and function the system must do has to be specifically defined. Table 8.15 identifies specific terms to avoid, and Table 8.16 shows examples of requirements using these terms.

2. **Built-in assumptions**

a. *Functional/environmental knowledge:* There is an element of assumed knowledge for the audience of a requirements document. Ensure that requirements are clear and specific and include an element of explanation for each technical item so that the broad audience of the document can understand it and sign off on it. One of the most common issues in requirements is the assumption that the reader has the same level of knowledge of the applications, internal

Table 8.14 Examples of requirements using ambiguous synonyms

Poor Example	The user shall be presented with several input fields for account information
Good Example	The user must have the ability to enter personal account information. The account information must contain the following fields: name, username, account ID, home address.

Table 8.15 Examples of ambiguous verbs

adjust	alter	amend
calculate	change	compare
compute	convert	create
customize	derive	determine
edit	enable	improve
indicate	manipulate	match
maximize	may	minimize
might	modify	optimize
perform	process	produce
provide	support	update
validate	verify	

Table 8.16 Examples of requirements using ambiguous verbs

Poor Example	The system shall compare the data in the user fields to determine if the entry is valid.
Good Example	The checkout function must validate the entered credit card details entered by the user against the bank system.

verbiage, processes, and units as the author. Assuming this means that a level of tribal knowledge, which is not readily translated by other business units, resources, and groups required to utilize the requirements in their tasks, has been built into the document.

b. *Use of jargon:* "Techies" and developers tend to use a lot of slang and jargon. Jargon includes abbreviated terms, such as "ASAP" instead of "as soon as possible," or "RUP" instead of "rational unified process".

If abbreviated jargon terms are used over writing out a full phrase repeatedly throughout the document, it must be defined in the glossary and the first time it is used. My personal preference is to use the full phrase, followed by the abbreviation in parenthesis, and to reuse this style, redefining the term at its first instance in a new section. This makes it easier for the reader to find and provides a reminder of the definition.

3. **Directive**

It is important to ensure that requirements clearly state whether the requirement is a "must have" or a "nice to have." It is important to remember that there is nothing polite about requirements. They are directions, not personal requests for favors, and they must be worded as such. Words like "should" and "may" have no place in requirements because requirements indicate a moral imperative or an invitation to include the requirement. However, the requirement could also be ignored because it is a moral imperative. Table 8.17 illustrates examples of good and poor requirements.

4. **Implicit cases**

Another common mistake is to imply other attributes and inclusive cases. While ambiguous implicit cases are acceptable in colloquial writing, requirements must be precise and must, therefore, be written in exacting language that leaves no room for ambiguity. This means that some sentences must NEVER appear in a requirements document. Table 8.18 identifies terms that create implicit ambiguity, and Table 8.19 presents examples of requirements that use implicit cases.

5. **Latin verbiage**

People often misuse and interchange terms they do not understand. Unfortunately, many people do not know that these Latin terms (e.g., i.e., and etc.) are *not* interchangeable. They are Latin phrases which have completely different meanings. Table 8.20 lists Latin verbiage to be avoided, and Table 8.21 shows examples of requirements using these terms.

6. **Negation**

a. *Scope of negation*

Scope of negation refers to specific boundaries for the negative item. It is important to be explicit about which item in the requirement is being negated. Table 8.22 provides good and poor examples of the scope of negation.

b. *Unnecessary negation*

Unnecessary negation refers to the author using more simplistic language. If the item can be written without negation to be clearer, then it must be written without the negative. Table 8.23 provides an example of good and poor requirements using unnecessary negation.

c. *Double negation*

It is common for people to use double negatives in colloquial (conversational) language. This is a bad habit which must be avoided in requirements. Table 8.24 provides examples of good and poor double negation.

Table 8.17   Examples of requirements using ambiguous directives

Poor Example	The system should calculate the sales tax of the total sale. The calculation may use the billing address entered by the customer to determine the amount of the sales tax paid.
Good Example	The system must calculate the sales tax of the total sale based on the billing address entered by the customer.

Table 8.18   Examples of ambiguous implicit cases

also	although	as well
besides	but	even though
for all other	furthermore	however
in addition to	likewise	moreover
notwithstanding	on the other hand	otherwise
still	though	unless
whereas	yet	as required
as necessary		

Table 8.19   Examples of requirements using ambiguous implicit cases

Poor Example	The system shall collect user information. Moreover, it should store this information in the database.
Good Example	All user profile details must be stored in the client information database. The profile details are: full name, home address, phone number and client ID.

Table 8.20   Examples of ambiguous latin verbiage

The follow Latin terms must not appear in requirements
i.e.—id est: Latin phrase for "that is"
etc.—et cetera: Latin phrase for "and including"
et al.—et alii: Latin phrase for "and others" but can also be short for et. Alia which means "and other things" or et alibi meaning "and other places".
e.g.—exempli gratia: Latin phrase meaning "for example"

Table 8.21   Examples of requirements using ambiguous latin verbiage

Poor Example	The system shall collect user information. The user information should contain: name, address, client ID, etc.
Good Example	All user profile details must be stored in the client information database. The profile details are: full name, home address, phone number and client ID.

Table 8.22   Examples of requirements using ambiguous scope of negation

Poor Example	If the administrator attempts to link a painting with an artist, and it does not already exist, he not only needs to create a new "Painting Information" for the painting, but also create a new "Artist Information" manually for that artist and provide suitable links between the two as described in the requirements above.
Good Example	All paintings must be associated to an artist profile. Artist information must exist in the system before a painting can be added and associated to an artist profile.

Table 8.23   Examples of requirements using unnecessary negation

Poor Example	If the administrator adds a new painting information with an artist whose entry does not already exist, he not only needs to create a new "Painting Information" for the painting, but also create a new "Artist Information" manually for that artist and provide suitable links between the two as described in the requirements above.
Good Example	All paintings must be associated to an artist profile. Artist information must exist in the system before a painting can be added and associated to an artist profile.

Table 8.24   Examples of requirements using double negation

Poor Example	Paintings must never be unassociated to artists.
Good Example	All paintings must be associated to an artist profile. Artist information must exist in the system before a painting can be added and associated to an artist profile.

7. **Scope of Action**

   It is important to ensure that requirements completely and fully define the actions to be performed under specific circumstances. Define what must occur when all of the criteria are met, some of the criteria are met, and none of the criteria are met. See Table 8.25.

8. **Time reference ambiguity**

   Time reference ambiguity occurs when the requirement makes vague references to time. An example of this would be "the transaction is to be repeated annually, after the last transaction occurred." Table 8.26 identifies specific terms to watch for.

Individual Requirement Structure

Requirements are directions, and therefore they must be worded as such. They must state the actor, the directive, the action to be performed, and the criteria

Table 8.25   Examples of requirements using scope of action

Criteria	• The user has an active bank account • The user inserts a valid debit card into the ATM • The user enters a valid personal ID number
Scenarios	**Requirement Sample**
All criteria are met	The user must have the ability to perform specific banking transactions. Banking transactions are defined as: withdraw funds, transfer funds, pay bills, and print account statement.
Some of the criteria are met Key combinations of criteria are met None of the criteria are met	The user must not be able to access account information AND the user must not be able to perform any banking transactions. Open ambiguities: Is there a prompt or an error message? Does the ATM keep the debit card for any reason? How many times can the user enter a personal ID number before the transaction is rejected?

Table 8.26   Examples of ambiguous time references

after	annually	at a given time
at the appropriate time	bimonthly	biweekly
daily	every other month	every other week
fast	in a while	later
monthly	quarterly	quickly
soon	twice a month	twice a year
weekly	yearly	next
former	latter	previous
quickly	slowly	

that must be met in order to successfully perform the action. An example of this structure is: "The user must have the ability to perform banking transactions from the web application." One of the biggest problems in writing requirements (and writing in general) is the author's inability to organize the content into an end-to-end flow. By utilizing the mind-mapping technique, the author is better able to organize the requirements into functional areas. This will make it easier for consumers of the requirements document to read and comprehend it.

When planning out how an organization will document requirements, bear in mind that what makes sense to one or two people may not make sense to others. It is also important to consider how easy it is to relay the format and standard writing organization to others as they join the team. If it takes a while for others to learn how to document the requirements into the standard template, reconsider how it is organized. Some of the predominant issues with organization are:

1. **Lack of traceability from requirements to business rules, process, and functional groupings.** It is important to remember that random requirements cannot be justified if there is no apparent rhyme or reason for creating them. Having to make assumptions is what causes products not to be built to specification and ultimate quality failures.

2. **Disconnected sub-requirements and technical details.** Remember that architects, developers, and testers have to be able to pick up the document and perform their tasks according to the information it contains. This means that specific details from single requirements must be documented as supporting information. This supporting information must be associated with, and must be documented immediately after, the requirement. This will make the requirement more readable and readily consumed by others.

3. **Random sequencing where there is no relation to the preceding or proceeding requirements.** As in disconnected sub-requirements, random sequencing of requirements occurs when requirements are not grouped by functionality but are listed in random order, and there is a disconnect between the information that would lend clarity to the overall requirements document.

4. **Mixed causes and effects.** This occurs when not all the causes and effects are easily distinguishable from one another because they are mixed together. See Table 8.27.

5. **Buried Requirements.** This occurs when requirements, sub-requirements, and supporting elements of requirements are not documented as requirements but are documented within the text of other sections of the project documentation (executive summary, business case, use cases, e-mails, etc.).

Updating Use Cases

Once requirements have been drafted and are ready for the validation stage, the analyst revisits the use cases and reviews them against the requirements to ensure

Table 8.27 Examples of requirements using mixed causes and effects

Poor Example	Both employees must be full time employees or part time employees in order for the shift trade to occur.
Good Example	Shift trades are restricted to trades between two employees of the SAME employment status. One of the following must be true:
	Both employees must be full time employees OR both employees must be part time employees.

that all up-to-date details have been captured and the use cases have been edited to reflect these updates. Within the context of the elaboration and specification stage, use cases can also be utilized to ensure that all requirements have been captured, and that there are no gaps between the user workflow and the requirements for the system that will manage this workflow.

Future State Definition Refinement

Within the context of the specification stage, the analyst may also edit or refine the future state documentation when appropriate and necessary. Any appropriate changes will be based upon new discoveries made during the analysis stage. These discoveries are often made when new and hidden (previously unknown) factors are exposed.

However, simply discovering or exposing new and hidden factors is not the only criteria for making changes to the future state. Changes to this documentation must be analyzed and determined to be both necessary and feasible. To determine necessity, the changes are assessed to determine whether or not implementing them will directly impact the team's ability to generate certain features or functionality. In this case, the business analysis team will be required to present the needed changes to the business stakeholders for approval. To present this documentation to the business, the future state documentation can be a marketing-style slide presentation, illustrating the solution and how it meets the business goals and objectives, needs, and drivers, and ultimately solves the business problem. The onus is on the business analyst team to provide enough information to the business stakeholders that they can make well-informed decisions about whether to approve the changes. If the business stakeholders opt not to implement the changes, the recommendations must be documented and recorded in the issues log, along with the supporting information.

Best Practices Unapproved Changes

It is important to ensure that all relevant information is logged with the recommended changes in the issues log—especially when those recommended changes are not approved for adoption. These could represent risks and gaps and should be well-documented so that, as it becomes feasible to adopt these changes, the business is free to do so. Be sure to include the potential risks and impacts of not implementing these changes so that the stakeholders can make effective decisions. It is equally important to document the decision made by the business, as well as the rationale for this decision (if available).

EXIT CRITERIA FOR SPECIFICATION

The key deliverable from the specification stage is the draft of the requirements document itself. This document must contain enough detail to allow the architects to create complete designs, the developers to generate complete code, and for the testers to be able to design testing and validate test results against it. This means that the content must be consistent, accurate, and logically complete. It also means that, while the requirements document describes (in great detail) what the system must do when all is well, it must also describe (in detail) what the system must do when specific criteria are only partially met or not met at all.

Best Practices Specification

The specification stage is the final stage in the requirements process. Here, the analyst finalizes the draft of the low-level requirements and refines the other documentation to present the differing audiences with the "story" of the new system or application. While this story remains consistent across all project documentation, the amount of technical details will vary in order to present the story in a way that each particular audience (or consumer) can readily understand and, in turn, utilize the documentation as the foundation for their own tasks and deliverables. It is important to recognize that the products of the specification stage are drafts, *not final documents.* They will further evolve and change over the next stage, and the analyst must remain detached from the document's contents to be able to accept feedback and criticism. The input and feedback of other team members enables the analyst to write the final version and then to present the final documents for sign off with confidence.

REFERENCES

1. Canter, James and Liz Derr, June 2001, "Extreme QA—A Case Study," International Institute for Software Testing.
2. Canter, James, 2013.
3. Maya Angelou, 2009, "I Know Why the Caged Bird Sings."

## 9

Validation

The validation stage is the final stage in the overall requirements development life cycle. This stage delivers the final and complete requirements to the architects, developers, and testers for the next steps in the project life cycle. It is, by far, the most critical of all stages in the requirements process, as it is the culmination of all of the requirements into a coherent form, the presentation to the audiences (consumers), the establishment of the future state baseline, and the negotiation point for the final requirements. The key here is that validation not only creates complete deliverables but also brings all team members to the point of mutual understanding about the expectations set out in the requirements for what is to be built. This mutual understanding is critical for the development process and testing activities to occur seamlessly and for the resulting products to align with the business needs.

INPUTS AND OUTPUTS OF VALIDATION

The primary entry criteria for starting the activities in validation are that the requirements have been drafted, business rules have been finalized, business processes are mapped, use cases are defined, and the future state is clearly identified. The primary inputs for validation are the requirements draft, the finalized future state, and the business rules. However, at this point the analyst must have access to all of the previous documents that were either utilized as sources of information or produced in the requirements development process. It is not only important that requirements trace back to the scope and to the business objectives but also critical they are consistent with the other deliverables that have been created.

The outputs for the validation stage are the finalized requirements, the ambiguity documentation and the user presentations. Earlier, I mentioned that the successful analyst does not ask the stakeholders what they want, but rather what they need and the solution to that need. These outputs are intended to articulate and communicate that solution. It was also mentioned that the audience of the requirements document is not the stakeholders. It is the architects, developers, and testers of the project itself. This means that the analyst must create and plan user presentation material that is easily consumable by the business. This material will articulate the solution in a way that the business can comprehend and will readily sign off on. Sign off should also be a formality, with no major surprises for the analysts, business, architecture, development, or testing teams.

WHAT ARTIFACTS AND DELIVERABLES ARE CREATED IN VALIDATION?

Ultimately, the goal of the validation stage is to produce verifiable requirements and obtain sign off on those requirements. The key work products and deliverables include:

- Signed off requirements document
- Ambiguity documentation
- User presentation material

WHO SIGNS OFF ON VALIDATION?

The validation stage culminates in the sign off of the requirements and functionality. While this is signed off by the business stakeholders and sponsors, the consumers are the remaining downstream project teams. By the time the sign off sessions arrive and are conducted, everyone should have a clear picture of what is being delivered and exactly how it will function. Sign off will be a formality when the business analyst has done a good job of engaging and working with the business and maintaining transparency throughout the process. It becomes a formality when the analyst has created an engaging forum for inputs into requirements, when the analyst has the trust of the business, and when the stakeholders are confident in the ability of the team to deliver. All of this takes skill and consistent application of the techniques prescribed in this book.

REQUIREMENTS TRACEABILITY

Traceability refers to the ability to correlate individual elements in both a chronological and meaningful way. Requirement traceability is an activity of management which enables the project team members to locate the original source and destination of every requirement. To this end, it links requirements from project scope to mid-level, finalized draft, architectural design, source code, test scripts, and executable (implemented) code. In addition, traceability tracks all changes made to these requirements. The full description and documentation of each of the changes are recorded within the change control mechanism for the project.

Requirements traceability focuses on mapping the relationships between requirements and development artifacts. It is intended to promote and facilitate:

- the ability to control and measure changes during development
- the ability to make calculated steps toward the improvement of the business situation
- full comprehension and transparency of the solution
- the quality of the solution being developed.

It is imperative that traceability be managed within a specific tool. Many requirements management tools are available for this purpose, though it is imperative to be sure that these tools actually provide and manage traceability—from scope all the way through the development and implementation life cycle. Remember, traceability is not from the requirement forward, but it is bidirectional and must link all elements, from the business objectives to the implemented solution.

If, however, the organization does not provide a tool for this purpose, it is important for the business analysis team to establish a tool that will support and enable the traceability and management of requirements. This could be as simple as a spreadsheet, listing all of the requirements in rows and mapping the other elements of traceability across in the columns. This must be updated throughout each stage of the development life cycle.

TASKS AND ACTIVITIES IN VALIDATION

The validation stage is all about validating requirements before they become part of design and development. The traditional models for project methodologies tend to be light in the validation process and rely heavily on testing to reveal any discrepancies and issues. This means that fixing problems in requirements can cost in excess of $1000 per requirement.[1] The reason for this is simple. Issues are found in testing, and the whole team must go back to the start of the process to fix the requirements, design, and developed solution, which must again be tested. Basically, it must go back through the entire project life cycle to fix the issues in requirements.

The approach presented here is agnostic toward project methodology and illustrates how requirements can be successfully validated before design and development even occurs. It reduces the amount of work and the overall cost because it reduces the costs associated with scrap and rework. There are two primary activity categories in the validation stage. Those activities are verification and validation.

Verification is the process of ensuring that the requirements are accurate, based on alignment of the requirements to the objectives and business needs. In other words, will these requirements create the functionality that will produce the results needed by the business? Are project teams doing the right things? Validation is the process of ensuring that the right things are being defined (and later designed and developed) in the right way. Are those project teams doing the right things right? This means that those teams must ensure the requirements are complete, consistent, accurate, feasible, and testable.

Each of these two primary categories applies two separate approaches. In order to verify requirements, the analyst must present the functionality to the business in a walkthrough, which focuses on the feature sets and how each feature will generate the needed results. However, in order to validate requirements, the business analyst must apply various techniques to "test" them and conduct a walkthrough with the architecture, development, and test teams in order to ensure that the defined requirements will actually produce the required functionality. Further, this validation will ensure that those requirements meet the criteria described as attributes of great requirements.

Assessing Business Criticality and Priority

One of the key elements of successful requirements management is the full and complete understanding of the impacts the functionality or features to be developed will have on the business. This is not as simple as documenting the preferences of individual business units. Criticality and priority are two completely different aspects for categorizing requirements. Where criticality is the assessment of how important the requirement is, priority is the timing sequence when the requirement must be implemented.

It is imperative that the analyst consider how important or critical each requirement is to the business units. In order to assess criticality, it is necessary to know the sources of each requirement. This would be uncovered by asking questions, such as: "Why is this feature or functionality needed?" Once this is known, criticality is assessed with the input and collaboration of the business team. On the other hand, to assess priority, the business analyst must consider the project factors that might restrict when a requirement can be developed and implemented. This assessment is done with the collaboration of the project manager, sponsors, stakeholders, architects, developers, and testers. It uncovers the restrictions by asking questions about the environment, which may limit the ability to implement specific features of the solution. It is particularly valuable when the project encounters major issues and is broken into multiple phases to accommodate these issues.

Untestable Requirements

A large insurance company was developing a new program that would adversely impact the premiums of subscribers for getting tickets while driving. One of the requirements was to assess a multi-year penalty onto the regular premium. Unfortunately, this feature was not testable because the testing environment at the company did not allow for changing system dates in order to follow a case after the current year.

In this example, it was recommended that the requirements be given a lower priority simply because they could not be tested and would actually draw time and effort away from the project team working on more important items.

TECHNIQUES FOR VALIDATING REQUIREMENTS

Validating requirements consists of use case definition, peer reviews, team reviews, and walkthroughs. It may also include logic modeling and cause and effect tabling. This degree of validation and review is intended to identify and remove ambiguities from the requirements and to bring the project team to the same understanding of the solution prior to development. Using the information from applying validation techniques, the analyst will finalize the low-level requirements, refine the use cases, communicate expectations to the rest of the project team, and obtain sign off from the necessary stakeholders.

In order to validate the requirements, the analysts will distribute the drafted document to the business analysis team for review and initiate the ambiguity log. Once the analysts have had a chance to review the requirements, to log and address ambiguities, they will work to correct the requirements in order to remove the specific ambiguities identified. Table 9.1 illustrates an example of an ambiguity log entry.

The requirements are then distributed for review to the architecture, development, and testing teams. Each of the individual members of the teams will review the requirements and log any questions and items that are unclear as ambiguities in the ambiguity log. During the course of this independent review, the analysis team members will address and make corrections to the requirements document and update the ambiguity log on a daily basis. The person who initiated the ambiguity item will close it, once satisfied that the resolution meets expectations.

Table 9.1 Sample ambiguity log entry

AID	Type	Location	Description	Date Entered	Resolution
9	Req	GLOB.WFM.NF.2	Can changes be scheduled for future dates/times—change request scheduled for mass changes—supervisor changes, pay rate changes	3/20/2013	Is this a possible enhancement?
10	Dom	BUSI.AC.NF.1.5	Change CC1 to not include Create or Modify	3/20/2013	4.2 WFM System Login Requirements added
11	Req	3.1.2	Include reason for changes in log	3/20/2013	Global Audit log
12	Req	3.1.1	Automatic notification when changes are made, turn notification on/off, include effective date of change	3/20/2013	
13	Req	3.1.3	Add to data displayed—supervisor & seniority date	3/20/2013	
14	Req		Include all existing IEX reports, ability to generate ad-hoc	3/20/2013	Reports review of existing reports
15	Test		Selection criteria needs to be more robust for filtering	3/20/2013	

After the independent review period, the analysis team will begin conducting a series of ambiguity workshops in order to review the function sets or feature groups and scenarios. Each of the workshops is a detailed walkthrough of the requirements as they relate to the functionality required by the business. In addition, each workshop lasts a minimum of four hours and should adhere to strict guidelines for achieving directed results and making the most of participants' time.

Cause and Effect (Decision) Tabling

The cause and effect table is a quick matrix-style view of the end-to-end transactions performed by a system. Again, it is used to map individual variations in the inputs as criteria or causes, coupled with the business rules and the resulting effects in processing and outputs created by the system.

Cause and effect tables allow the business analysts to identify and map complete input-process-output processing in order to expose logical inconsistencies and incomplete requirements, processes, and process controls. The purpose of cause and effect tables is to validate requirements in a quick and efficient manner. It provides the business with an opportunity to identify issues with the processing that are exposed by the table early in the requirements process.

The main benefit of using the cause and effect table as both a technique and a tool is that it takes the requirements validation from the testing phase of the project life cycle and moves it to the requirements phase where it belongs. It is the key to the success of validating requirements before the design and development of the system occurs. It reduces the size and scope of the resulting break-and-fix cycles.

Scenarios

Scenarios are used in validation in the same way that cause and effect tables are. They are used to map how the process will work from start to finish and how the users will perform specific work functions. Scenarios map out the detailed steps in the performance of the work, regardless of the system or person performing the work. By utilizing the scenario-based approach to validating requirements, the analyst, the business, and the project teams gain a solid understanding of workflow and are better able to ensure that requirements are complete and logically consistent.

Use Cases

In validation, use cases provide the foundation of a valuable technique called logic modeling. While logic modeling is more commonly performed by the testing team, it models use cases that have been developed by the business analysis team. In addition to logic modeling, use cases also present features and functionality, which are represented by requirements back to the business in a way that is easy for the average non-technical person to understand. They are not mandatory but present a level of validation that leads directly to more complete requirements. However, use cases are strongly advised when the system is complex because they will add a level of validation from the user perspective that may not be present in other formats. Finally, quite simply, they are easier for the business to understand.

Ambiguity Reviews and Tracking

The ambiguity review is first conducted with the business analysis team as an independent peer review. Later, the ambiguity review is conducted in collaboration with the architecture, development, and testing teams as part of the independent review period. Finally, it is conducted as a group session (again in collaboration with the architecture, development, and test teams) to ensure that all ambiguities have been exposed so that they can be addressed before the design and development work begins.

Tools and Techniques for Ambiguity Reviews

During the independent review period, all project team members receive a copy of the requirements document and access to the ambiguity log in a common file location, such as Microsoft SharePoint. The team members proceed to read the requirements document and log any questions they have about the contents and any issues found, which correlate to the guidelines in the peer review checklist (adapted from Richard Bender's "Requirements Based Testing Ambiguity Review Checklist").[2] As this process continues, the analysis team addresses the identified ambiguities in the log, updates the log, and corrects requirements to fix the ambiguities. At the end of the independent review period, the analysis team releases the next draft of the requirements document and schedules ambiguity workshop meetings.

In general, the rules for ambiguity review are:

1. Provide teams a minimum of one to two weeks to perform the independent review.
2. The primary ambiguity meetings should be conducted in four hour blocks.
3. Provide access for all to the ambiguity log.
4. Provide access for all to the ambiguity review checklist.
5. All ambiguities are documented by the reviewers and logged into the ambiguity log for management.
6. NO ambiguities are ever documented outside the ambiguity log (such as e-mails or meeting minutes), as they cannot be managed and addressed appropriately outside of this central log.
7. Ambiguities are risks to the project and must be recognized and managed as such.

While writing great requirements is an art, it is not open to interpretation. Ambiguity is the leading cause of requirement issues and failure. In requirements, ambiguity is anything that can be interpreted in more than one way, language that is inconsistent, use of jargon, and incomplete logic.

Multiple Interpretations

When reviewing requirements, pull out words like would, should, could, some, few, and many. In fact, pull out any terms that cannot be measured or quantified.

Terms would, should, and could mean the item is nice to have because they indicate a moral imperative and not a directive. Be assertive. If the tool must do something, write that the tool "must" do it, without trying to be "polite" about it. On ham radios, operators use special language to get a clear message across. These operators say "correct" instead of "right" and "roger" instead of "yes." Requirements need to follow similar guidelines. Use explicit and simple language, and remember that the more a thought is embellished, the more unclear it becomes.

Inconsistent Language

In addition to embellishing requirements language (some requirements fall just short of "thou shalt . . ."), many requirements documents also use terms interchangeably, as though they mean the same thing. But ambiguity creeps in here. While many terms might be interchangeable in general conversation over the water cooler, they are not interchangeable in a requirements document. Using terms interchangeably in a requirements document only confuses the audience. In related meetings, trying to follow the discussion could be as much fun as the "Who's On First?" skit by Abbott and Costello.

A product typically has a full name and a nickname. This same product might be part of a suite or a product line and it is also associated with the company which owns it. These terms of reference are not interchangeable names! At the start of the requirements document, the terms and names that will be used to describe the product must be defined. These must be used—consistently—throughout the document. Define it with the full company name, product line, and product name. Adopt one shortened name and stick to it. Use that one name everywhere that the product is mentioned.

> ### Who's On First?
>
> A number of years ago, there was a project to enhance a web application for making travel reservations on a commuter ferry. Two of the more common terms, which were being used interchangeably by the project team, were "reservation" and "booking." However, "booking" is the process of making a "reservation" on the ferry. In fact, the term "reservation" refers to the record that has been created by the booking process.

Use of Jargon

The trouble with jargon is that many terms used in one context have a completely different meaning in another context. This means that the reader probably will not understand how the terms are being used, and a miscommunication will be created. Another problem with jargon is that it assumes a level of "intimate" knowledge on the part of the audience. By intimate knowledge, I mean knowledge that may be common within the company, or even within the industry, but only insiders know about it. The problem here is that not all teams are made up of resources privy to the meaning of the term. Coupled with context jargon, there is a real problem in understanding what is being built. On top of the miscommunication, it takes longer for any resources to be ramped up and limits the available talent pool to those who would understand the terms. This is a contributing factor to the idea that resources must be recruited for domain knowledge.

> Warning: *Excessive use of jargon may cause business*
> *users and stakeholders' eyes to glaze over.*

If a person is sitting in a meeting and does not have a clue what is being talked about, it is pretty hard to contribute. If people cannot contribute, they get bored. If they get bored, they become disinterested and are less likely to ask questions, which add value to the quality of the end product by challenging the features and requirements being presented. And guess what: ambiguity creeps in because people lose the ability to pay attention and really care.

Incomplete Logic

Far too often, people focus on defining what the software has to do under a given set of circumstances (let's call this positive functionality). Unfortunately, people most often forget to explore the negative and combination functionality. Negative functionality is what the system should do when none of the criteria or circumstances are met. Combination functionality is when only some of the criteria are met in various combinations.

Peer Review Checklist

If William Shakespeare wrote requirements, no one would be able to understand them. The good news is that William Shakespeare has never written a single requirements document. The peer review checklist is a simple, back-to-grade-school approach to reviewing the individual requirements for grammar, completeness, and ambiguity. The peer review checklist summarizes the most common terms and phrases that cause ambiguity. These are:

- Arbitrary grouping and structure
    - Are all requirements grouped appropriately by functionality?
- Ambiguous phrases
    - Are all requirements, with numeric values and other calculations, measureable and quantifiable?

- Do any requirements use unclear logical operators, like "and," "or," and "nor?"
- Do any requirements refer to other requirements by number, location in the document, or proximity to the current requirement?
- Do any requirements use an unclear task order?
- Do any requirements use adjectives, like "efficient," "frequent," and "improved?"
- Do any requirements use adverbs, such as "accordingly," "commonly," or "rarely?"
- Do any requirements utilize general terms in place of definitive names?
- Do any requirements use verbs that do not clearly identify the actions and the outcomes?
- Integrated assumptions
  - Do any requirements imply a certain level of domain knowledge?
  - Do any requirements use jargon?
- Directive
  - Do any requirements use terms such as "should" or "may?"
- Implied cases
  - Do any requirements imply inclusion or exclusion of any items, without directly stating the inclusion or exclusion?
- Latin verbiage
  - Do any requirements use Latin terms, such as "etc.," "e.g.," or "i.e.?"
- Use of negative terms
  - Do all requirements clearly identify the item or items being negated, and under which circumstances they are negated?
  - Do any requirements use any negative terms that are unnecessary?
  - Do any of the requirements use terms that negate other terms within the same requirement?
- Scope of action
  - Do all requirements have the appropriate and associated positive, negative, and combination functionality defined?
- Time reference ambiguity
  - Do any requirements make time references using terms such as those listed in Chapter 8 ("frequently," "bi-weekly," "monthly," "annually," etc.)?

Best Practices Ambiguity

The best solutions come from the marriage of ideas from different sources. Many great documents, such as the *Declaration of Independence*, the *Constitution*, and the *Charter of Human Rights and Freedoms* were created this way. Requirements are no different. Ambiguity is best addressed with peer and team reviews. All ambiguities should be tracked in an ambiguity log which contains metrics for measuring statistics against them. After giving the team members a chance to read the requirements against the identified ambiguity criteria (tell them what those criteria are *AND* post them in a common file location!), host an ambiguity walkthrough.

Ambiguity Workshops

The purpose of an ambiguity workshop is to conduct a full walkthrough of all of the high-level functions described within the requirements documentation. This provides the analysts with the opportunity to describe the intended functionality, ask whether that meaning has been conveyed by the requirements document, and provide clarification where needed. Ambiguity workshops are conducted with the architecture, development, and testing teams after the independent review period. These workshops are a series of facilitated sessions in which the analysis team walks through the overall functionality or feature sets of the new solution and elicits feedback from the other teams. The workshops are meant to help determine whether the document, as written, is consistent with this description, and outlines the end product effectively.

The inputs to the ambiguity workshops are simple: requirements documents. On the other hand, the outputs from the ambiguity workshops are increased team communication, a higher degree of understanding about the functionality defined in the requirements document, and a more complete and accurate set of requirements.

According to renowned expert, Richard Bender, the biggest benefits of conducting ambiguity reviews are: "All members of the project team can work from one clear set of requirements, thereby reducing the chance of scrap and rework throughout the software development lifecycle;"[3] and "the cost of correcting defects is at its lowest point in the software development lifecycle."[4] To be effective, the ambiguity workshops must be attended by the analysis team, architects, developers, and testers—*all of them*, not just the team leads. Each of these team members will play a crucial role in the validation and communication of the requirements expectations into the final document.

Guidelines for Hosting an Ambiguity Workshop

There are some best practice guidelines for hosting ambiguity workshops that will make these sessions more effective and will reduce the time that it takes to gain understanding, identify ambiguities, and to obtain sign off. These guidelines include blocking enough time for each session, providing enough notice, inviting the appropriate resources, managing time, and managing the agenda. It is important to remember that people need time to focus, time to process conversations, time to respond, and time to make decisions. Let's face it: one-hour meetings are better used for status reporting where no decisions have to be made (especially in groups). The average attendee was probably not working on the specific topic or focused on the sub-topic to be covered in the session. In other words, the average participant was working on something else.

According to an article in *Fast Company*, once a person has been interrupted, "it takes an average of 23 minutes and 15 seconds to get back to the task."[5] This means that participants may be coming in to the ambiguity workshops with their minds on another task, and they will now have to redirect their attention to the topics on the agenda. This is especially true when it comes to business stakeholders: stakeholders may have a mental block in relation to the subject simply because they may not understand all of it. This mental block will prevent them from listening and participating as fully as possible.

This will be further complicated by politics and power dynamics. All of this means two things: provide more time within the meeting to get work done and maintain control of the ambiguity workshop at all times. This being said, each ambiguity workshop should be a minimum of four hours, especially at the start of the process. Multiple sessions could be scheduled over the course of up to two weeks. If breakout sessions are needed, they are best held in two-hour sessions but should also be scheduled when booking the workshops. The breakout sessions may be removed if it turns out that they are not needed. I strongly doubt people will be disappointed about decreasing the number of meetings!

It is important to provide enough notice about impending ambiguity workshops and to distribute a copy of the requirements so that the team may review them before the sessions. One of the key factors in getting people to be engaged in this process is cultivating good working relationships. Getting the document well in advance may not matter if they do not have buy-in and trust. Another key factor is setting the tone for priority of the sessions and being assertive (not aggressive or demanding) about getting this participation. Tone is a huge problem when it comes to e-mails (and other documents, for that matter). People need to understand why the meeting is important, why they need to be there, what they need to do to prepare, and how they will be involved. Remember that each invited person will have to plan separate tasks and schedules for the day. Many attendees have to choose between project meetings and other meetings on their agenda. Look at it this way: if you had to choose between a meeting invitation from your notoriously rigid manager (e.g., the chief information officer) or an invitation from a project team member, which would you choose? Consider these scenarios:

> *Scenario A*: that same rigid manager's invitation does not have an agenda, nor does the project invitation from your team member.
>
> *Scenario B*: that same rigid manager's invitation has an agenda, which includes chatting about your career plan, and the project invitation has an agenda, which describes the requirements review.

In Scenario A, most people would be likely choose the manager's invitation because the manager has more importance in your everyday work life. In Scenario B, most people would ask the manager to reschedule, unless you could see from the project invitation agenda that you were *not* going to be important to the meeting about the requirements review. The agenda allows for prioritization.

Let's look at a third scenario. Scenario C: the manager's invitation does not have an agenda, and the project invitation has a very detailed agenda describing your role in the meeting and why attendance is necessary. In this case, many would ask the manager to reschedule, even without knowing what the manager wants to talk about. Most would accept the project meeting because you can see exactly how and why you will be involved, and would know why it is important to attend.

What happens when there are participants who do not agree with the project, the direction, or the solution? These people still need to be involved, but they may avoid the team and consistently decline invitations to meetings. In this case, it is important to remind these people that their participation is the only way their voices will be heard, and their needs will be met.

One of the major issues pertaining to ambiguity workshops (as in many other project meetings) is that everyone who is remotely associated with the project gets an invite. Is it really necessary for absolutely everyone to attend the meetings? It is important to remember that only appropriate resources should be invited to the workshop. If the focus will be on the business stakeholders, then invite the stakeholders and not every tester or even the sponsor. Yes, it is important to keep them informed, but this is how the RACI matrix (Responsible, Accountable, Consulted, Informed) guides the business analysis team. Decision makers should be invited to breakout sessions to support the finalization of key decisions and to keep them in the loop. Only people who will actively be involved in contributing to the discussion should be invited to the workshop. By inviting too many participants too often, the meeting, the team, and the project loses credibility.

Again, it is critical to remember that the business analyst in the ambiguity workshops fills the role of the facilitator. This means the analyst is responsible for managing time, the agenda, and the process of the session. As the facilitator, managing the process means setting rules that make the sessions go faster and smoother. Some of the most effective rules, which I have used, are:

1. Everyone is there to participate, and everyone deserves to be heard.
2. No idea is stupid or dumb.
3. If it will take longer than 5 minutes to discuss a topic or resolve an issue, if the topic requires more analysis, or if the topic requires input and decisions from someone who is not in the meeting, then these topics are moved to breakout sessions.

Ambiguity workshops could take longer than necessary if the granular details are discussed for every single function or feature. Do not forget that people have already had time to read the document, and this—mostly technical—audience is more likely to have read the requirements line-by-line (especially after they had the chance to log questions into the ambiguity log). Ideally, the ambiguity workshops are best started at the high-level and only dive deep into the individual requirements where clarity is needed. This means the analysts should talk about the requirements from a functional perspective. As an example: "this feature is intended to provide the functionality for check-out. The basic processing is x, y, and z. Did anyone see anything in this section that does not make this clear?"

Trust, Respect, and Collaboration Comes From Feeling Heard

A number of years ago, there was a project that was overdue and over budget. The team was barely speaking to one another, and there was little coordination and cooperation. They would not even have coffee together! After some digging, it turned out there was a developer who had a habit of going directly to the business and making changes on the fly. Sitting down with this developer revealed that her concerns over the feasibility of some of the requirements had consistently been ignored. Ultimately, she felt unheard and had serious concerns about the quality of the product being produced.

An ambiguity log was introduced, and all developers were instructed to log their concerns and questions in the log. It did not take long for the mood to improve. The log was a formal record of the concerns, and each concern had to be addressed by the business analysts. Nothing got lost in e-mails after this point. By the end of the project, team lunches were common. They even laughed and joked with each other during meetings!

Many people seem to hold the belief that analysts complete the requirements with the business in a vacuum and toss those requirements over to the rest of the project team for design, coding, and testing. However, when architects, developers, and testers provide the kind of 360-degree feedback that comes out in this ambiguity forum, the end result is that the requirements more fully define the needed solution. Not only will this solution align to the business objectives and drivers but it will also have more of the target functionality, fewer bugs, and fewer defects, and this feedback will decrease the overall break-and-fix cycle! On top of this, all team members will feel that they have been heard, they have had their concerns addressed, and they have contributed to a quality product. By utilizing the ambiguity management techniques outlined in this book, two things will happen: the quality of the product will increase, with greater alignment to the project objectives (defects will drop), and the project team will learn to collaborate on an unprecedented level.

Best Practices Ambiguity Workshops

These workshops are a minimum of four hours in length and are designed to limit conversation to the immediate functionality. Remember, the rules are:

1. Overall functionality is discussed for each feature set; it is not a line-by-line reading of the requirements.
2. If the discussion is going to be longer than five minutes, it will be tabled to a breakout session.
3. If the key decision makers are not present, it will be tabled to a breakout session, and the decision makers must be invited.
4. After each feature set has been described by the analysts, the other teams are given the opportunity to provide feedback, ask for clarity, and point out errors or omissions.
5. All ambiguities are documented by a scribe, logged into the ambiguity log, and *managed*.

Numbering Requirements

Do everyone on the project a big favor and *DO NOT NUMBER THE REQUIREMENTS UNTIL THE DOCUMENT IS READY FOR SIGN OFF!* Why? Delaying the numbering will reduce housekeeping and confusion in requirements. In the same way that reference creates ambiguity in requirements, having numbers in place while the requirements are still being edited and changed can cause a tremendous headache. Remember, ambiguity of reference means the requirements use terms that relate those requirements to other requirements or physical placement in the document. What happens when those requirements change? Imagine this: You are in the middle of an ambiguity workshop, and you want to talk about requirement number 76. When you talk about it by number and functionality, the other attendees get this funny look of confusion on their face. They printed the last requirements document that was sent, but you added one requirement, bumped the numbers and did not resend the document to them. Now everyone is confused and frustrated.

From a practical perspective, it is important to remember that requirements are not associated with a number until the document has been completed and signed off. It is amazing to think how many countless and pointless hours can be spent formatting and renumbering a document every single time there is a change to the requirements. You should think twice (or more) before assigning numbers. If there are more than 10% of changes to the requirements and the requirements document, DO NOT ASSIGN NUMBERS! How are those 10% of changes going to be handled? Simply use the following basic rules for easier management and control of the requirements:

1. Wait until changes to requirements will be minimal before assigning numbers.
2. Never change the numbers once assigned.
3. If a requirement is added, use a new number.
4. If a requirement is removed, the number will NOT be reassigned to any other requirement.
5. Requirements should not be numbered consecutively (for example: 1, 2, 3, 4 . . .).
6. Number the feature or the function and use it to set the numbering for the corresponding requirements (for example: feature—"12. Edit;" requirement—"12.1 Solution must allow cut and paste of content into all user input boxes.").

FACILITATED SIGN OFF OF REQUIREMENTS

The final step in validation is getting facilitated sign off. One of the most significant challenges, faced by every analyst, is how to get the stakeholders to read the requirements document. First of all, assume that stakeholders will not read it or will not read it all of the way through, even though they have plenty of time to do so. If some stakeholders actually do read the document, they will generally not read it thoroughly enough to understand the details. In truth, there are probably one or two stakeholders who will actually read the full document in all its dry and boring glory, and this is okay. The truth is that they do not need to. However, every stakeholder *must* understand all of the functionality represented by the requirements. The best way for them to really understand it is to participate in a facilitated walkthrough of the functionality and sign off on this.

Best Practices Requirements Sign Off

Utilizing a marketing style presentation, which outlines the high-level functionality and features of the new solution to the business users and stakeholders, and giving them the chance to ask questions about the full functionality enables them to make informed decisions about the solution and how it aligns to their needs. In this presentation, ensure that topics—such as risks, user maintenance, security, and compliance issues that may be faced—are covered. It often helps to include screen mock-ups or screenshots if you have them available.

EXIT CRITERIA

The primary exit criteria for the validation stage are having consensus and agreement on the requirements from the business, developers, architects, and testers. This agreement is in the form of formal approval and sign off. Getting this sign off and approval is not simply a matter of putting a requirements document in front of the business and tossing it over to the rest of the project team for consumption. The whole point of sign off is to ensure that everyone is on board, and that the solution is feasible and fully defined before the business spends any money developing it.

REFERENCES

1. Ritscher, April, 2010, "Excerpt from PNSQC 2010 Proceedings."
2. Bender, Richard, circa 2005, "The Ambiguity Review Process."
3. Ibid.
4. Ibid.
5. Pattison, Kermit, July 2008 at http://www.fastcompany.com/944128/worker-interrupted-cost-task-switching.

SECTION IV

APPLYING PROJECT AND ARCHITECTURE METHODOLOGIES

## 10

Implications of Agile on Requirements

Agile is an iterative process for the software development life cycle. It was intended to deliver functionality in small increments within shorter time frames than more traditional life cycles. It is based upon the principles put forward by Watts Humphries of IBM and Hadar Ziv of the University of California that requirements are uncertain until people have had the chance to work and play with the solution.

> "Uncertainty is inherent and inevitable in software development processes and products."[1]

The Agile process runs in short iterations, called "sprints," and each sprint is guided by a person in the role of a "scrum master." These sprints can be anywhere from two to four weeks. Figure 10.1 illustrates the agile process.

The Agile process begins with the road map to value. This road map provides a high-level view of the overall project and identifies several stages that will enable the project to progress from concept to product in a clearly defined manner. These stages are product vision, product road map, release plan, sprint planning, sprint review, and the sprint retrospective. Figure 10.2 illustrates the agile road map to value.

In the first stage (also known as initial planning), the product vision is defined in collaboration with the product owner. This vision clearly defines the product, how it will support the business and its strategy, as well as who will use the product, and how this product will be used.

In the second stage (also known as planning), the product road map is defined in collaboration with the scrum master and the product owner. This road

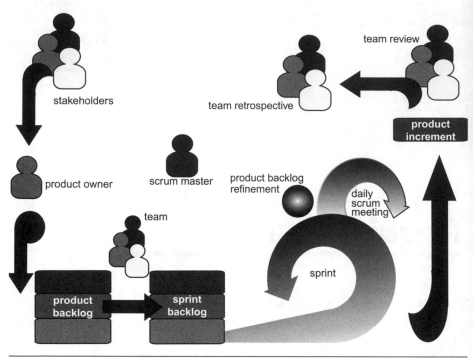

Figure 10.1 Agile lifecycle

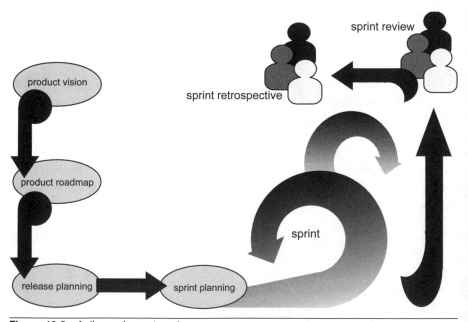

Figure 10.2 Agile road map to value

map provides a high-level view of the requirements, with a rough time frame for developing and delivering those requirements. The road map is only effective when it contains details about the product and the effort required to develop and implement this product. In this case, these details include requirements, prioritization of those requirements, and an estimation of the effort to develop and implement those specific requirements.

In the third stage (which is an extension of planning), the release plan is defined in collaboration between the scrum master and the product owner. The release plan lays out the high-level schedule for the release of a functioning product, such as software. While an agile project will have many releases, this release plan does not replace or substitute a formal scheduling and release plan. The release plan is limited to the life cycle of the project, and maps out the launch of the features in priority order, with the highest-priority features launching first. A typical release plan crosses approximately three to five sprints, and a new release plan is created at the beginning of each release.

In the fourth stage, the scrum master and the development team plan the sprints in collaboration with the product owner. As with release planning, sprint planning sessions take place at the start of each sprint. In these sprint planning sessions, the team determines the specific requirements that will be in the forthcoming iteration.

Once the sprints have been planned, the team starts creating the product within each of those sprints. Each sprint is managed on a daily basis through the daily stand-up meeting. The daily stand-up meeting should not be more than 15 minutes, and participants are there to discuss the work that was completed the day before, the work to be started or completed today, as well as any barriers to getting this work done.

The basic tasks for each sprint include requirements, analysis and design, implementation, deployment, and testing. Whereas a traditional project model creates as many of the features that have been identified by the needs analysis, the Agile project model focuses on individual sets of features, and the tasks required to create the functionality needed for each feature. Requirements in Agile start with identifying and filling a requirements backlog. The requirements backlog is a list of features that need to be defined in order to address the product backlog.

Using requirements planning criticality and prioritization, the business analysts determine what needs to be defined and developed. This determination is based on the business strategy and objectives. As with the development team, the business analysts plan the requirements sprint, perform the requirements definition, and then review the outputs. If those outputs are verified and validated, they can be moved into the product backlog. All of this is done at a pace that keeps the business analysts and the requirements development activity about two steps ahead of the product development work.

There are two crucial elements to requirements definition and management in an Agile project. These elements are process control and decomposition. In some cases, businesses create control-specific documentation. These documents are required to control the process itself. These process control documents can be entered into the requirements backlog, but they should not be entered into the product backlog. Instead, these documents will become reference materials for the project team as it develops the product in each sprint. Traceability from the product backlog to all these documents is an important factor in ensuring project continuity across all sprints. Within Agile, the analysis of requirements begins early in the process, when features are being prioritized and put into the requirements backlog. The techniques for collaboration, analysis, and valida-tion all have to be met in order to produce quality results. Remember: "garbage in—garbage out."

Another crucial element in the requirements definition and management on an Agile project is decomposition. Decomposition is the way in which the product backlog items are both communicated to the development team and refined in collaboration with them. The only significant difference between requirements on an Agile project or any other project is the limited amount of time that the business analysis team has to apply the techniques mapped out in each of the stages. On an Agile project, therefore, the team will only choose one or two techniques, based on which of these techniques will give the most value in the deliverables.

The techniques, outlined in Section 3, must be used and applied throughout the Agile project in order to get great results. Due diligence does not change or diminish simply because of the project methodology; it gets scaled back. Requirements still have to be complete, consistent, and accurate. This means that the requirements process must apply the same refined techniques that produce such results in requirements.

In the fifth stage of the road map to value, the team conducts a sprint review. During this review, the team demonstrates the working product, which has been developed during the sprint, to the business stakeholders. The sprint review is held at the end of every sprint. The results of the review help the team determine the requirements for the subsequent sprint when the product does not match the business needs.

In the final stage, the team conducts the sprint retrospective. This retrospec-tive is a meeting wherein the team discusses the lessons learned and plans for improvements to the subsequent sprints. As with the sprint review, the sprint retrospective is conducted at the end of every sprint and enables rapid integra-tion of the lessons learned.

MISCONCEPTIONS ABOUT AGILE

Some of the most common misconceptions about Agile are that Agile is a requirements methodology, requirements are not necessary, Agile teams deliver more functionality faster than other project models, Agile teams are self-organizing and do not need to be managed, and Agile can be applied to every project. Agile is not a requirements methodology. To be clear, Agile is a project methodology, which describes a process for the entire life cycle of the project, including requirements. A requirements methodology only describes the process of the requirements life cycle. It is also a mistake to assume that when using Agile, requirements are not necessary in an iterative project. While the Agile Manifesto values "Working software over comprehensive documentation,"[2] this does not remove the need to have documented requirements before development begins.

To Document or Not to Document, Part 2

Remember the story about the online retailer from Chapter 8? In this instance, the requirements had never been documented, so the re-architecture of the website took additional efforts to define the exiting processes and business rules that would be the foundation for the new website requirements. One of the problems was that the team was trying to apply the principles of Agile in the development of the original website. They developed features, in iterations, as they were needed. To compound this approach, there was a consistently high employee attrition rate. After two short years, no remaining staff understood the functionality, new iterations developed by new team members created overlapping functionality, and above all, the system functionality was delivered as separate mini-applications. This resulted in thousands of errors every day, which swamped the support team. In this situation, the cost for support rendered the company unprofitable and put partnerships with other software companies at risk.

Another common misconception is that using the Agile life cycle means that teams deliver more functionality, more often than other project methodologies. This idea comes from the delivery of parsed functionality in limited iterations. This means that, after the first iteration, the business could have working software, even though the functionality is limited. One of the keys to Agile success is the concept of continuous integration. However, resources are required to support continuous integration, test automation, peer reviews, and end of sprint reviews. Many perceived gains in cost, scope, and time are spent on these activities and are not gains at all during initial projects applying the Agile methodology. Continuous integration is not to be mistaken for, nor does it replace, scheduling and release management of active products. A project is still the development process with a defined start and end.

The concept that self-organizing teams do not need to be managed is a misconception based upon the principle in the Agile Manifesto which states:

"Build projects around motivated individuals. Give them the environment and support they need, and trust them to get the job done."[3] However, trust, support, and management are three entirely different things. While management provides guidance and direction, it also frees up the team members to focus on the tasks without having to also focus on reporting back to the business and ensuring that the project is on track. Management also enables the business to identify and prioritize the features to be developed in each sprint through planning. Trust only means that team members will not be micromanaged to complete the tasks and will be allowed to utilize their own judgment in the completion of those tasks. Support requires that obstacles to the completion of the tasks be managed and minimized. This ensures that the tasks are completed in a timely manner.

The last major misconception is the idea that Agile can be applied to every project. Consider this: methodologies are techniques to be applied to achieve a specific outcome in the development process. This is similar to the use of specific techniques in any other construction process: for example, the method for installing home flooring will vary according to the attributes of both the home and the flooring type to be installed. In other words, the subfloor, the load-bearing structures, and the type of flooring to be installed will determine the application and approach used to install the flooring.

According to Mike Cohn, a leading Agile author, consultant, and practitioner: "The most appropriate projects for Agile are ones with aggressive deadlines, a high degree of complexity, and a high degree of novelty (uniqueness) to them."[4] This refers to projects with a high degree of urgency, intricacy and/or complexity, as well as some elements of newness or uniqueness to the development team. He means that projects with one or more of these attributes are great candidates for applying the Agile methodology because of the way in which the sprint delivers functionality. He does suggest, however, that complexity alone is not a determining factor in the application of Agile, but complexity is the one attribute that must occur in combination with any of the other attributes for Agile to be successfully applied.

According to noted Certified Scrum Master, Mark W. Timmis, project size, requirements stage, and ability to increment are also factors in the selection and application of the Agile methodology. For project size, he suggests that "Medium to small system projects that are relatively independent of other systems are easier to leverage with an Agile approach."[5] While he does not state why project size factors in, one can assume it relates back to the complexity of the project, as suggested by Cohn. In reference to the requirements stage, Timmis suggests that Agile is better suited to high-level requirements than those that are more granular and well-defined. The concern is that using Agile for granular requirements leaves room for invalidated requirements and features. Agile does not alleviate the problems of unused software features and does little to curb the costs associated with scrap and rework. Finally, Timmis suggests: "If it can roll out incrementally, and continuous improvement is feasible, then it is absolutely a good candidate. If not, but all of the other elements meet the Agile criteria, then this can be worked out."[6] In other words, while the ability to increment is a factor, it is not a make-or-break factor in the application of Agile to a project.

IMPACTS OF AGILE ON REQUIREMENTS

Let's face it: uncertainty in software comes from our inability to predict user actions. This is increasingly true with the advancement of object-oriented programming, which allows software to be driven by user events. It can be hard to predict the thought process of human beings because everyone is different and may perform any one task in multiple ways. Fortunately, technology professionals do not have to predict what the user will do. It is more important to deliver events that will produce the results than it is to predict what users will do and how they will do it.

As Timmis points out, one factor that makes an Agile project successful is high-level and not well-defined requirements. Again, a major concern here is that this means requirements are not validated and could leave room for assumptions by architects and developers. The issue is that others downstream must interpret what the business needs. This alone renders it more difficult to adequately test the features as they developed because there will be little to tie down the exact functionality. As illustrated in Figure 10.3, the agile project

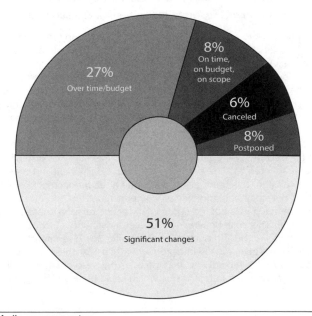

Figure 10.3 Agile success rates

success rates, reported by Planit Software Testing in 2012, are a mere 8%, while the volume of projects that report significant changes is an overwhelming 51%.[7]

In order to truly fix the industry issues of failing projects, unused functionality, and unpredictable costs, the team must produce testable requirements. These requirements will deliver the needed results and achieve the business objectives of the project.

STRENGTHS OF AGILE

Agile does have an upside, in spite of the perceived risks of leaving ambiguity in requirements. For those projects with aggressive schedules, projects that cover new technological ground, and even for projects with parceled budgets (the funding comes in increments instead of one lump sum), Agile can create and deliver much-needed functionality to the business as time, money, and resources permit.

Having shorter delivery time frames means that the business is able to be more agile in obtaining or maintaining a competitive edge. The business can literally develop functionality on demand, if it can master the delivery of Agile projects under the right circumstances.

Agile Success Story—contributed by Tony White, Lead Senior IT Consultant, Olenick & Associates

"Several years ago, a project was initiated at a large company to replace the existing underwriter risk assessment tool and to change how the underwriters kept track of notes on client accounts. Agile was chosen as an alternative to using traditional waterfall as the business felt it would take too long, consume excessive resources, and really not deliver exactly what the business wanted. The team was small: there was one project manager, one architect, one solution lead, one development lead with five developers, and a single test lead with three testers. The team was supported by one business sponsor and one business lead.

The majority of the leads on the team were generally co-located in one central location (at least the majority of the time). The team also maintained a disciplined calendar, which everyone adhered to. The calendar included a daily stand-up meeting with the entire team. In addition, this team also established a team document, which contained the solution, the development, and the test components.

In this case, the team was able to successfully decommission a legacy application in roughly six months. This solution already had user buy-in and a low defect rate. On top of this, the solution was built in such a way that after any given iteration, the resulting application could have been moved into production as a fully operational product. One of the main strengths of this project was that the team had also created a solid foundation of requirements and associated test cases, which could be used for any future changes or modifications."[8]

There were several factors in the success of this project. The entire breadth of the solution was predetermined; the team established timed iterations based on the input of the entire team; they utilized a single reference document; and they used individual iteration prototypes. In addition, the project team was co-located, had a great dynamic, and leveraged engagement and feedback mechanisms.

In spite of misconceptions and issues with implementation, this story is not unique. According to the Planit Testing Index, produced by Planit Software Testing (as shown in Table 10.1), over half of the survey respondents cited that Agile had been more successful in the categories of team collaboration, time to market, addressing requirements, and overall success. Among the strongest results, team collaboration reported a 74%[9] improvement, and only a fraction of them reported a negative result.

It is interesting to note that, in spite of the increases made to team collaboration, 40% of these respondents reported only moderately higher improvements to requirements. The truth is that regardless of the project process, requirements must still be developed by utilizing a process of due diligence and validation. Even when the project team has more access to the users, and the users feel more involved, the need for the processes utilized to develop quality requirements remains.

Further still, this same survey reported that when comparing Waterfall, V-model (named for its distinctive "v" shape), and Agile methodologies, the most significant changes to requirements were reported by Agile projects. In fact, a whopping 51%[10] reported completing "projects with significant changes to scope."[11] Remarkably, this can be directly attributed to the increased access and involvement of the business stakeholders in the development process. Without a means to validate inputs before incorporating them into a new product, this will not change—for many of the reasons cited in the Chapter 2 discussions on stakeholder management.

Table 10.1   Agile success statistics for 2012

Success	Team Collaboration	Time to Market	Addressing Requirements	Overall Success (ROI)
High	34%	18%	15%	14%
Medium High	40%	33%	40%	34%
Medium	19%	30%	27%	28%
Medium Low	7%	11%	13%	18%
Low	0%	8%	5%	5%

RISKS OF AGILE

Despite the strengths Agile presents and the various critical success factors already discussed, the biggest risks in applying Agile arise from the interpretation, misconceptions, and incomplete applications of the Agile methodology by the resources themselves. In reality, people interpret, understand, and apply techniques based upon their own experiences, education, personal beliefs, and even their other skills. Exposure is not the same as experience, and experience is not the same as expertise. Simply having exposure to a given methodology does not necessitate that a resource will obtain any levels of experience. It also does not mean that having experience in something will automatically make the resource an expert. This means that when resources come together to apply Agile techniques on a project, they are all working at it from different angles and degrees of exposure. This is true on every project; however, remember that in Agile a degree of ambiguity already exists because the team is working from high-level requirements instead of more refined specifications.

REFERENCES

1. Ziv, Hadar at http://www.techrepublic.com/blog/tech-manager/the -roots-of-agile-project-management/1491.
2. Agile Manifesto, 2001 at http://agilemanifesto.org.
3. Ibid.
4. Cohn, Mike, 2011, "Deciding What Kind of Projects are Most Suited for Agile" at http://www.mountaingoatsoftware.com/blog/deciding-what -kind-of-projects-are-most-suited-for-agile.
5. Timmis, Mark W., 2011, "Is Agile Right for Your Project" at http://www .pmforward.com/is-agile-right-for-your-project/.
6. Ibid.
7. Planit Software Testing, 2012, "Planit Testing Index 2012: Project Outcomes" at http://www.planit.net.au/resource/industry-stats-project -outcomes-based-on-primary-methodologies/.
8. White, Tony of Olenik & Associates, 2013, "Agile Interview with Barbara Davis."
9. Planit Software Testing, 2012, "Planit Testing Index 2012: Project Outcomes".
10. Ibid.
11. Ibid.

Implications of Waterfall on Requirements

Waterfall is the most common and prolific project methodology in the information technology industry. In fact, in the fall of 2011, Planit reported that Waterfall was still being applied to 36%[1] of all projects, and by 2012, that number had remained unchanged (as illustrated in Figure 11.1).

In reality, broken, misunderstood, poorly implemented or not, technology firms and resources are averse to risks and slow to implement new methods, even if those methods promise bigger, better, and faster results. This book is not intended to pitch one methodology over another but to educate companies and resources about how these methods will impact requirements, and what they should look like in order to more effectively produce those requirements. This being said, the basic Waterfall process (as illustrated in Figure 11.2) is as follows: project planning, requirements definition, design, development, test, and implementation.

Each of these stages is conducted in sequence, and subsequent stages typically do not start until the previous stages have been completed. This "gated" approach is intended to ensure the completion of necessary deliverables and artifacts that will serve as inputs to subsequent stages; however, completion does not guarantee quality, any more than an iterative approach does. What matters most for quality is the tasks and the level of due diligence within the tasks, as well as the skill of the resources in performing those tasks. Within each stage, the tasks and the due diligence are crucial to ensure success, but each task must still be benchmarked, and metrics applied in order to prove that the expected results are being achieved.

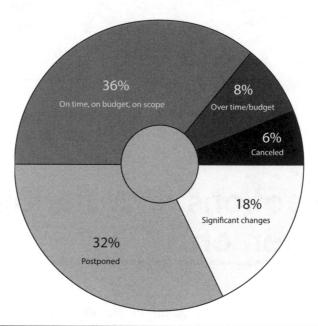

Figure 11.1 Waterfall success rates

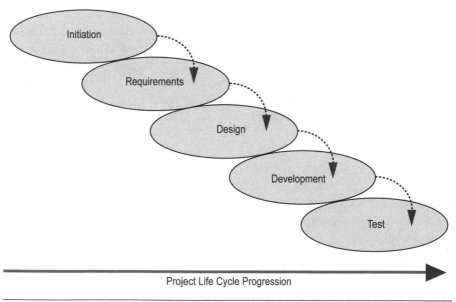

Project Life Cycle Progression

Figure 11.2 Waterfall life cycle

Lessons learned, and the triple constraints of projects (scope, time, and cost) are not the only measures to demonstrate quality or to understand what is going on within a project to impact quality. Project resources and teams will also need to look at those attributes, outlined in chapter 5, about estimating and benchmarking requirements (numbers of ambiguities and defects, e.g.) as well as lines of code (in thousands), numbers of integration points, volumes of transactions, and types of defects. Table 11.1 illustrates the proposed alignment between the life cycle stages of Waterfall and Agile.

MISCONCEPTIONS ABOUT WATERFALL

The greatest misconception of Waterfall is that it is broken and ineffective. However, like every other methodology or project approach, its effectiveness lies within the due diligence and the application of the tasks performed by those who use it. Unfortunately, the vastly different interpretations of the methodology, the tasks, and the skills of the resources involved within the industry create the main quality problems in use of the Waterfall development cycle. In some cases, this leads to excessive back and forth between the teams and the business about what to expect, when to expect it, what the deliverables should look like, and ultimately, issues with quality.

Another misconception about Waterfall is that Agile is either better than or worse than Waterfall. Again, the important thing in both of these approaches is really the tasks, due diligence, and the resources in the application. Look at it this way: a different hammer or saw doesn't make anyone a better carpenter; knowing how and when to use those tools is what makes one better at doing the job and leads to quality results. According to the Planit Testing Index, 36%[2] of survey respondents reported projects that were delivered on time and on budget by utilizing the Waterfall methodology. When compared to 42%[3] employing the

Table 11.1   Waterfall and Agile

Waterfall Life Cycle Stage	Agile Life Cycle Stage
Project Planning	Roadmap To Value, Product Vision, Product Roadmap, Planning
Requirements Definition	Sprint (Requirements) Planning
Design	Sprint (Design) Planning
Development	Sprint (Development) Planning
Test	Sprint (Test) Planning
Implementation	Sprint (Implementation) Planning, Sprint (Project) Review, Sprint (Project) Retrospective

V-model and 8%[4] of projects applying Agile, it is clear that Waterfall is still a contender.

In reality, Waterfall is merely a tool, the same as any of the other methods and approaches. While many may argue that it has had its day and is no longer valid, the truth is that in the right context and under the right circumstances, Waterfall can be—and still is—as valuable as ever. That does not mean that it is perfect, or that it does not need to continue on the road of consistent improvement. Any tool, technique, or approach that is utilized must be continually improved and managed towards increasingly better results.

IMPACTS OF WATERFALL ON REQUIREMENTS

The most significant impacts on requirements from Waterfall come from the inconsistent application of incomplete tasks. As I pointed out in *Managing Business Analysis Services*, the biggest issue is the inconsistent application of techniques between resources and between projects utilizing the same resources. While associations, such as the International Institute of Business Analysis, provide a loose framework, resources are really on their own when it comes to the application of those techniques, so this framework can come across as "suggestions." Without proper corporate standards, requirements processes, and management of resources, these suggestions could be misinterpreted or ignored altogether. Thus, the processes outlined in this book must go hand in hand with appropriate operational infrastructure and management in order to be effective and for real differences to be seen in projects—regardless of whether the approach is Agile or Waterfall.

USING WATERFALL TO MANAGE CHANGE

Change management is not the same as change control. Change management helps employees, customers, and vendors to cope with change and adapt to new methods and tools. Change control manages changes made to requirements, document versions, and other deliverables. Change control dictates requirements traceability.

Change Management

Managing change on any project is a delicate challenge. In technology, the biggest challenge can be getting people to buy-in. Getting buy-in takes skill and intuition. This skill enables the team to set up communication plans, feedback mechanisms, and other tools to support change. However, intuition enables people to understand and predict how others will react and to be able to read their unspoken needs for security and control.

The difference between Waterfall and Agile, when it comes to managing change, is that the iterative nature of Agile lends to smaller changes, which would be easier for the business to accept, and that Agile is designed to have constant input and close collaboration between the project team and the business. In Waterfall however, the project team must rely on the skill of the change management, the business analysis team, or the project manager and stakeholders. The length of time it takes to manage a project from start to finish can be multiple years, and the new functionality and processes can impact multiple business units. This means that managing change is more crucial and more complex in a Waterfall project.

The establishment of a RACI matrix (Responsible, Accountable, Consulted, Informed), communications architecture, a frequently asked questions website, and a designated point of contact are going to be critical to supporting the business through change. The biggest misconceptions about change management are that employees do not need to be coddled (they should simply accept change), people will want to follow better processes, anything will be an improvement on the broken tools that have been used to date, and people do not need time to prepare for change. Change management is not a haphazard, shotgun approach to preparing people, nor is it a reaction to angry employees. Change is a carefully planned process, following a simple strategy: inform, involve, evolve, maintain, and observe.

In short, this is a change process that supports employees, teams, customers, and vendors through significant changes. These stages align with the basic principles behind the sales process: attention, interest, desire, and action.

Both the "inform" and "attention" stages are designed to let people know about the product and what is going on. It's like a "heads-up" for the business, its vendors, and its customers to ensure that they each have a chance to understand what is going to happen and how it will impact them (if at all) and to mentally and emotionally prepare for the changes. Both the "involve" and the "interest" stages are designed to get people interested in what is happening. It is the start of buy-in and is based on the principles that people will want it once they have been a part of it, and that they support what they help build.

Whatever change management techniques are applied, remember that change is scary and exciting. It is scary when people feel a loss of control and confidence, and exciting when they feel in complete control. In every change, people need to know how it will impact them. But change must also be managed to ensure that buy-in is maintained throughout the process. In order to manage buy-in, communication vehicles must be planned and usages measured, and lessons learned must be applied in new projects. It comes down to ensuring that people feel in control, heard, and *important*.

Despite the fact that change management is a soft process, supporting the emotional and mental sides of business resources, it is necessary to manage the process and understand the implementation through a carefully planned approach. When change management is ad hoc, it leads to a lower level of confidence and decreased feeling of control—a general feeling of chaos. This will directly impact the length of time it takes to elicit requirements and implement the new solution.

Again, the reason that change management is a more crucial consideration when it comes to the Waterfall methodology is because of the considerable length of time between initiation, development, and implementation, but also because the process does not require specific interactions with the business throughout the life cycle. In an ideal world, all project resources would recognize the importance and their own role in managing change through every single conversation and interaction with the business.

Change Control

Change control is most commonly managed through a combination of governance and change advisory boards. While the project manager is more heavily involved in the change process, where change requests must be drafted and submitted, it is primarily the business analyst who supplies the bulk of the supporting details for the change request. At the stakeholder and sponsor level, the changes are presented by the project manager, who expresses the rationale for the changes and awaits the board's decision. The reason for the change advisory board is not only to prevent scope creep but also to restrain the project budget within acceptable means.

This means that the board recognizes that scope is associated with additional funding requirements. The decision rendered will reflect the company's tolerance for the additional costs to achieve the business objectives. It is only once these change requests have been approved that the analyst must proceed with the changes to the requirements. These changes will then cascade down through the life cycle and will impact the deliverables utilized by other teams. As such, maintaining traceability across changes is critical.

STRENGTHS OF WATERFALL

The strengths of Waterfall are often swept aside in the rush to dismiss it with, or as the source of, project failure. When people buy those pieces of modular furniture from box stores, take them home, and open them up to try putting them together, they often dismiss the instructions because they are difficult to interpret. When the project is completed, there are usually extra nuts and bolts and sometimes various other parts. To throw away the furniture, merely because the instructions were hard to understand or there were extra parts, would be silly. To disregard or ignore the good attributes of anything, simply because there may be areas that need clarification or the person applying the techniques or utilizing the tools cannot understand something, would be equally silly. Remember: it may not be the process that is defective. The primary source of issues in any given process is poor implementation. If inventor Thomas Adams had thrown away the "chickle" because it did not suit the implementation (and, consequently, failed as a rubber substitute), the world would not have bubble gum today.

The strengths of Waterfall are that it utilizes a systematic approach to projects and does require control gates between stages. A systematic approach lends to the ability to govern and manage the project. In addition, other strengths of Waterfall include the application benchmarks and subsequent quantification of results against the benchmarks. It is important to know what Waterfall is and is not, in the same way that it is important to know what Agile is and is not. Using the right tool for every job is as critical as choosing and managing the process and the resources applying it.

The Capability Maturity Model illustrates the need for a managed and optimized approach to processes in order to see consistent delivery and enable success in applying those processes. One of the key factors in Waterfall, which aligns to this model, is the delineation of roles across these managed processes. While this delineation and role definition are still evolving and changing, by and large the industry is making an effort to manage these roles to produce better results. Approaches—such as extreme programming—that attempt to remove layers and role definition, so every resource is more accountable and delivery can occur more rapidly, demand more of the allocated resources, and in the long run, the industry will see that this is not the answer.

A systematic approach works best when everyone is on the same page and knows what to do and when to do it. Control gates throughout the process manage those pieces to ensure that key criteria are met before products with massive defects are released. However, control gates also require clear criteria, enforcement, and buy-in to be effective. Properly regulated and managed control gates allow projects to be held accountable for delivery standards at every stage of the development process and forces the team to justify the work being done with hard evidence. These controls play no favorites and are intended to prevent failing projects from advancing.

RISKS OF WATERFALL

The biggest risk from Waterfall is that there is no governing body, such as The Open Group or the Institute of Electrical and Electronics Engineers for Agile, to educate people and companies which choose to utilize it and to certify "levels" for practitioners. Furthermore, governance is left to companies to determine and manage. Again, resources—who may be full time employees or contract resources—apply the methodology inconsistently. It is important to note that the risk is primarily people-based, which results in inconsistent quality or requirements and a host of other project issues. These people-based issues result in problems from two perspectives: limited vision (scotoma) about how to change and overloading the resources, which reduces their ability to deliver quality outcomes.

According to Bloor Research practice leader, Martin Langham: "The problem with the Waterfall model is that it has become hardwired into the thinking of project planners."[8] What this means is that people have trouble thinking outside of the box because the box is all they can see. This is evident in any process that calls for validation of requirements in any other phase than requirements. Validation is not specified in the Waterfall model—then again, nothing beyond "requirements" is identified, which provides no solid understanding of what validation means or what it takes to be successful in developing requirements. However, in order to think outside of the proverbial box, all technology resources, stakeholders, and proponents must let go of the past ways of doing things. This letting go is really the only way to support new methods for conducting business analysis tasks. It is then that the redefinition of the requirements process can occur outside of that context.

All these decades later, technophiles the world over are still wrestling with this understanding and trying to look at the requirements process without seeing this process through the Waterfall box. All requirements steps—elicitation, research, analysis, specification, and validation—should occur within the requirements stage. End of story. To do any of these activities after the requirements process has ended will only lead to ambiguities, issues, defects, and low quality project outcomes. So long as the analysts, project managers, stakeholders, and even chief information officers review and scrutinize the requirements process through the lens of the project methodology, all they will see is the project methodology.

In the process of maturing business analysis, the information technology industry has also wrestled with how to hone, manage, and leverage their skills for increased project success. When resources like business analysts are tasked with other duties, such as project management or testing, this only reduces their time and attention for quality outcomes. In this case, it is not the desire or drive to deliver results that matters, but the fact that people can only be really proficient in some key areas—especially when the list of tasks to be completed is so diverse that it requires competing skill sets and levels of attention to detail.

REFERENCES

1. Planit Software Testing, 2011, "Planit Testing Index 2011: Project Methodologies," at http://www.planit.net.au/resource/industry-stats-project-methodologies-2011/.
2. Planit Software Testing, 2012 "Planit Testing Index 2012: Project Outcomes" at http://www.planit.net.au/resource/industry-stats-project-outcomes-based-on-primary-methodologies/.
3. Ibid.
4. Ibid.
5. Langham, Martin, 2005, Bloor Research http://www.it-director.com/technology/productivity/content.php?cid=7865.

## 12

Implications of WAgile on Requirements

WAgile stands for "Waterfall–Agile" and represents a blended approach to applying a combination of both Waterfall and Agile techniques. There are several reasons an organization would use a blended WAgile approach, including: project realignment, inability to let go of familiar techniques, inability to perceive a difference, unclear instruction in applying Agile, and the application of Agile to inappropriate projects.

Many teams that claim to be using WAgile are actually utilizing Waterfall. These teams only utilize a handful of Agile tactics when they need to get a struggling project back on track. Depending on the need, these teams may utilize daily stand-up meetings, breaking the project into iterations and on-the-fly release planning. Further, teams may also attempt to reduce the deliverables and the artifacts in an effort to flip from Waterfall to Agile. However, when this happens the project sinks deeper into trouble, and failure becomes imminent. When projects change the expected deliverables and artifacts, it creates a sense of chaos and miscommunication, which leads the team deeper into compounded challenges.

In other cases where organizations claim to be using WAgile, it may be due to the fact that technology organizations are attempting to move from Waterfall to Agile. However, resources have problems letting go of the Waterfall techniques because, broken or not, these techniques are what they are most familiar with. In other words, resources are deliberately attempting to apply Waterfall techniques to the Agile approach because they are most comfortable in performing those specific techniques.

Claiming to use WAgile when the team is, in fact, using either Waterfall or Agile, poses a tremendous difficulty. It illustrates that individual team members cannot differentiate between the techniques of either of the two methodologies and the approach becomes convoluted and chaotic. Resources are looking at Agile through Waterfall and interpreting it from a Waterfall perspective. It is like a type of color blindness.

In still other cases where WAgile is being claimed, it turns out that the confusion amounts to poor and incomplete instruction in how to apply the Agile process and its methods. In other words, the organization provides some instruction, and the responsible resources learn about 75% of what is important, remember about 25%, and make efforts to apply about 15%. In reality, these numbers could be much lower because of the ways in which people learn. According to Edgar Dale's research,[1] knowledge retention, from the various types of learning methods, can be charted in a "cone of learning," as illustrated in Figure 12.1.

In addition, Dale cited knowledge retention rates of 85% after four months, 80% after eleven months, and 75% after twenty-four months, as illustrated in Table 12.1.[2] This means that people who attend training programs, such as Agile training, or those who only read about it in books will learn only about 10%, and they will lose about 75% of this ten percent over the course of the subsequent twenty-four months.

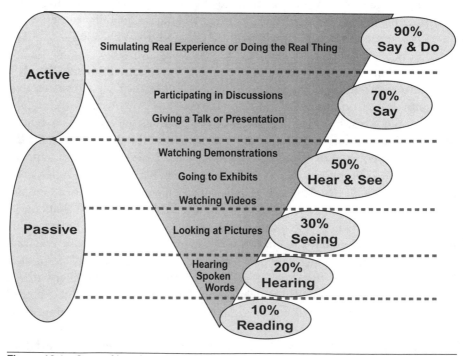

Figure 12.1   Cone of learning

Table 12.1   Percentage of knowledge retention after time period

Time Period	Percentage of Knowledge Retained
4 months	85%
11 months	80%
24 months	75%

Lastly, the blend of Waterfall and Agile projects could also come from attempting to apply Agile to inappropriate projects. By applying the Agile process to the wrong projects, teams find they will have to either flip back and forth between Agile and Waterfall or revert back to Waterfall when the Agile approach fails.

MISCONCEPTIONS ABOUT WAGILE

The biggest misconception about WAgile is, in fact, that it is a valid project approach. This is more of a defensive position than a true statement of fact. In other words, the person is merely attempting to rationalize the chaos and the haphazard approach being taken by giving it a name, which is a derivative of Waterfall and Agile. It is, rather, the "Jackalope"—the mythical jack rabbit and antelope combination—of project methodologies.

IMPACTS OF WAGILE ON REQUIREMENTS

It goes without saying that a reactive approach to the project life cycle ultimately has disastrous consequences on requirements. Let's face it: technology organizations have not really mastered any consistent techniques in requirements. Without metrics and benchmarking, there is not a single organization that has any evidence to prove otherwise. That means that between Waterfall and Agile, what is already broken, misunderstood, and poorly communicated in requirements is being further damaged by attempting to blend the two approaches without a solid plan for doing so.

STRENGTHS OF WAGILE

If WAgile were indeed a valid approach, and it were well planned, there could be some serious benefits to using it. Like any other approach, this would mean that WAgile would have to move from reactionary to proactive, it would need to utilize consistent steps and benchmarks, and the resources would all have to be well versed in its application. For example, Waterfall could be vastly improved if it utilized more collaboration and the roadmap to value from the Agile approach. Agile, on the other hand, could be vastly improved with a more consistent degree of due diligence in requirements.

In this case, WAgile would essentially be a systematic process for the development of the product utilizing highly collaborative sessions for the definition of the value roadmap, project planning, requirements elicitation, validation, product coding, and the subsequent implementation reviews. WAgile, as a well-planned systematic approach, would utilize the most effective techniques from each methodology and deliver exceptional and well-refined results to the business.

RISKS OF WAGILE

The biggest risk for the application of WAgile is that it may become either a knee-jerk reaction, which is enacted to correct the course of a challenged project, or a poorly planned approach, which does not clearly identify the techniques to be used, the deliverables, the artifacts to be created, or the results to be achieved. Unfortunately, poor planning of the approach usually signifies poor process control and management. This means inconsistent deliverables, unpredictable results, and an inability to utilize consistent improvement methods. The best approach is to select either Waterfall or Agile and simply focus on doing it well. By learning and understanding each of the requirements techniques specified in Section 3 of this book, project teams can successfully manage either approach and still achieve dramatic improvements to project outcomes.

REFERENCES

1. Dale, Edgar, 1969, "Audiovisual Methods in Teaching".
2. Ibid.

13

Implications of TOGAF Enterprise Architecture on Requirements

The Massachusetts Institute of Technology Sloan Management Center for Information Systems Research defines enterprise architecture (also known as enterprise information technology architecture and enterprise information systems architecture) as:

> *"The organizing logic for business processes and information technology (IT) infrastructure reflecting the integration and standardization requirements of the company's operating model. The operating model is the desired state of business process integration and business process standardization for delivering goods and services to customers."[1]*

The United States government, on the other hand, defines the term "enterprise architecture" as the documented results of the examination process, not the process itself. Specifically, US Code Title 44, Chapter 3601, Sub-section 4 defines it in this way:

- Means:
    - (i) a strategic information asset base, which defines the mission;
    - (ii) the information necessary to perform the mission;
    - (iii) the technologies necessary to perform the mission; and
    - (iv) the transitional processes for implementing new technologies in response to changing mission needs; and

- Includes:
    - (i) a baseline architecture;
    - (ii) a target architecture; and
    - (iii) a sequencing plan."[2]

This being said, there can be no results without undergoing the process. In order to create these results, architects use various tools and techniques to illustrate the structure and dynamics of the enterprise. These include the creation of deliverables and artifacts, such as taxonomies, diagrams, models, and documents. These deliverables and artifacts illustrate the organization of business functions, capabilities, processes and systems, employee architecture (people) and communication infrastructure, information resources, assets and applications, computing capabilities, and data and information exchange within the enterprise.

According to Chris Curran, thought leader and Chief Technologist at PwC:

> *"A good EA [enterprise architecture] program starts with a representation of what the business units and functions want to do (objectives, metrics, a strategy of some kind) and uses it as a basis to understand what business capabilities are needed and then build a business and technology blueprint and plan."*[3]

EA is a crucial element of the governance structure of information technology. It is the primary role for overseeing the systems framework and ensuring the interoperability of those systems in the fulfillment of the business objectives. The Open Group Architecture Framework (TOGAF) is an approach to EA, or an architecture development method (ADM). As illustrated in Figure 13.1, this approach defines the process and outcomes for planning, designing, implementing, and governing enterprise information systems architecture.

According to subject matter expert and chief technology officer, Udayan Banerjee, the architecture development method is a series of four basic steps. These basic steps are:

> *"Tailor TOGAF to suit your need;" "Define scope of work and prepare plan for rollout;" "Oversee development and implementation;" and "Manage post-implementation change."*[4]

MISCONCEPTIONS ABOUT TOGAF

In researching common misconceptions about TOGAF, all but two of the myths and misconceptions identified would have been inherited from EA in general.

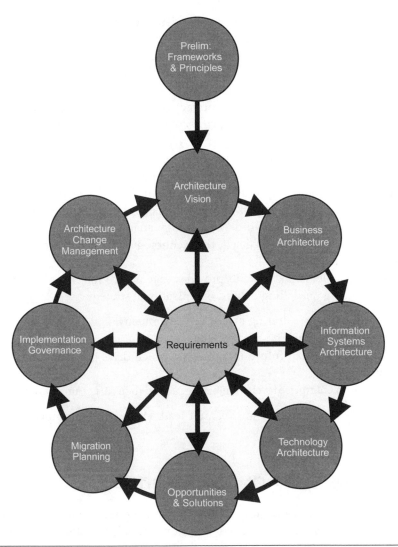

Figure 13.1 TOGAF architecture development method

The two misconceptions, which would not have resulted from EA, still speak to misunderstandings and misinterpretations that exist within EA, but, in this case, they do have a direct impact on the interpretation of the TOGAF approach.

First and foremost, as Banerjee succinctly puts it: "TOGAF is NOT a methodology for managing software development."[5] Rather, TOGAF is a framework for the process and outcomes within a project methodology for planning, designing, implementing, and governing information systems architecture within the context of the business. This process must define the appropriate technology to meet the objectives and strategic goals of the organization. A project methodology, on the other hand, is the process by which a specific project is planned, designed, implemented, and governed within the context of the EA. Whereas the TOGAF ADM is a comprehensive strategy (the high-level view) for meeting multiple objectives and goals, a project is a more detailed perspective (the low-level detailed view) on a particular solution and how it fits into the existing architecture to meet specific goals.

The second myth uncovered is that information technology organizations utilize EA to plan the technology (uses and applications) for the business. If this were the case, technology would be leading the business. The truth is, no matter how advanced technology is, it must meet the needs of the business and support its core functions. In other words, technology enables the business. So, unless the business *is* the technology itself, the technology must be determined by the business and its objectives.

Thought leader Thakur Sahib provides sage advice for ensuring that IT is neither outpacing nor falling behind organizational strategy:

- Figure out the operating model of the company.
- Design EA for the current scenario.
- Identify and map future IT products, which drive growth in an organization . . .
- Create an enterprise level architecture . . . and then carry out an execution.[6]

This is not to say that technology cannot lead. However, it is simply not EA in this case; it is the business.

IMPACTS OF TOGAF ON REQUIREMENTS

TOGAF's greatest, and certainly best impact on the requirements process lies in requiring the capture of detailed business architecture documentation. As discussed in Chapter 1, "Identifying the Solution," this documentation is crucial for getting requirements through both the elicitation and the research steps. By utilizing such detailed articulation of the business architecture, (which in many ways would far exceed what a business analyst has the time and inclination to develop) the analyst is able to develop a more complete understanding of the overall architecture. This, in turn, gives the analyst (and the business) more complete information for the development of requirements.

Remember that business architecture provides the big picture view of the "who, what, where, and which" of the company's operating model. As pointed out in Chapter 1, this information is not only necessary, it is crucial to the development of more complete and detailed solution requirements. It reminds me of something Glenn Brule of ESI International recently said at a conference. He suggested that there are only two questions he starts with when approaching the business. These are:

- What is it?
- Why should I care?

The analyst can learn a lot from the business by asking these two questions. "What is it" elicits information about the business, the architecture, and the problem; "Why should I care" elicits information about why each of these things is important.

It is not enough to think in terms of why something is important to the business. The analyst should also be thinking of it in relation to the problem, the architecture, and the solution. Consider this scenario:

Question: "What is it?"

Answer: "The customer information management system (CIMS) that handles all of the customer accounts for our company."

Question: "Why should I care about this system?"

Answer: "Because it handles all of the customer accounts for our company and because of impending changes from an upcoming merger with one of our smaller competitors which we have recently acquired."

From here, the analyst can request further details and probe the stakeholders for critical information about the two systems that have been identified. The two systems, identified in this example, are the existing CIMS and the one from the newly acquired company.

The point is that this is the starting point for great conversations, which will enable the analyst to elicit better information about the business architecture. This architecture will provide the framework and context for the artifacts to be used and for the deliverables to be produced during the entire project.

The second mandate from TOGAF that has a tremendous (and equally positive) impact on requirements is to create a requirements management repository. Far too many projects "make do" without any real repository for requirements. Unfortunately, this only leads to excessive time to manage, lack of traceability, lost requirements, miscommunication, and ultimately, scope creep.

If there were any negative impacts from TOGAF, they would stem from a misinterpretation of the method, an inconsistent application of the techniques, and a lack of experience from the resources. Of course, these negative impacts span multiple processes, methods, and methodology in business—that is, they are not unique to TOGAF. This is exactly why it is critical that businesses, technology organizations, and project teams utilize management and governance techniques that include performance management, quality control, and consistent improvement principles.

STRENGTHS OF TOGAF EA METHODOLOGY

Again, the greatest strengths of TOGAF EA methodology come from those areas that also have the largest and most positive impacts on requirements. These are: a comprehensive view of the business architecture through its detailed deliverables and artifacts and the use of a requirements management repository. It is because of the positive impacts on the requirements deliverables and efforts that these are TOGAF's greatest strengths (from a business analysis and, arguably, a project perspective). From a business analysis perspective, these strengths lend the most to the effective and efficient delivery of requirements that are complete, consistent, and accurate (and testable!). It is also these strengths that lend the most to effective and efficient management of requirements. The fact is that great requirements are only truly useful when they are managed. Management enables traceability for change, verification, validation, and access by other teams, from the earliest to the most current version. Further, it also enables teams to benchmark, govern the process, and to improve the process by applying key performance indicators.

RISKS OF TOGAF EA METHODOLOGY

Negative impacts of the TOGAF EA methodology stem from misinterpretation of the TOGAF method, its inconsistent application, and the lack of experience from project resources (there are risks associated with each). The risks presented by these impacts include disjointed understanding and disconnected expectations, missed milestones and incomplete details, and excessive time to produce deliverables. As with any other process or method that is not clearly articulated, managed, and staffed, these risks increase exponentially. In the end, if these risks are not managed appropriately, the project faces challenges. Many of these challenges will come directly from requirements that have been built upon the foundation of deliverables that were created according to the TOGAF application development method.

Business analysts and teams will see the old adage, "garbage in—garbage out." The quality of requirements is wholly dependent upon the quality of the information that can be extracted through the elicitation and research stage and on the ability of the analyst to extract this information. If the business does not know what the business architecture looks like, it will not matter how capable the business analysts are in the elicitation: they will have to generate the missing documents for themselves in order to create a complete set of requirements and to verify and validate those requirements.

REFERENCES

1. Weill, Peter, 2007, "Innovating With Information Systems: What Do the Most Agile Firms in the World Do?" presentation at sixth e-Business Conference, Barcelona, Spain.
2. US Code Title 44, Chapter 3601, Sub-section 4 (44 USC 3601 (4)), 2002 at http://us-code.vlex.com/vid/sec-definitions-19256361.
3. Curran, Chris, 2010, "Busting 5 Enterprise Architecture Myths" at http://www.ciodashboard.com/architecture/5-enterprise-architecture-myths/.
4. Banerjee, Udayan, 2011, "What Is TOGAF—Without Jargon" at http://setandbma.wordpress.com/2011/01/25/what-is-togaf-without-jargon/.
5. Ibid.
6. Sahib, Thakur, 2009, "IT as Business Strategy" at http://www.thakursahib.com/2009/08/it-as-business-strategy/.

## 14

How Business Analysis Can Leverage DO-178C Aviation Engineering Specifications

While the discussion here is not intended to replace the DO-178 guidelines, it is intended to illustrate an alignment between the due diligence of these guidelines and the due diligence in commercial software applications, in order for business analysts to understand requirements development within the context of multiple types of development environments. It is hoped that, while this chapter provides an overview of DO-178 and is not intended to enable or support certification applications, this information will help business analysts understand the big picture. That is to say, the goal is to articulate the real significance of requirements and how they contribute to project success.

The importance of the DO-178 guidelines for business analysis lies in their relevance to verification and validation of requirements. This approach enables analysts to be able to verify and to validate requirements in the absence of user stakeholder technical knowledge. Hence, it helps the analyst to answer the key question, "how can requirements be validated when the user does not know enough detail?"

RTCA/DO-178C: Software Considerations in Airborne Systems and Equipment Certification is a documented set of guidelines, produced by the Radio Technical Commission for Aeronautics (RTCA) and the European Organisation for Civil Aviation Equipment (EUROCAE), for ensuring the quality and safety of software systems that are utilized in airborne applications. RTCA/DO-178C is recognized by the aviation industry and its certification authorities as an appropriate approach for ensuring the safety of all software that is embedded and implemented within airborne systems. Further, it ensures that all relevant equipment has been developed in compliance with the safety objectives of federal regulations. (Note: For clarity, DO-178 is the framework established by RTCA. There are many elements which are not specific to a particular version of this document. For these elements, I use DO-178. The framework is released and updated in versions: DO-178A, B, & C.)

In the United States, the Federal Aviation Administration officially recognized this framework in its published Advisory Circular, AC 20-115B, in January of 1993. This advisory circular provides formal guidance toward applying for, and achieving, airworthiness certification of products that employ software. While the RTCA/DO-178C software considerations are not the only means of achieving certification, prospective applicants must document and prove the equivalence of any alternate approaches to meeting the safety objectives of the regulations when they apply.

The DO-178C software considerations provide a framework that utilizes the Design Assurance Level (DAL), also known as "Item Development Assurance Level" (IDAL), to assess the risk and impacts of varying degrees of failure in software applications. This DAL is determined by conducting the safety assessment process and hazard analysis. The impact of failure is categorized according to the following five levels:

- *Level A, Catastrophic:* Software failure may result in aircraft crash and loss of life. The loss of these critical functions is considered catastrophic because these systems are required in order to safely fly and land the aircraft.
- *Level B, Hazardous:* The failure of these systems will have a significant adverse impact on safety or aircraft performance; it will reduce the capability of the aircrew to operate or control the aircraft as a result of physical distress; or these errors could causes serious (even fatal) injuries.
- *Level C, Major:* The failure of these systems will have a significant impact on the functioning and operation of the aircraft or the ability of the flight crew to perform their duties.
- *Level D, Minor:* The failure of these systems is noticeable; however, it will not cause injury or death. Occurrence would likely cause inconveniences to the crew of the aircraft or a slight increase in workload.
- *Level E, No Effect:* The failure of these systems will have no impact on passenger safety, aircraft operation, crew workload, or passenger comfort.

The framework also provides considerations for traceability between the software, design, and requirements. These are intended to ensure alignment between the system and the operational and safety-related requirements. In addition, the DO-178 framework outlines a process for the decomposition of system requirements into high-level software requirements, which are then verified by utilizing the software verification process. This process is intended to establish two primary characteristics of the software being produced. These are:

1. The software functions according to the directives of the requirements.
2. The software does not demonstrate any of the irregular functionality described in the safety assessment.

DO-178 FRAMEWORK

The DO-178C software considerations specify detailed sets of activities[1] that are categorized into three basic process areas across the product development life cycle. As depicted in Figure 14.1, these process areas are software planning, software development, and the correctness, confidence, and control (software verification) process areas. Figure 14.2, however, illustrates the flow of safety-related information across the development process itself.

Within each of the process areas, there are several subprocesses that result in key documentation, which is produced through the prescribed activities. The

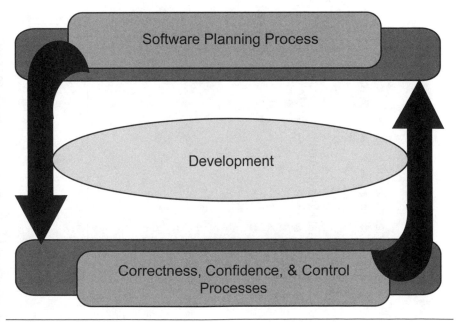

Figure 14.1 DO-178 life cycle process

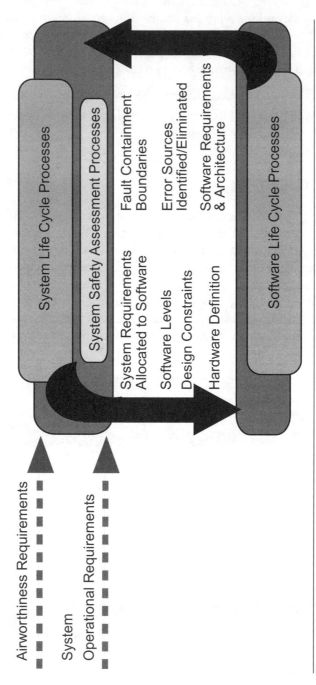

Figure 14.2 Software and systems flow

intent is that these documents, in combination, provide an accurate picture of the rigor applied throughout the development life cycle and a level of assurance about the quality and safety of the resulting product.

Software Planning Process

The first process in the DO-178 framework is planning. The objective of the planning process is to plan all activities that will be undertaken in order to develop safe, requirements-based software. During the planning process, the primary activity is to coordinate the development, management, and revision of each particular plan. This essentially means that the planning for the project is to be accomplished up front—before any designs, prototypes, or codes are ever developed.

The planning process encompasses planning for the development life cycle environment (including methods and tools), identified software development standards, as well as the software plans and their compliance with DO-178. Furthermore, the planning processes identify the interrelationships between processes, process sequencing and feedback, and process transition criteria. The planning process produces several key plans for use throughout the subsequent stages in order to ensure that due diligence is incorporated into the process. These plans include: plan for software aspects of certification (PSAC), software development plan (SDP), software verification plan (SVP), software configuration management plan (SCMP), and software quality assurance plan (SQAP).

The PSAC is the detailed plan that provides specifics about how the software development will be accomplished in compliance with DO-178.

The SDP describes the software development life cycle. This includes the methodology or approach, techniques, and the tools within the development environment. The SVP illustrates how the selected verification method to be utilized will satisfy all objectives of the software verification process. To accomplish this, this document must outline what those objectives are and demonstrate alignment to the proposed approach. The SCMP outlines the proposed method for configuration management of all software artifacts. This configuration management plan outlines both the tools and techniques to be utilized. In addition, this document defines the process for making revisions to the specified configurations and the escalation process for any software issues which may arise. The SQAP describes the strategy for meeting the objectives of the software quality assurance process. It describes how the applicant's software quality assurance process confirms that the documented plans have been followed. To accomplish this, this document must outline what those safety objectives are and illustrate alignment between the product and the objectives.

Each of these documents is intended to: identify the objectives of the project and product; outline the plans for the overall development life cycle; and articulate what approaches, tasks, and tools will be utilized to achieve those objectives. In addition to these planning documents, the planning process for all software levels, except Level D, identifies the following standards that are utilized for the project: software requirements standards, software design standards, and software code standards.

Each of these planning documents and standards is utilized throughout the development, verification, configuration management, and quality assurances processes, but is also required to be submitted with the certification application to the regulatory certification authority. They are used both to guide the process and to prove the elements of rigor and due diligence that give the certification authority confidence in the resulting system.

One of the inputs to the planning process is the system requirements document (SRD). This document contains a statement of the operational premise that will form the basis of the system being developed; a definition of the impacted external systems; a statement of the operational requirements; justificatory evidence for the engineering version of the requirements in terms of analyses, expert opinions, and stakeholder meetings; the traceability from every single requirement to previous documents or other documentation; and finally, the description of the anticipated test plan for each requirement. Throughout the planning process, it is expected that the team will identify and plan the approach toward effectively and safely satisfying those system requirements.

Software Development Process

DO-178 software considerations are not intended as an aviation software development standard. Instead, the DO-178 process provides software assurance by identifying a set of specific tasks to meet objectives and demonstrate levels of rigor throughout the development life cycle. The software development process is further broken into four manageable subprocesses: the software requirements process, the software design process, the software coding process, and the integration process.

Software Requirements Process

The objective of the software requirements subprocess is to develop high-level software requirements related to software function, performance, interface, and safety. This process utilizes the outputs from the system life cycle processes in order to generate the high-level software requirements. The specific activities of this process are to analyze and decompose the system requirements and the interface system architecture. This process also refers to the software development plan and the software requirements standards in order to define and meet the criteria prescribed in these planning documents. Once the transition criteria are satisfied, the requirements are developed from the input materials.

Software Design Process

The objectives of the software design process are to develop the low-level requirements and software architecture, and then provide those to the system safety assessment process for review. To that end, the high-level requirements (in addition to the planning documents) serve as the primary input to this process, and will be utilized as the basis for the low-level requirements. During the software design process, the team works to decompose the high-level requirements into low-level (also known as design-level) requirements and the software architecture. These design-level requirements must be easily traceable, directly from the implemented source code. These requirements will be utilized to implement the source code.

Software Coding Process

The objective of the coding process is to develop source code that satisfies the low-level software requirements. That code must demonstrate key attributes and characteristics, which are:

- Consistent
- Traceable
- Verifiable
- Accurately aligned (implemented according to the low-level requirements)

The software coding process begins when the low-level requirements and the software architecture are understood. In essence, it is the generation or development of the individual lines of source code that have been identified from the design process. It is important to remember that all source code must be traceable back to the requirements and the system-level requirements in order to comply with DO-178.

Integration Process

Finally, the integration process is where the team transitions the object code from the development environment to the target hardware environment, with its related hardware components. It includes building the object code from the source code. The objective of the integration process is to integrate the hardware and software components. This is accomplished by loading the executable code onto the specific hardware. The basic process for this integration is the process of loading itself. It takes the source and object code, derived in the software design process, and loads it onto the hardware component. It utilizes the software architecture as the blueprint for this integration. The outputs from the integration process are the executable object code and the linking and loading data from the integration process.

The collective outputs from the software requirements, design, coding, and integration processes are the software requirements data, software design description, implemented source code, and the executable object code. These documents and codes are provided as a means to demonstrate traceability and alignment from the start of the process, the process objectives, the processes applied, and the resulting tangible product outputs. In this way, the documentation supports the assertion that the product was developed by applying due diligence and rigor in order to meet DO-178's safety objectives.

Both the source and executable codes are delivered to the certification authority in order to demonstrate consistency between the requirements and the resulting code. This code and documentation alignment ensures traceability across the solution—right from planning to implementation. It also proves to the certification authority that what was built aligns with the documented requirements.

Throughout the development process, the most common methodologies or approaches utilized are Waterfall, Spiral, and the V-model (or verification and validation model). In Chapters 10 and 11, both Agile and Waterfall were discussed. While Agile is not as common, it has reportedly been applied in some instances; however, the skill of the team involved and the interpretation of Agile have often meant gaps in the ability to prove that the product has met the DO-178's objectives and safety mandates. As depicted in Figure 14.3, the Spiral model is a type of software development process that combines some of the elements of Waterfall and prototyping (prototyping is the method of building and testing a scale version of the product to identify issues and challenges). The Spiral model is also referred to as either the Spiral lifecycle model or Spiral development model, and is conducted in stages.

While the model was originally designed for projects from six months to two years in length, it appears to be most effective when size, cost, and complexity are significant factors. This application's dependency on these factors is especially true, with the industry trend towards Agile adoption for smaller projects. Both Agile and the Spiral model are similar, in that each is intended to provide continuous improvement of the features and requirements through cycles. Where Agile utilizes "sprints," Spiral utilizes "spirals." Each approach is intended to provide and support incremental product releases. In this manner, incremental refinement is achieved at each pass around the spiral.

The other most common project methodology utilized within the DO-178 development process is the V-model. As illustrated in Figure 14.4, the V-model is an approach to development that represents the relationship between each stage in the development life cycle.

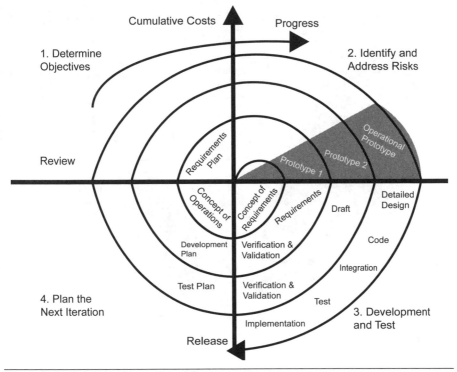

Figure 14.3 Spiral development model

This approach may be considered an extension of the Waterfall model. However, the model bends upwards after the coding and implementation stages to illustrate the feedback loops and the linkages between testing at the various stages of the life cycle. Hence, it is merely a graphical representation of the work to be done throughout the life cycle. Those steps are represented in the specific sequencing and further describe the activities to be performed in each of those steps.

The model moves from left to right, in the order of project progression or completion, as well as according to the level of abstraction or granularity. In addition, where the left arm represents the collection, decomposition, and analysis of requirements, as well as the generation of architecture design specifications, the right arm represents the integration of the product and its validation across this integration. As depicted in Figure 14.5, the V-model has a project success rate of 42%,[2] which stands in stark contrast to the mere 8%[3] success rates of Agile.

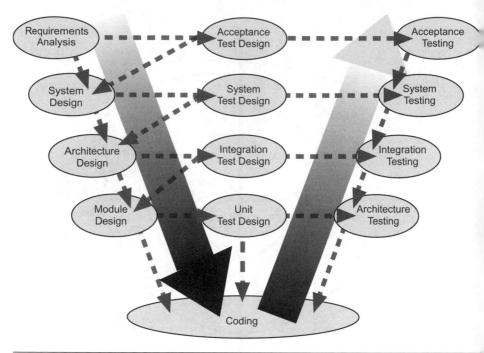

Figure 14.4 V development model

Traceability

The DO-178 software consideration also provides clear guidance for the traceability of requirements throughout the entire process. These guidance areas are:

- Traceability between both system and software requirements is provided. This supports the verification activities and proves the accurate implementation of the system as designed.
- Traceability between both low- and high-level requirements is provided. This supports the transparency between decomposed requirements and decisions made for architectural design elements.
- Traceability between both source code and low-level requirements is provided. This verifies that all source code has been documented.

Correctness, Confidence, and Control Process

The correctness, confidence, and control process is merely a convenient way to describe and package the verification and quality assurance processes. These processes are designed to verify that the software product meets the plans and requirements and to ensure that the safety objectives are met and upheld. In

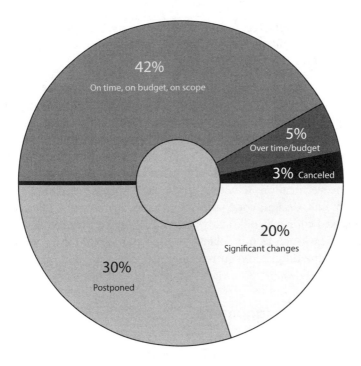

Figure 14.5   V-model success rates

addition, they are designed to ensure that the process is deliberate, measured, and controlled along the way. This ensures that the resulting product operates as planned, meets the DO-178 directives, and can be reproduced in exacting detail.

Verification

After the development stage has concluded, the DO-178 framework moves through verification. Verification is the stage wherein the product is verified against the requirements and design to ensure that the objective of consistency has been achieved. The general objectives of the verification process are to confirm that:

- Applicable system requirements have been built into the high-level requirements
- The resulting high-level requirements have been decomposed into architecture and low-level requirements
- These low-level requirements and architecture have been developed into the resulting source code
- The executable object code produced meets the defined software requirements

- The methods utilized to meet these objectives are logically complete and accurate and align to the appropriate software level (A, B, C, D, E) identified for the DO-178 standard.

Traceability is crucial to the successful completion of this stage because it will enable the development team to clearly establish the alignment between requirements, design, and code. This documentation will be utilized in support of the certification application. Specifically, the documents to be produced for this purpose are: the software verification cases and procedures, software verification results (SVR), and the traceability matrix. The SVR document captures the results of the verification activities. These activities are: a complete review of the requirements, design, code, and integration outputs; test cases; procedures and results; and code coverage analysis. In addition, verification dictates specific testing activities—such as unit, black box, acceptance, and integration testing—as part of the due diligence required to ensure the alignment of the product to requirements and design.

Configuration Management

One of the key components of the DO-178 framework is configuration management. Configuration management includes the detailed version control for the product, once it has been produced and has passed through the development process. The objectives for configuration management under this framework are:

- To supply controlled and predetermined configuration of the software
- To have the ability to consistently replicate the executable code in an exact manner (i.e., all potential variables are exactly the same)
- To deliberately control the process inputs and outputs in order to ensure both consistency and exacting replication of the process
- To provide a baseline for review, status assessment, and change control
- To supply an urgency-control mechanism for prioritizing and addressing problems and for ensuring that resulting changes are appropriately recorded, and approval status is documented and implemented where approved
- To provide evidence of the required software approvals and control of the software development artifacts
- To support the software compliance assessment
- To provide the means for the secured archival and recovery points, which are housed in a physical location

The configuration management process must capture detailed descriptions of the exact documentation (versions and file locations included) utilized in the development, as well as the versions of all tools utilized during the development process. The intent here is to ensure that the results can be duplicated *exactly* as first achieved by repeating the development process in its entirety. The configuration management process is also responsible for managing problem reports, changes, and other associated activities. Further, configuration management is designed to manage and maintain the software configuration index and the software life cycle environment configuration index. In addition, the process provides archival and versioning control for the source code development environment, other development environments (such as test and analysis tools), software integration tools, and all other related documents, software, and hardware.

Quality Assurance

The DO-178 framework also mandates a specific set of activities for quality assurance (QA). The overall objectives of the QA process are to ensure that:

- The development and integration processes align with the approved standards and plans
- All transition criteria between processes have been satisfied and met
- The software has undergone a conformity review

The quality assurance process in this case is designed to ensure that the planning documents have been followed. To accomplish this, the quality assurance process requires the development and management of the software quality assurance records and the software accomplishment summary, and it requires accomplishing a conformity review of the code. Each document contributes to the application for certification process by identifying the specific rigor and due diligence employed in the audit and review process, which demonstrates DO-178 compliance.

TRANSFERRABLE DO-178 ELEMENTS (APPLICABILITY AND IMPLICATIONS TO COMMERCIAL SOFTWARE)

While the DO-178 framework provides processes and techniques for project planning, development, configuration management, and quality assurance, the most important elements are those processes and techniques that are specified for requirements development and verification. These elements can be adapted and transferred to commercial software application development projects. The benefit of adapting DO-178 to commercial applications is that it would generate more effective results and significantly decrease the current statistics of failed projects that are produced by The Standish Group.

DO-178 software considerations provide a view of requirements that flows from system-level to high-level and down to the low-level requirements. In this transition from state to state, very specific activities and outputs are described. When business analysts on commercial software projects perform requirements elicitation, analysis, and documentation tasks, they ultimately produce a single document (albeit with multiple versions). Requirements are not considered to be a part of an evolutionary process that drives out increasingly granular details through the analysis and decomposition of requirements.

By applying the concepts of the evolution of requirements (as described in Chapter 3), business analysts will gain clarity about the process and the activities, which create requirements that are complete, consistent, and accurate. As long as the process and its respective outputs remain an ambiguous blob, requirements will remain vague and riddled with ambiguities that directly lead to defects. Further, in the verification of requirements, the team must not only apply rigorous techniques for the verification of the product but also provide evidence of traceability across the entire project, from vague concept to detailed product output and executable code. In commercial software applications, business analysts could learn much about what it really takes to validate and verify requirements.

In *Managing Business Analysis Services*[4] I describe common responses from business analysts about the process they employ in requirements. This is more than a simple assessment of their abilities and their openness to new concepts; it is a statement about the lack of applied techniques throughout the requirements development process. The first question I ask is "how do you [the business analyst] gather requirements?" The most common answer (about 90%[5]) is "I [the business analyst] go to the user." In follow-up, I will always ask, "how do you [the business analyst] validate requirements?" Again, the most common answer is "I [the business analyst] go *back* to the user." The concern here is not that the user is so heavily involved. It is important for users and stakeholders to be involved. What is of grave concern is the dependence, and almost exclusive reliance, on user input when generating requirements. Requirements are better and demonstrate greater clarity, completeness, and accuracy when they are developed from a "what if the user doesn't know" perspective.

The DO-178 software consideration framework provides a level of due diligence and rigor, which enables the verification and validation of requirements from this perspective. This framework supports the development of the right requirements for the right solution by utilizing a process that will demonstrate alignment and support the business analyst in performing the work. If someone wanted to build a log cabin but had never built one before and had no blueprints or plans, it would be necessary to learn how to build it before starting. I would want to know how to do it and where to start. I would also want to know how to make sure it was not going to collapse on me one night while I am enjoying dinner in front of the fireplace. This preparation is akin to validating the requirements for the cabin.

STRENGTHS OF DO-178

The primary strength of the DO-178 software considerations framework is its detailed structure for the levels of certification. Each level represents both a degree of safety consideration and indicates the amount of due diligence and rigor that must be applied to achieve this level of certification. While commercial software developers do not have to concern themselves with airborne software safety levels (at least not for certification by a transport authority), they do have to understand the due diligence associated with each of those levels in order to understand how to generate a better product through the application of modified techniques, and how those techniques contribute to the end quality of the product.

Simply because the software being produced may not cause fatalities in the event of a catastrophic failure, it does not follow that commercial information technology projects should not incorporate elements of the framework into the development life cycle. The reality is that commercial projects impact the quality of work that a business can accomplish, as well as its ability to service its customers, its compliance with external regulations, and ultimately, its profitability. While commercial technology projects may or may not need to classify levels of software, they should include consideration of greater up-front due diligence in the process.

DO-178 can be viewed as concerning more than safety and due diligence. It is about a work ethic and a commitment to taking pride in the work that is done. Knowing that the product is not going to cause a mid-air crash helps. Okay, it helps a lot. It is not that people in technology do not take pride in their work. I believe they all take pride in their work. But I also believe that people "don't know what they don't know." Wanting to change is only half of the change process. Knowing how and what to change is the other half.

Within the DO-178 software considerations framework, requirements are developed by applying techniques for software development, verification, and validation. These techniques, which enable the creation of complete and accurate requirements for safe aviation systems, protect millions of air travelers every year. It is this process and these techniques that were adapted within the requirements section of this book to ensure that commercial software could benefit from the DO-178's high degree of due diligence and rigor without adding unnecessary cost, resources, and time to the project. One of the most common justifications utilized by project resources in defense of a lack of controlled rigor is that it is simply not needed. The truth is that with the business and its reputation on the line, controlled rigor does need to be applied.

At the end of the day, DO-178 software considerations provide a view of a framework that implies requirements success. This framework provides assurance, through a controlled, repeatable, measureable process replete with process-based key performance indicators, that the resulting software products will contain the appropriate level of quality for the system application.

REFERENCES

1. De Mattos, Alessandro Nicoli, 2012 at http://upload.wikimedia.org/wikipedia/commons/4/4f/DO-178B_Process_Visual_Summary_Rev_A.pdf.
2. Planit Software Testing. 2012. "Planit Testing Index 2012: Project Outcomes" at http://www.planit.net.au/resource/industry-stats-project-outcomes-based-on-primary-methodologies/.
3. Ibid.
4. Davis, Barbara. 2012. *Managing Business Analysis Services: A Framework for Sustainable Projects and Corporate Strategy Success*, J. Ross Publishing.
5. Ibid.

APPENDICES

Writing Effective E-mails

Ever notice how some e-mails get opened and others do not? Why is an employee more likely to open nonwork e-mails than work e-mails? How and why do people determine the order for opening e-mails? The ability to write effective e-mails—those that are opened, read, and answered in a timely manner—is partly marketing, but it is mostly about respecting the reader. These helpful guidelines will get project e-mails opened in the appropriate priority order and will get the reader to respond because the e-mail author informs the reader in a well-crafted e-mail. This e-mail formula respects the reader's time and recognizes that people receive numerous e-mails throughout the day which need to be sifted through, prioritized, and made sense of. This is especially critical when there are action items buried within the e-mail or any type of response is required within a specific time frame.

The general rules for effective e-mails are: to make the subject clear and use it to set priority; to set the tone; to be precise, to tell the reader exactly why you are e-mailing; to set expected actions and timelines within the body of the e-mail; and to conclude the e-mail with supporting information.

Subject Line

1. Priority Level: state the priority that the reader should give this e-mail
   a. For Your Information or FYI
   b. Urgent
2. Tag Line: state the level of action the reader is expected to take
   a. Response (indicates that the author has a question)
   b. Action (indicates that the reader must do something)
   c. Assistance (indicates that the author would like the reader's help)

    d. Information (indicates that the author would like information from the reader)

  3. Need for the Information: state the need for specific information.

    a. Requested (indicates that the author would like information or assistance)

    b. Required (indicates that the author must have this information or assistance)

  4. Subject: state the subject the reader must address

Examples of Effective Subject Lines

Urgent Assistance Requested—Technical Interview of Candidate J. Doe
Urgent Response Requested—Technical Interview of Candidate J. Doe
Urgent Response Required—Technical Interview of Candidate J. Doe

Body of E-mail

  1. Salutation: "Hi or Good Morning/Afternoon" and the person's (recipient's) name(s)

  2. Set Tone: the author should thank the reader or share something that they appreciate about the reader

  3. Purpose: tell the reader EXACTLY why they are being contacted in *one* sentence

  4. Action requested: tell the reader WHAT action is expected and by WHEN (when more than one reader is included in the e-mail, specify WHO is to take the action)

    a. Request additions/contributions to the agenda

    b. Solicit contributions to discussions—cite topics

    c. Identify prepared topics and discussion leaders

    d. Give notice when brainstorming activities will be performed

  5. Detail the type of preparation the reader is expected to perform before the meeting

    a. Send documents that need to be read before the meeting far enough in advance that the recipient has time to read them

    b. Send samples of documents and artifacts the reader will contribute to

    c. List demonstrations and exercises to be done in the meeting

    d. Include agendas for meetings

Important Tips

1. Set a flag in the e-mail to remind the reader of when assigned tasks need to be completed (this flag is optional, unless there have been consistent issues with getting items on time)

2. Set the "Flag To," "Due By," and "None" fields by selecting from the drop-down lists in the e-mail invitation

3. Almost ALWAYS respond when someone sends an e-mail! The only exceptions are after the final "thank you" e-mail has been sent and an FYI e-mail

   a. Let the reader know when you have received an e-mail and when you will have a request completed

   b. Thank the reader for any submissions or suggestions

   c. Thank the reader for participating in the last meeting

Sample Document Templates

Ambiguity Log Content Sample

See Table B1 on the following page.

BA Deliverables And Artifacts Index Content Sample

See Table B2 on the following page.

Business Rules Content Sample

Prepared By: [name]

Project Name: [project name]

Business Unit/Area: [business unit or area]

1. Rule ID [identification code assigned]
2. Rule Name [name of the business rule]
3. Description [description of the business rule]
4. Impacts [list of the processes impacted by this rule]

Table B1 Ambiguity log content sample

AID #	Code	Requirement & Location	Ambiguity Description	Entered By	Entered On	Resolution	By	Resolved On	Source Updated
1									
2									
3									
4									
5									

Table B2 BA deliverables and artifacts index content sample

ID#	Deliverable/ Artifact ID	Document Name	Document Description	Inputs	Outputs	Dependencies	Author	Status	Audience

Table B3 Change control log document content sample

ID#	Requirement ID	Requirement Name	Change Description	Date Submitted	Approved Y/N	Business Criticality	Priority	Assigned To

5. Activity Performer [identification of the performer of this rule in the processes—if applicable]
6. Dependencies [list of the dependencies of the business rule]
7. Prerequisites [list of any prerequisites for this rule to occur]
8. Control Type [identification of the specific control for this rule—financial, regulatory, operational, business unit]

Change Control Log Document Content Sample

See Table B3 on the previous page.

Current State Document Content Sample

Business Problem Statement

Business Processes Affected

- The following business processes are affected by this problem: [list business processes]
- The following business processes are in scope and will directly or indirectly be addressed by this project: [list business processes]
- The following business processes are out of scope and will not be addressed by this project: [list business processes]

Systems/Applications Affected

- The following systems and/or applications are affected by this problem: [list systems/applications]
- The following systems and/or applications are in scope and will directly or indirectly be addressed by this project: [list systems/applications]
- The following systems and/or applications are out of scope and will not be addressed by this project: [list systems/applications]

Assumptions/Constraints [list assumptions/constraints]

Risks [list risks]

Related Documents

- [project plan]
- [project scope]
- [project charter]
- [cost–benefit analysis]

- [statement of work]
- [existing system architecture document]
- [existing technical design document]

Business Process Flows [business process name]

Current State Process Flow [high-level diagrams or process descriptions]

Future State Definition Document Content Sample

Project Overview
- [project overview]
- [high-level problem statement, project goals, and objectives]

Business Problem Statement [describe the business problem]

Business Process Changes
- The following business processes will be changed during this project: [list business processes]
- The following business processes will be added by this project: [list business processes]

System/Application Changes
- The following systems and/or applications will be changed during this project: [list systems/applications]
- The following systems and/or applications will be added by this project: [list systems/applications]

Assumptions/Constraints [list assumptions/constraints]

Risks [list risks]

Related Documents
- [current state document name]
- [business process models name]
- [high-level requirements name]
- [gap analysis and assessment name]
- [change and implementation plan name]
- [existing system architecture document name]
- [existing technical design document name]

Business Process Flows [business process name]

Future State Process Flow [insert high-level diagrams or process descriptions here, highlighting changes in red or yellow]

GAP Analysis Content Sample

Prepared By: [preparer's name]

Project Name: [project name]

Phase: [project phase or document name]

Process: [process name: gap analysis]

- Definition [process definition]
- Key work product/deliverable [deliverables]
- Activity performer [actor]
- Dependents [dependents]
- Prerequisites [prerequisites]

Gaps

Gaps	Type
• [gap]	• [Routine, Realignment or Peripheral]
•	•
•	•

Issues

Issues	Risk/Impact
• [issues identified by this gap]	• [risk of not closing this gap]
•	•
•	•
•	•
•	•
•	•
•	•
•	•

High-Level Requirements Document Content Sample

See Table B6 on the following page.

Requirements Document Content Sample

1. Introduction
   a. Document Purpose: *This document will describe the low-level requirements for x*

Table B6 High-level requirements document content sample

Business Requirement Description	Priority **M–Must Have** **N–Need to Have** **L–Like to Have**
Functional Requirements	
Input and Output Requirements	
The system or app has to take Data X and process it into information for System or App Z	
Nonfunctional Requirements	
Security Requirements	
The system or app has to meet standard security protocol. List any potential questionable areas of concern	
Portability Requirements	
The system or app has to be available on or off the network	
Operational Requirements	
The system or app has to be used by Department X to manage stored data for X-Y-Z processes	
Technical Requirements	
Architectural Requirements	
The system or app has to interact with X-Y-Z systems and environment to function	

    b. Audience: *Detail users and the application of this information*

    c. Document Scope: *Describe the scope of this document*

    d. Assumptions: *Detail the assumptions made during requirements activities*

    e. Constraints: *Detail the constraints to requirements activities or about the solution or development process revealed during requirements activities.*

2. Naming Conventions and Definitions

    a. Naming Conventions

    b. Glossary

Term	Definition
List the terms here...	Define the terms here...

c. Acronyms

Acronym	Full Terminology
LDAP	Lightweight Directory Access Protocol
PMM	Portfolio Merchandising Management
SME	Subject Matter Expert
TEM	Trade Event Management

3. General Description

   a. System Definition

      ■ *System Narrative and/or Context Diagrams*

      ■ *Future State Narrative and/or Context Diagrams*

      ■ *Gap Analysis Summary*

4. Requirements

   a. Business Requirement *[List the business requirement here]*

   b. Functional Requirements *[List the related functional requirements for this business requirement here]*

   c. Data Requirements *[List the related data requirements for these functional requirements here]*

      ■ Inputs [Detail System Inputs]

      ■ Outputs [Detail System Outputs]

   d. Non-functional Requirements *[List the related non-functional requirements for this business requirement here]*

   e. Data Requirements *[List the related data requirements for these functional requirements here]*

      ■ Inputs *[List and describe the system inputs]*

      ■ Outputs *[List and describe the system outputs]*

Requirements Risk Assessment Document Content Sample

Client Name

Project Name [Project]

Document Title:	Requirements Risk Assessment	File Name:	
Prepared by:		Create Date:	
Status	Version	Status Date:	
Test ID		Due Date	

Impact Table

Impact	
High	Will have severe impact on the delivery schedule, environment, number of known defects, testability break and fix volume and time spent and Service Level Agreements of delivered product and could result in scrapping application, lost return on investment (ROI) and greater than 25% application downtime
Moderate	Will have moderate impact on the delivery schedule, environment, number of known defects, testability break and fix volume and time spent and Service Level Agreements of delivered product and could result in lost ROI and 10 to 25% application downtime
Low	Will have low impact on the delivery schedule, environment, number of known defects, testability break and fix volume and time spent and Service Level Agreements of delivered product and could result in minimal ROI loss and 0 to 10% application downtime

Probability Legend

Probability of Occurrence	
High	70 to 100% chance of occurrence
Moderate	30 to 70% chance of occurrence
Low	0 to 30% chance of occurrence

Test Priority

Testing Priority	
1	High probability of occurrence + High impact
2	Moderate probability of occurrence + High impact High probability of occurrence + Moderate impact Low probability of occurrence + High impact
3	Moderate probability of occurrence + Moderate impact Low probability of occurrence + Moderate impact
4	Moderate probability of occurrence + Low impact
5	Low probability of occurrence + Low impact

Requirement

1. Risk Event Table

Risk Event/User Scenario	Probability	Impact	Risk Strategy

2. Requirement Test Priority

Testing Priority
[# assigned value]

Use Case Document Content Sample

1. Introduction
   a. Document Purpose [This document will describe the full step-by-step interactions between the user (actor or task performer) and the system or application. This document is intended to communicate scenarios that depict circumstances under which the system and the user will interact and how the system will respond to user inputs.]
   b. Audience [The audience for the use cases includes the business sponsors, the business leads, and the project team.]
   c. Document Scope [This document contains complete details of the main work flow, the alternate work flows and any extension points as well as the list of actors.]
2. Brief Description [Briefly describe the use case without including requirements.]
3. Requirements

Requirement ID	Description

4. Domain Experts/Sources [Name the subject matter experts (SMEs) who provided the information documented in this use case.]
5. Actors [Name the actors (by role) who initiate and perform the major activities in the use case. This should match the use case model exactly with the exception of the actors. These should be the actors listed for your project.]

6. Preconditions
   - <Precondition one>
   - <Precondition two>
   - <Precondition three . . .>
7. Postconditions
   - <Postcondition one>
   - <Postcondition two>
   - <Postcondition three . . .>
8. Flow of Events
   a. Basic Flow [This section contains the ideal path for the actor by describing what the actor does and how the system responds to that action. These statements will serve to illustrate the functional requirements of the system.]
      - Actor step 1 and System response a.
      - Actor step 2 and System response a.
   b. Alternate Flows [This section contains the pat, or flow of the system, when only some or none of the conditions are met during the processing of the main path or basic flow. Describe what the actor does and how the system responds to that action. These statements will provide the basis for handling errors as well as for illustrating the functional requirements of the system.]
9. Alternate Flow 1
   a. At Step X in the Basic Flow, what happens, why? and System response a.
   b. Actor step 2 and System response a.
10. Alternate Flow 2
   a. At Step X in the Basic Flow, what happens, why? and System response a.
   b. Actor step 2 and System response a.
11. Special Requirements [First Special Requirement]
12. Extension Points [Name of Extension Point] Extension points include any related use cases that describe post-completion paths (extends) or are executed entirely, much like a subroutine (includes).

Index